POISONED CHALICE

THE INSIDE STORY OF
KEVIN KEEGAN
AND ENGLAND

BRIAN WOOLNOUGH

EBURY PRESS
LONDON

Dedicated to Linda, Emma, Ben and Jack.
With all my love.

First published in Great Britain in 2000

1 3 5 7 9 10 8 6 4 2

Copyright © Brian Woolnough 2000

Brian Woolnough has asserted his right under the Copyright, Designs and
Patents Act 1988 to be identified as the author of this work.

Ebury Press
Random House · 20 Vauxhall Bridge Road · London SW1V 2SA

Random House Australia Pty Limited
20 Alfred Street · Milsons Point · Sydney · New South Wales 2061 · Australia

Random House New Zealand Limited
18 Poland Road · Glenfield · Auckland 10 · New Zealand

Random House (Pty) Limited
Endulini · 5A Jubilee Road · Parktown 2193 · South Africa

The Random House Group Limited Reg. No. 954009

www.randomhouse.co.uk

Papers used by Ebury Press are natural, recyclable products
made from wood grown in sustainable forests.

A CIP catalogue record for this book is available from the British Library.

ISBN 0 09 187403 3

Designed by Lovelock & Co.

Printed and bound by Clays Ltd, St Ives plc

CONTENTS

I knew the moment I walked out at Wembley before the game with Poland that I had to take the job full time. I made up my mind there and then. It was a big moment for me in my life. I had to take it. And one thing I know, I am not scared of you lot.

Keegan talking to the national newspaper media at one of his first press conferences.

PREFACE

My first real memory of covering England was standing in the players' tunnel at Wembley and waiting for Alf Ramsey to emerge. England had just drawn at home to Poland and we were out of the World Cup. It was Wednesday, 17 October 1973. There was disappointment in the air. Ramsey appeared to be surrounded by about twelve media men. He offered some excuses until one reporter shouted at him accusingly. 'You have just lost us the World Cup.' Ramsey turned on his heels, pushed his way out of the scrum and disappeared back into the dressing room. Ramsey's reaction had a lasting impression on me. A few minutes later one of the senior England players popped his head around the door and asked if anyone was heading into the West End for a drink. I will never forget that either.

I tell these stories because, although times have changed dramatically when it comes to covering England, the outcome is the same. It is the manager who takes the blame, the players who get the pleasure. Kevin Keegan, surrounded by security guards and Football Association staff, sitting at an official UEFA Press Conference and peering into camera lights, was in exactly the same position as Ramsey, 27 years on. It was an hour after the Euro 2000 defeat by Romania and England were out. This time there were no accusing questions for the manager. Instead Keegan held up his hands and blamed himself and the players' inability to pass, keep possession and carry out instructions.

'I just could not get the team to do what I wanted them to do,' he said. It was the greatest admission of failure I have known from any England manager I have covered, from Sir Alf to Keegan.

When an England side goes out of a major tournament it is usually met with a mixture of frustration and anger from the now hundreds of journalists who follow England around the world, especially if it has been a penalty shoot-out, as in 1990, 1996 and 1998. This time with Keegan it was different. There was no frustration or anger. Just depression: from the realisation that under Keegan England had gone backwards; that, compared to the best, we are hopeless.

We knew that Keegan was good at man management and motivation. That was never going to be enough. Terry Venables, when his methods were questioned on the approach to Euro 96, always said: 'Judge me in the finals.' We did and it was outstanding. Keegan had to be judged at Euro 2000, that was only fair, and ail the fears about him were justified. England were a team without a purpose. They played like a bunch of strangers who didn't seem to know what they were doing, or what was expected of them. It is no good blaming the players. Any coach worth his £1 million a year salary should be able to organise a team into a pattern. A side difficult to beat even if they are not good enough to win it. Twice at the European Championships England lost a decisive lead. Yes, it was just like watching Keegan's Newcastle. Entertaining yet empty.

It is clear now that England has a cheerleader as much as a coach. The FA say they will back him and support him all they can. You can not blame them for that. Keegan is a passionate man who cares deeply about his country and there is nothing wrong with the FA's support. Deep down, however, when it comes to tactics he will need help if he is to last. The chairman, Geoff Thompson, seemingly indicated as much soon after England's exit. His was an honest view and yet, understandably, Keegan will never work with anyone forced on him. He is his own man. He will sink or swim by his methods. What are those methods? He said that he had learned a lot from England's three matches at Euro 2000. When asked what, he could not really tell us.

Part of Keegan's management skills are treating players like friends. He is close to them, allows them freedom and there are continual stories of race-night games, where the manager loses money on silly bets just to keep the squad amused, or stories of card games for high stakes. After the defeat by Romania at Euro 2000 some of the players stayed up until 8 am drinking. It was not the first time we had heard of all-night boozing. It is all very well, just as long as you are a successful manager. Be a failure and such incidents come back to haunt you. The players will laugh with him but there is more than that needed.

Respect comes from knowledge, the ability to change things mid-match, to spot something to improve the side. It comes when players realise that the manager has seen things that they hadn't. Hitting the three lions on the chest with your fist and calling for more passion is not enough. Keegan said: 'If I ever lost the respect of the players I would walk into Lancaster Gate and resign.' It might be a phrase that comes back to haunt him. Players will laugh with you face to face. Their mood changes when you are not there.

By the end of the European Championships there were claims of questions being asked within the squad. In the build-up to the Romania match Keegan practised with a three-man defence and a different formation. Gareth Southgate played alongside Martin Keown and Sol Campbell and the players were surprised and pleased. Then a training ground injury to Steve Gerrard allowed Keegan to change his mind and return to his tried and trusted 4–4–2 formation.

This time the players were disappointed. There were raised voices in the dressing room at half time as manager and players tried to sort out what was happening, despite England's 2–1 lead at that stage. Keegan did make a change at 2–2, sending on Southgate. But not in defence, in midfield alongside Paul Ince. Southgate had not played there all season. He was surprised to say the least. Soon after England returned home Martin Keown went public over England's tactics and called them inept. It poured more pressure on the manager. He was joined by a collection of senior voices in football. It all pointed to one thing. That Kevin Keegan is not good enough tactically.

February 1999 to June 2000 is not a long journey for an England coach. In 16 months, however, there should be the development of a side. A picture should emerge. What has Keegan left English football with after the first period of his career as England career? Let us peer inside the cupboard and take a look. Not much. An ageing side with the manager insisting that he will again pick his tried and trusted players for the new season. Not a full back to our name. Steve Gerrard is a bonus and offers the game hope for a new decade. David Beckham and Paul Scholes are here for a long time, Sol Campbell too, although his form has dipped alarmingly...and now I am struggling. Michael Owen is only 20 and yet, incredibly, we are already asking 'Will he be the same player again?' But it is about the manager that the biggest questions are being posed. Is Kevin Keegan the right man for this job?

The game in England did not need such questions. We wanted a period of stability, of success and smiles, of hope and real forward planning. Journalists are often accused of too much criticism of the England manager, of trying to topple the man with the biggest job in football. Not so. We want success just as much as the fan in the stands. We are fans. We can't, however, ignore the facts when they are put before us. At the moment the facts tell us that Kevin Keegan may not be the man to lead England to the kind of success this country has searched for since 1966.

Kevin Keegan arrived on a white charger, the manager to save the game after the controversy of Glenn Hoddle. The FA went on their bended knees for him. They were desperate. Hoddle was out and there was no-one else. Keegan said yes for four matches and then fell in love with the job. The FA could not get him under contract quickly enough. That seems a long time ago now.

Behind the scenes at Lancaster Gate there is a lot going on, from grassroots through to senior level. Howard Wilkinson, the technical director, has a five-year plan that should see England make a challenge for the World Cup. Keegan is part of that plan. If the new system starts to produce talent there always has to be a manager to mould it together into a winning combination. Again we have to ask. Is Keegan the right choice?

Football has changed dramatically. You can no longer rely on passion and pride. They are Keegan qualities and they are honourable. But football today is a science, of mind games and techniques. England, on the evidence of the European Championships in Holland and Belgium in the month of June 2000, are failing the exam. We are getting left behind. We were one of the worst teams in the Championships. The football of the Dutch, French, Portugal, Italians – most of them – was far superior to England. Some of them were on a different planet. We gave the game to the world. They will not give it back any more.

Germany were beaten but we know that they will come back again under new management. Maybe in October 2000, when they play in the last match at Wembley before it is pulled down and rebuilt. Wembley want to turn that occasion into a night to remember. Winning will do. Forget the fireworks.

Keegan spent the summer after England's Euro 2000 exit on holiday and reflecting. He would have thought a lot about the job. Some of us were left behind at the finals, enjoying one of the greatest tournaments of skill and talent. The match between Spain and Yugoslavia was a classic and Holland's stunning victory over the same opposition will not be forgotten. They showed us how football should be played. Italy in the semi-final were masters of organisation, tactics and concentration. The final, France against Italy, was a dramatic and fitting end to a magnificent tournament of football. France were the first World Champions to win the European Championships at the same time – and were worthy winners.

Another season ends. No Euro glory, no vote to stage the World Cup in 2006 and the same old problems. I thought it might be different under Keegan. I was captivated by his enthusiasm and capacity to build up expectation. There were other journalists who welcomed him into the job. Keegan's boasts were not a con because he believed it too. I am sure he still does. His pride will drive him on to the World Cup in 2002, when his contract expires. If we make it and England are successful, then he can still be a hero. The signs are not good. He admits that if England do not beat Germany and Finland in the two opening qualifying games he will probably be sacked. It was another extraordinary statement and one that may well have been frowned upon by more than one senior figure inside Lancaster Gate.

Sacking Keegan is not on the agenda for the FA. They don't want it. Another change of management would only emphasise the problems we have in English football. If it did happen I believe that they would have to break with tradition and go for a foreign coach, a man like Arsene Wenger. He is on record as saying he would never be interested in the job because of the aggravation. It is also what Kevin Keegan said when Hoddle was sacked.

He was persuaded. He was chased and signed by the FA. They celebrated when they got him. They could not believe their luck. Keegan lifted the nation with his talk. The British Bulldog had arrived. The tail is between the legs at the moment and he has slipped off into the corner. He will be back but for how long? This is an incredible job that no-one seems to be able to make a success of. The FA thought they had the right man. They know that being manager of England can be a Poisoned Chalice, yet they believed that Keegan had the character to make a success of it.

The waves of criticism for Keegan after Euro 2000 hit the FA hard. They did not realise how strong the feeling against him would be. It is not against Keegan personally. The criticism was almost out of sympathy, that here is a man without the tactical awareness to go all the way. It was a cry of frustration. When you watched Holland and France at the European Championships it was like looking at a different game. I suspect the rock-hard support for Keegan from inside

Lancaster Gate may begin to splinter. There were suggestions that some senior men now share the same concerns as the critics.

Keegan has his heart set on a long England career. He desperately wants to make a success of this job. Football knows that if he is pushed too hard, if the criticism became too fierce, he could walk away from it. He has done it before.

This is exactly what the Football Association didn't need. When they decided after the Hoddle sacking that it was to be Keegan, they fought so hard to get him. They believed that he was the only choice. The top man. Keegan lifted the nation. Lifted hopes. The atmosphere changed over nine days at Euro 2000, the period it took England to go out. The biggest nine days of Keegan's career. The build-up had been so long and positive, the fall so quick and painful. By the end of Euro 2000 the atmosphere had changed again. It was a familiar stink of failure. The longer the tournament went on the worse it became as the realisation set in deeper. One FA International Committee member admitted: 'We have a lot of work to do.' It was an understatement.

Can Keegan do it? The FA thought he would. So did he. That is why they went for him. That is where this story begins. No one knows now where it will end.

Brian Woolnough
Surrey, July 2000

CHAPTER 1

ENGLAND CALLING

Both men laughed. It was more of a spontaneous chuckle, an embarrassed giggle. No joke had been told, no one-liner delivered. The men did not know each other particularly well and they were not face to face. It was not even an amusing situation. But it was funny because both had been expecting the contact. They knew it had been coming. Knew it was inevitable.

The date was Friday, 12 February 1999 and the telephone call that took place at around four o'clock in the afternoon was to prove one of the most significant in English football's recent history.

The telephone call was made by David Davies, then the Football Association's acting Chief Executive, to Laurie Mayer, the press representative and right-hand man of Mohammed Al Fayed, the owner of Harrods and, more significantly, the owner of Fulham Football Club. Fayed had something the FA wanted and needed badly. Kevin Keegan.

England was calling Keegan to take over from Glenn Hoddle, who had been sacked in humiliating fashion after his ill-timed comments about invalid people to *The Times* newspaper. Hoddle was suddenly history and the old game needed lifting, inside and outside the dressing room. The morale of the England team and the football-loving nation was depressingly low because of Hoddle. It had happened quickly. Most of the media had turned on him; many of the players either didn't like, trust or understand him; and the fans, the most important people of all, did not have a clue what he was trying to achieve with his public thoughts about faith healing and his stubborn and determined relationship with Eileen Drewery, the faith healer who hardly left his side in those last months. It was a relationship that was to help bring him down. The FA, therefore, needed someone to repair the damage quickly. After all, they were in the middle of a European Championship qualifying group. In fact, you could say they were desperate.

They needed someone with charisma, style, a figure the public loved and trusted, a man who could end the gloom with one wave of his magic wand. There was only person for it as far as the FA were concerned. It had to be Keegan – KK, King Kev, the Mighty Mouse, the little man with a huge personality who had taken Newcastle so close to winning the Premiership in the kind of attacking style that usually only dreams are made of. Newcastle had persuaded him to manage when he had said many times that it was not for him. Fulham had done the same thing, bringing him out of retirement when, again, he said that he would never be persuaded back. Now it was the FA's turn to find some way of making Keegan alter his thinking. They relied on the pull of the nation. They let the public do their job for them.

There is no one prouder than Keegan when it comes to flying the flag. The International Committee inside Lancaster Gate, the home of the FA just off London's Bayswater Road, believed that if Keegan was offered the job he would find being manager of England too big a situation to turn down. He will say yes when he gets a smell of it, they said. When he realises that it is England and the country wants him to be the manager, he will say yes, the men in suits all agreed. There was no doubt it in their minds. And they were right. One hundred per cent, they were right.

Hence the phone call from Davies to Mayer. It was the first port of call. 'I rang Laurie because I had known him through working for the BBC, and then when he was with Sky Television,' says Davies. 'He was my contact inside the Fayed empire. When he picked up the phone I said who I was and he laughed. We both laughed. I suppose it had been an inevitable conversation and, deep down, we were both expecting it to happen. I said that I wanted to speak to Mohammed Al Fayed and he laughed again.' The ball was rolling, as they say. And how much the FA wanted Keegan to run with it.

They knew that if Fayed had said no, or indeed if Keegan had been adamant that he did not want the job, then they would have been in a huge predicament. Keegan was their first choice, and the outstanding one, but the reality was that under him the cupboard was too bare for comfort. Mayer recalls the conversation like this: 'We chuckled and I said, "I wondered when you would call, David." I knew that, effectively, David was trying to come around the back door. But the Kevin Keegan thing had nothing to do with me and I was certainly not involved in any negotiations. I simply passed on the message. David said more than once that he was trying to clinch the deal for England and, because we had known each other professionally, he may have thought that I could influence matters. It was a good natured call, with a meaning. They wanted to speak to Mohammed before they approached Keegan. They were going about it in the right way and all I could do was relay to Mohammed that the Football Association had been in contact and wanted to talk to him.'

The role of Davies throughout the sacking of Hoddle and appointment of Keegan is interesting. He had his finger on the pulse of both matters. In fact his involvement was total. Following the sacking of FA Chief Executive Graham Kelly and chairman Keith Wiseman for the votes for cash scandal it was Davies who led the FA through one of their darkest periods. His role and power was ironic considering that he had ghost-written the infamous *Hoddle World Cup Diary*, a book that was to help get Hoddle the sack. Davies survived his own goal to become captain of a ship that almost went under in its scandal after scandal. Davies now regrets his involvement in the book and wishes he had never written it. It was a big mistake and one that helped split the England dressing room. Some players could not trust Hoddle after he had commented in the book on private conversations and matters, particularly involving David Beckham and Paul Gascoigne. The book was serialised in my own *Sun* newspaper and got huge publicity. It was ironic then that here was Davies trying to persuade Keegan to come and be the Pied Piper of a happy England band again.

It was on the Wednesday before that Friday phone call, 10 February, when the FA's International Committee had decided that it had to be Keegan. They had met in the morning, a few hours before England lost to France at Wembley in a friendly International. Hoddle had gone and Howard Wilkinson, the FA's technical director, took temporary control for one match. He didn't enjoy himself, especially when Nicolas Anelka, then of Arsenal and now Real Madrid, scored two goals for World Champions France. Wilkinson may have had a glimmer of a dream about taking the England coach's job permanent control, but he soon forgot the idea. The International Committee of chairman Noel White, Geoff Thompson, then the FA's vice chairman, David Sheepshanks of Ipswich, Arsenal vice chairman David Dein, Sheffield Wednesday chairman Dave Richards and Davies knew who they wanted. They had met at the then White's Hotel in London, just around the corner from Lancaster Gate and a favourite watering hole of England's top brass; Davies recalls: 'It was clear pretty quickly that the group had Kevin as their number one choice. It was amazing that here the committee were again asking the same questions that had been discussed before Terry Venables and Glenn Hoddle.' The big question, as always, was 'Who is there?'

In the search for Venables the FA had employed Jimmy Armfield, a former England player and former Leeds and Bolton manager, to go out into the country and ask the professionals, the managers, coaches, staff and even the players, who the best man was for the job. This time they had to act much quicker. Davies adds: 'Everyone felt that, this time, we had to move rapidly. For a start, the European Championship match against Poland was only weeks away and that game was going to be vital to our chances of qualifying for the finals.'

Davies had no idea whether Keegan would want the job or not. But he recalled comments made by him in his autobiography.

> I remember reading Kevin saying that one day he would like the England job. That inspired me somewhat. I felt that he should be approached sooner rather than later. Kevin had made comments about the England job since writing his book, and was on record in the national media insisting that he did not want it. But there is a great deal of difference in saying no to a newspaper and saying thanks but no thanks to the FA after actually being offered the position of national team coach. Deep down I thought he might take it, if we were given permission by Fulham to make the official approach. I have to say that I was more optimistic than the other members of the committee.

White, the Liverpool director who had been so instrumental in the resignation of Venables, was even on record as saying that the country was in danger of scaring off anyone else to do the England job. At the height of the pressure on Hoddle, self-inflicted in my opinion, White said: 'The media in this country does not allow the England manager to manage. We are in danger of making this the impossible job. It could easily become the Poisoned Chalice.'

There's always someone who will take the biggest and best job of all though. Of course there is. To become manager of England is the ultimate position for any manager to be offered and accept. Those who say no are lacking something in their makeup and ambition.

How can anyone not be interested in having 'Manager of England' next to their name? Yes, it takes a 'big' man to do it but the bottom line is ability and gaining the respect of the players and public. What about the media? is the obvious question. We are the easiest people to handle in the world, if you know how to do it. Hoddle was useless at public relations, Venables clever and Keegan is brilliant. But results are all important. The media's role is king making. Yes, we can be king sackers, especially in the Hoddle saga, but the coach has his destiny in his hands. If he is successful and clever he gets huge publicity and massive backing. If he fails he has to accept criticism. There is not much grey in newspaper coverage these days, it is black or white.

All along it was clear that Keegan wanted the job, despite the denials and claims otherwise. Davies, to his credit, felt that Keegan would say yes if offered it. It was in his book, *My Autobiography* (Little, Brown & Co, 1997) and once Davies had the green light from the committee he went after it. Keegan had written:

> There is a part of me that will always be tempted by the idea of coaching the England football team. It looks an unlikely prospect now, even if things should not work out with Glenn Hoddle.
> I have a five-year contract with Fulham, and when that comes to an end it will probably be too late for me to serve my country. Football is a young man's sport, and I will be in my fifties by then.
> Nevertheless I would be lying to myself if I didn't admit that at the back of my mind the thought lurks that one day it might happen. I won't push for the job – I didn't when the job was mine for the taking. But you never know. I don't think it was any secret in the game that if I had approached the FA when Terry Venables left in 1996 it would have been hard for them not to have given me the job. I don't mean to disparage Glenn Hoddle, or anyone else for that matter, there were plenty of candidates whose credentials stacked up, but at the time there was a massive antipathy towards the role for a variety of reasons. Not the least of them was that a lot of good

young managers were frightened of taking it on, having seen the immense pressure placed on previous managers, Bobby Robson, Graham Taylor and Terry Venables.

It is no use having someone managing England who is scared of the job or of picking big names. Poor Graham Taylor undoubtedly had a problem in that area, because he seemed to find it difficult to handle the star players. I thought Terry Venables was a good choice, and likewise Glenn Hoddle. For me it was all a question of timing, and that moment it just wasn't right. That's life. And if it was wrong then, if there is a next time maybe it will be wrong again. There are doubtless those who think I would be too up-front and too open to be England manager. Some people can not relate to that attitude, particularly in the ranks of the press, but I do not see it as a fault. Openness can on occasion leave you exposed, as Bobby Robson discovered. It was something I learned at Newcastle, where the press knew me so well they knew when I was lying. But that said, give me honesty every time. Even in 1996, a part of me wanted that job. There must be a piece of every English manager that wants to be the England coach. It is the same for players. If he does not want to play for his country then he is not worth taking seriously.

Interesting views and Davies had logged them at the back of his mind after reading the book. When Keegan was the name the FA's International Committee decided upon, he knew, deep down, there was a great chance of getting him, even if he was employed by Fulham. Davies just hoped that this was the right time for Keegan.

There was another FA meeting, this time on that Friday morning, between Davies and Wilkinson at the new offices of the Premier League in Connaught Place, London, at the junction of Oxford Street and Edgware Road. Had Wilkinson said that he could not possibly work with Keegan then the FA would have abandoned their bid to get their first choice, such is the power of Wilko inside Lancaster Gate. Davies admits:

'I had to know if there was an issue. I wanted Howard to know what the committee had decided and whether he had any objections. Howard had to be involved because the two of them were going to have to work closely together. If Howard had been opposed, if he said that he would not have been able to work with Kevin, then we as a committee would have had to have discussed the whole situation again. Howard had no objection. He said that he could work with Kevin, and went as far as to say that had he drawn up a short list then Keegan would have been on it.'

It left Davies on his own to do the business. The Committee had every confidence in him and left him to make the contact, gain permission and set up the first meeting between Keegan and the FA. Davies walked back from the League Offices to Lancaster Gate. He hardly noticed the chill February weather because there was a lot on his mind. And his mind raced. The rest of the committee thought that he was going to make that call to Mohammed Al Fayed the following Monday morning. 'Why wait?' he asked himself over and over again as he strode the short distance back to Lancaster Gate. 'I suppose I was bursting,' he said. 'My natural reaction was to do it there and then. If this is what people want, why not now? The one thing I was determined to do was go through the front door. It was very important that the FA did things in the right way. By the time I got back to my office I had made up my mind. I was going to make the call now, and not wait. I could not find a reason to delay.'

Davies didn't. He made the call. And both men laughed. When the pleasantries were over Davies asked for permission and urged Mayer to give him an answer as quickly as possible. 'I told him to ring back soon because the FA were keen to get on with it,' Davies recalls. 'I told Laurie that I would come over at any time during the weekend.' Davies didn't have to wait long. Meyer was soon back on the phone. This time there was no laughter. Can you be here at six? was the message. Davies spent the next hour and a half clearing admin for the weekend, answering his post and throwing instructions at his secretary. But his mind was not really on the job. He had a bigger fish to fry. He had Kevin Keegan to capture. The next England manager. He was on the string, could Davies reel him in?

CHAPTER 2

PLEASE, MR FAYED

Davies did not go in the Harrods front door. He went around the side. He was told to report to the receptionist at door 10 in Hans Crescent and ask to be shown to the chairman's office. Davies felt very conspicuous as he walked towards the door, mingling with the public, a commissionaire doffing his peaked cap. Keegan for England. It had been the talk of the newspapers and his own picture had appeared regularly on the back pages as the speculation mounted. Had he been recognised then the secret would have been out. One phone call from a football fan to a newspaper would have blown the gaff. No one did. On the fifth floor he was met by Laurie Mayer, more smiles, a little laughter, a warm handshake and he was shown to Fayed's private offices.

The first thing that struck Davies about the owner of Harrods was his waistcoat. It was brightly coloured and the acting Chief Executive of the Football Association could hardly keep his eyes off it as he asked for permission to talk to Fayed's Fulham manager, Kevin Keegan.

'You will not be surprised I'm here,' Davies said as he explained why the FA wanted Keegan. Fayed wasn't and he was not in the mood either to stand in the way of the FA. His attitude was simple. 'It has to be Kevin Keegan's decision, not mine,' he told Davies. 'If he wants the job then ... so be it.' The multi-millionaire made it clear that he would not stand in Keegan's way. It sounded simple but, as Davies later discovered, these things never are.

The 40-minute meeting between the two men at which they sipped white wine – Harrods' own brand of course – was just the start of a long saga of meetings and negotiations between the parties that went on long into the night. There were many secret discussions. The key, Davies knew, was Keegan. If he wanted the job this time then he would find a way of taking it, despite his contract with Fulham, despite the pressure, the media and huge expectancy that would surround him. But the first door had been opened and Davies was encouraged as he slipped out of Harrods by the same side-street exit. Deep down he knew that he would get his man. He found his excitement hard to control.

Mohammed Al Fayed had been courteous to Davies, the perfect host. No anger about the approach. No bitterness that he might lose his man. 'The one thing he didn't do,' recalls Davies, 'was give me any indication of what Kevin might say to us. If he knew then Mohammed Al Fayed was not telling. I left Harrods with permission to make the approach but unable to gauge what might happen when I did.'

There was one stipulation from Fayed. That was the FA must not make any approach or statement until after Fulham's FA Cup fourth-round tie at Manchester United on the Sunday. It was a huge match for them with Keegan the centre of attention and the club knew that if word was out that the FA had permission to talk with him, then it could easily take away the concentration of the players and staff. Let alone the supporters. 'Mohammed Al Fayed was strong on that,' says Davies. 'He stressed that nothing must be done until after Sunday.'

It was frustrating for Davies as he reported back to the committee with an update. He was impatient to get things moving, and out into the open, especially as the speculation continued to roll.

Keegan was in the bath at his hotel on the outskirts of Manchester when Davies made his telephone call to Mayer. He knew about the speculation and had even done an exclusive interview in the *Sun* when Hoddle was sacked, saying that he definitely did not want the job. He had to say that, didn't he? He was employed by Fulham and had a huge job on his hands taking them into the Premiership. It was a five-year plan and he was hardly half-way through it. Yet behind the comments he gave to the *Sun* was a curious interest in what was going on at Lancaster Gate, and who they might choose to replace the disgraced Hoddle.

Keegan has amazing capacity to cope, mentally and physically, with a number of situations. Nothing fazes him. He can do different jobs with the same concentration and success rate. He was woken from his warm tub and private thoughts that Friday afternoon by a knock on his door. It was Neil Rodford, the Managing Director of Fulham, one of Fayed's men who had been given the job of working alongside Keegan and making Fulham great again. They had started on the same day and become good friends. Rodford was in Manchester with the team and Keegan, planning Sunday's big day. There was a bigger one around the corner for them. Rodford had just been rung by Mark Griffiths, a Fulham director. He told Rodford down the line, 'The FA have rung, they are coming in at six.' Shit, thought Rodford. He half expected the contact but didn't want it. Like Davies, he thought deep down that Keegan wanted the England job. He certainly feared he did.

Before putting the phone down on Griffiths the two men had discussed who should be at the meeting with the FA. At that stage they did not realise that it would only be Davies going to Harrods that afternoon. Even so, at the meeting there was Fayed, Griffiths and another Fulham director, Tim Delaney, waiting for Davies. It was a huge situation for Fulham. Fayed had invested heavily in the club and Keegan carried the dream. Without him it might just collapse.

Rodford popped along the corridor to knock on Keegan's bedroom door. 'The FA have made the call,' Rodford said when Keegan eventually opened the door. Rodford says: 'The phone call from Davies to Mayer was the first official approach we knew about, and in Kevin's room that Friday afternoon it was the first time that we had discussed it.' Keegan's reaction was interesting. He told Rodford that if he was allowed to go he wanted to talk to the FA.

Rodford says: 'Kevin said that he wanted to know what Mohammed Al Fayed's reaction was as soon as a decision had been made. I can say without any doubt in my mind, that had we been rung back and told that Fayed had turned down the FA approach then that would have been the end of it as far as Kevin was concerned. He is tremendously loyal and there would have been no question of his breaking away when Fulham had said no to England.

'My non-Fulham head told me that Kevin was the right man for the job. Yes, I feared there and then that he might go, that we would lose him. I feared that inside Kevin, the call from the country would be too great.'

Keegan and Rodford waited for the Davies meeting to take place at the other end of the country – it was hardly the best build-up to Fulham's huge FA Cup tie - and for the next phone call to come. 'I knew the meeting would not be a long one because Fayed does not have long meetings,' said Rodford. 'When the call came I was told that the FA had been given permission but nothing would be done, from them, or us, until after the game on Sunday. I told this to Kevin and he agreed. Both men, Davies and Kevin, gave their word. After all, we had a big football match to play. There was a circle of people who knew about it and it was up to us all to keep it quiet.'

It remained a secret until the Sunday night. Davies, who had watched the match on television (Fulham lost 1–0) and had been in London because he had to front the FA Cup fifth-round draw live on television, was out to dinner with his wife Susan. It was Mothering Sunday and they were enjoying a quiet evening together at a restaurant in London when his mobile phone rang. The voice at the other end said 'Mohammed Al Fayed has just announced at a Fulham party that the FA have permission to talk with Kevin Keegan. Is this true and what are your comments?' Davies froze at the sound of the media man's voice, then recovered his composure and made his excuses and ended the conversation. He had to go into action immediately and left his wife sipping her wine to go out on the street to make a series of important calls.

'I decided to get on with it there and then,' Davies says. 'Standing outside the restaurant I rang Noel White and Howard Wilkinson. I told them what had happened and prepared them to get up to Newcastle, where Keegan lived, first thing in the morning. Then I rang Keegan himself with the official approach. Yes, the first official approach to Kevin was made with me standing on the pavement, mobile in hand and being passed by members of the unsuspecting public.'

Davies knew that had he not made the calls then the story would have hit the papers and Keegan would have read about it and felt it strange that no personal contact had been made. Within half an hour Davies had arranged to see Keegan the following morning, booked his travel and confirmed the details with Wilkinson and White, who were to go and see Keegan with him. Then he went back to finish his meal. Like most journalists, the acting chief executive of the FA has an understanding wife. 'As soon as I took that unexpected call I knew that seeing Kevin as quickly as possible was vital,' said Davies.

Every move Davies and the FA made, Fulham were not far behind. And in the background Mohammed Al Fayed was kept in touch with everything that went on and everything that was said. He is not hands on but likes to be told. He logs it away in that incredible brain of his. Fulham knew that they were in danger of becoming two-time losers. If they fought it then they would be known as the club that stopped the country having Kevin Keegan. If Kevin wanted the job then they would lose anyway. Their only hope was that he would say no. No one at Fulham expected him to say that however. Not even Fayed. It was a crucial time for the club. Since Fayed had invested heavily in its development there had been real hope for it. Which is why Rodford, once he heard the news of the Monday morning meeting, made his own arrangements to be there. He says: 'We believed one hundred per cent in Kevin. We had been together for two years and seen what he had done for us. We had discovered that here was a man who gave 150 per cent.

'At that point we had a lot to lose. Since Mohammed had taken over he had invested more than £30 million into Fulham, he had chosen Keegan and part of that financial investment was based on Keegan delivering success. The investment and Kevin went together and that is why the changeover, if there was to be one, had to be done properly as far as we were concerned.'

Picture the scene that Monday morning, 15 February 1999. Davies travelled alone by train from London and White and Wilkinson journeyed from their respective homes. Rodford was ahead of them, inside Keegan's house, before the FA got there. Looking for a glimmer of hope that Keegan was going to say no. He couldn't find one. But Keegan had already made up his mind what he wanted to do, and it would be a surprise to everyone.

The role of Davies in the signing of Keegan and, indeed, the running of the Football Association becomes more interesting as this story unfolds. He joined them from the BBC early in 1994, and immediately discovered that the biggest body in football was not all it should have been. The FA had been criticised heavily, and still is, by media who are often appalled by the lack of decision-making, the councillors who get out of their bath chairs to make decisions and the general lack of leadership. While doing his job as press officer, Davies realised that there was a much bigger job to take on. A revolution was needed inside Lancaster Gate. A complete turn around. A streamlining. Top managers were being invited to run the national team, but it was not a top-run organisation. From day one it is obvious that Davies had other ambitions, good ones, and ones much higher than press duties.

Davies says: 'There have been changes, and changes will continue to happen, and I thought that if Kevin came he would like what he saw. It is vastly different now than when, for instance, he was the captain of England. If he had reservations about the FA in the past I believe that he would be encouraged this time. We are progressing. I am here to see things change. When I arrived I never thought that I would stay for more than four years. Now I am committed to bringing this organisation through to something exciting. As a football fan I want to be part of that. I don't think it is unreasonable. There are some decent people here now, some good characters.

'The one thing that has changed is that the place is more relaxed. It is not stiff. People talk to each other, swan in and out and it will get better as long as I have something to do with it.' Davies has had three roles within the FA: Press Executive, a job that he was paid a reported £170,000 a year salary; then acting Chief Executive after the sacking of Graham Kelly; and now Executive Director, which carries a reported salary of £300,000 a year. The FA, in many ways, are lucky to have him. The International Committee, and other executives, lean heavily on him. He is certainly one of the best Public Relations man they have. The Press Office, which he has left behind, is certainly one department that could be improved. The Football Association is a massive organisation, and big business. The press office is small-time in comparison. Some people inside the department are excellent, real unsung heroes and heroines, others need a personality bypass and to discover what the media need in this era of mass publicity. Davies knows who the good and bad are around him but, as yet, chooses to do nothing about it.

He adds: 'It matters to me what people think. Everyone has an idea what their ideal England coach should be. I am no different. My job is to be one hundred per cent supportive to people, when they are here. I got on well with Terry Venables and Glenn Hoddle, and still do.

'We have humdingers of a row here at the FA and I have those with the managers. But we are all pulling in the same way. Once the rows are over, you get on. That is healthy.' Davies emerged from one row unscathed, well, almost. He helped Hoddle write that *World Cup Diary*. It was Kelly who gave him permission, seeming to overlook the possibility that the players would feel mistrust and an invasion of their privacy. The dressing room is sacred. Things go on in there that should never be told or written about. Hoddle overlooked that principle and Davies should have known better.

'I would do things differently now, of course I would,' says Davies. 'I regret the book in more ways than one. It came too quickly. It was a mistake. It was politically wrong. If I could have my time again, I would not do the book. It was a secret diary, but no ... it was never that. I still speak to Glenn. Sure I do.'

Davies in a way got off lightly with the Hoddle book. He could easily have been sacked over it. Indeed, he should have known better. Writing a book in the middle of a World Cup was a basic error of judgment. Any good public relations man would have advised his client, 'I don't think you should be getting involved with this.' To actually write it for him was a serious error.

Hoddle. The mistakes made, the regrets, they were all behind him as Davies travelled to Newcastle by train for the meeting with Keegan. He wondered what would happen. He knew that if he could persuade Kevin Keegan to change his mind and manage England, then those mistakes over Hoddle would be forgotten. The country, not just the FA, wanted King Kevin. He was a people's champion. It was one of the most important meetings in the FA's history.

CHAPTER 3

HODDLE SACKED, KEEGAN BACKED

Glenn Hoddle had everything – a childhood sweetheart, Anne, for a wife and three lovely, healthy children; the job of his dreams as England coach and he had just qualified for the World Cup Finals by getting the point the country needed in Rome against Italy. Indeed Hoddle was on top of the world. Immediately after that result in Rome we spoke and you could tell he was walking on clouds. He was proud and happy and the smile told the story. Hoddle does not often relax in the company of the media. This was different and, deep down, he was convinced that England were going to win the World Cup in France 1998.

Then Glenn Hoddle blew it. Big time.

Dare anyone accuse the media, particularly the newspapers, of forcing Hoddle out? Hoddle shot himself in the foot. He held the gun, he pulled the trigger. It was the most blatant case of self-destruct that English football has known from the man in the most important job of all. I am not going to pass any judgement on the break-up of his marriage. That is personal and only he and Anne, perhaps, know the reasons. What we do know is that Hoddle had reached a period in his life when he had been taught that negatives played no part in his motivation and feelings. The story goes that when he returned from Rome on a professional high Hoddle sat in his living room that Sunday afternoon afterwards and thought deeply. Something was not right and within days he had announced the split. The decision, naturally, received huge amounts of publicity. We all wrote our articles and I recall saying that how incredible that Hoddle should be able to hide such personal torment when he was making the biggest professional decisions of his career over the game in Rome. There had been not a hint from him in Italy that something else was dominating his thoughts. It takes an interesting kind of public figure to be able to blank out a marriage break-up.

As the months evolved and a new season started it became more obvious that Hoddle was changing as a person. He retreated inside a mind that had started to discover different things that interested him. Religion, alternative medicine and, perhaps, the most dominating factor of all, his faith-healing friend Eileen Drewery. Nothing wrong with that, Eileen and many other faith healers do wonderful things for people throughout the world, but it began to change him as an England coach, which is when the media got involved. You are public property as England coach. Hoddle could never cope with that. Here was a private man who hated the publicity that went with the job he loved and wanted so badly. Rome was the turning point of his career. He thought he'd cracked it. He believed that he could do no wrong and began to treat his players differently and eventually committed the greatest sin of all. Not only did he lose some of his players, he lost the public.

In the end, England as a nation did not understand Glenn Hoddle. In a way this is a very sad story, the decline of a rich talent who had so much to offer. He was never understood or respected enough in England as a player by the coaches that controlled him. He went abroad to be appreciated. He found Arsene Wenger, his mentor in Monaco who is now the Arsenal manager. It was Wenger who persuaded Hoddle to become a manager when injury ended his playing career. He was sacked as England coach with no one understanding him. Hoddle went full circle and it was almost a magical mystery tour: the fantastic player who had to go to France to find mental and professional satisfaction, a man who wanted to be treated properly. A man who returned to England to become national coach but who then forgot the basic rule of management. Earn the respect of your players.

The ironic thing is that at the height of his criticism certain sections of the media were attacked for being so hard on him. Yet when he was sacked by the Football Association it materialised, over the following days and weeks, that Hoddle's bosses had been feeling exactly the same. We had been right. I say certain sections of the media because there were a few journalists who sided with Hoddle. This is not new and when an England manager is having a bad time there are always 'sides' in the media. They do this probably because it could lead to a story, more than out of any deep feeling for the coach. But one lesson I have learned in journalism is that you must say and write what you really feel. What you really believe. Don't go silent because you know the person well, or think that it might embarrass them. And the rules have to apply to everyone.

I knew Glenn Hoddle well. Glenn and Anne and my wife, Linda, and I had been out socially and I had always stuck up for him, especially as a player. But when a friend becomes England coach and starts making mistakes you have to say what you feel. Hoddle didn't like my criticism and let it be known, through third parties. He never once had the bottle to pick up the phone and have a go back. Sadly, we are no longer friends. Let's call it a football split. The relationship between Hoddle and the media got so bad that, in his last weeks, he held a secret lunch with hand-picked journalists to offer them titbits of stories or interviews, all given off the record, seemingly just to have a go back at the media men he disliked. I thought it was quite pathetic and certainly not the behaviour of an England coach. What Hoddle and those journalists did not know is that the FA, Hoddle's bosses and the men who would eventually sack him knew exactly what was going on. They were appalled.

Hoddle's mistakes. The biggest was his decision to involve Mrs Drewery with the inner sanctum of the England camp. A room was put aside for her in the England team's Burnham Beeches Hotel, near Maidenhead, and players were told that she was available if a player thought his injury could be cured by faith healing. Hoddle also said that players should go and talk to Drewery if they needed counselling for any problems. There were indeed England players, like Darren Anderton of Spurs, who were helped by Mrs Drewery. He believes. But a majority of the players became intimidated by her and by Hoddle's relationship with her. It led to a feeling that they would not be selected by Hoddle for the squad if they did not co-operate and visit Mrs Drewery. A number of players spoke about this although never for public consumption. One in particular made fun of her behind Hoddle's back and another was not comfortable in Drewery's company and couldn't get out of her house quick enough.

Mrs Drewery is undoubtedly a very sincere person. Her influence on Hoddle was staggering. I believe that she changed him as a person. Changed his feelings, outlook on life and beliefs. She denies this strongly and has voiced her opinion about me and other journalists. Sadly, her influence, in my opinion, did not assist his job as England coach.

Then there was his decision to write a World Cup diary. An unwritten law in football is that the dressing room is a no-go area for everyone except the players, the manager and his staff. Hoddle, with his book, broke the rules. He allowed secrets to be written about and comments made which appeared in the serialisation in the *Sun* and in the hardback publication. Players began to distrust Hoddle. They lost respect for him and once you lose the respect of your players then you are finished. Why did Graham Kelly, then the FA's Chief Executive, agree to the book? And why did David Davies agree to write it? Both men should have said, 'Glenn, this is not a good idea. Don't get involved.' Simple.

The book is a crucial part of Hoddle's downfall. It is incredible that Hoddle did not see the problems mounting up behind and in front of him. Maybe he did. Maybe they will be in another book. Soon after France had won the World Cup an interesting meeting took place at the Royal Berkshire Hotel, near Ascot. At that meeting Hoddle, his agent Dennis Roach and Davies met with Alex Fynn, who had helped Roach with some of Hoddle's business activities, and representatives of the publishers, André Deutsch. There was an August deadline for the book and Hoddle was asked whether he shouldn't answer some of the questions that had arisen during the tournament, in his book. Like the dropping of David Beckham, not playing Michael Owen, Paul Gascoigne's exclusion and, of course, Beckham's sending off against Argentina. Hoddle understood he needed to deal with some of these issues within the book. He, maintained, however, that criticism came from people who had never played the game. One of the things he also wanted to say in his book was that his biggest World Cup mistake was not taking Mrs Drewery with him to France. He was convinced that she would have made the difference, that England would have won the World Cup with her. Can you believe that? In my opinion it sounded suspiciously like a man who had lost control of the plot.

The serialisation is also interesting. It has always been said by Hoddle that he had no control over his book appearing in my own newspaper, the *Sun*, where it got massive headlines and coverage in return for a fat fee, which went towards earning back Hoddle's advance. But it has since emerged that back in January 1998 the publishers asked Hoddle and Davies if there were papers they did not want to run the serialisation and they said there were a couple they did not think suitable, but that the *Sun* was not one of them. All this time members of the FA's International Committee could not understand why a book had been authorised. Hoddle was wrong to suggest later that he did not want the serialisation in the *Sun*, when he knew full well that had he said so the publishers could not have sold the book to the paper.

There were so many own goals by Hoddle, such as his criticism and handling of Beckham. In training, it was alleged, he humiliated the Manchester United star by showing him how to hit a free kick. 'You are not very good at this, are you,' he was said to have told him in front of the England players. He revealed that Beckham was not focused when he left him out of his World Cup starting line up. It is also alleged that he said that if Beckham had not aimed his kick at Argentina's Diego Simeone then England would have won the game. It led to huge public hype and criticism of Beckham. For a period he became public enemy number one. There is a story that when Beckham attended a fashion shoot for a national newspaper he was asked, off the record, about Hoddle, and the reply was: 'Oh, that wanker!'

During the World Cup Hoddle told players to feign injury in training to confuse any spies from opposite camps, and requested others not to tell the media about injuries. It led to these kinds of interviews at press conferences.

'How is your injury Sol [Campbell]?'

'What injury?'

On top of the diary and all the other questions now being raised against him, Hoddle desperately needed a good start to the European Championship campaign. He did not get it. There was a 2-1 defeat in Sweden, followed by a desperate goalless draw with Bulgaria at Wembley. England did win 3-0 in Luxembourg, but there were rumblings in the dressing room and from inside Lancaster Gate. It was around this time that Hoddle got a big pay rise. He had a clause in his contract confirming a substantial increase and he duly got it after a meeting with the FA's International Committee. Here was the FA's opportunity to pin their coach down on all the things that troubled them. They bottled it completely. Mrs Drewery had been tentatively raised but Hoddle had been stronger than his bosses. 'If she goes, I go,' he told them. She stayed, so did he. It was after the FA had confirmed Hoddle's pay rise that Kelly and Noel White, chairman of the International Committee, held a press conference to discuss the coach. It was Nigel Clarke of the *Daily Mail* who challenged them hardest of all as we sat around a shiny conference table inside Lancaster Gate.

'How can you consider giving Hoddle support and a pay rise when he is a lame duck as an England manager?'

They looked surprised. Kelly blinked, White swallowed hard. The truth hurts. Deep down they knew that Clarke was right. Nigel has always been one of the bravest of journalists when it comes to forthright views.

The Hoddle mistakes rolled on. His treatment of the media now appeared to be at the contempt stage. He did not like the newspapers and they did not like him (apart from the chosen few) and it even led to a press conference being held to explain the book. Then Tony Adams, the Arsenal skipper, criticised Hoddle in his book, and the two were brought together by the FA at a press conference to talk about their relationship. It was quite bizarre. Then Hoddle made his final and biggest mistake, the error of judgment that was to bring him down. In an interview with Matt Dickinson of *The Times* Hoddle was asked about his religious beliefs, particularly the concepts of karma and reincarnation. When he was asked about disabled people and how they fitted into his karmic philosophy, he answered in a way that caused country-wide criticism. He said that invalid people were paying a karmic price for sins committed in a previous life.

The article appeared on the front page on *The Times* on Saturday, 30 January 1999. By the Tuesday he had been sacked.

Hoddle, ironically, had made the same views public on BBC Radio Five's Sunday morning sports show when he spoke live to Brian Alexander. But he had said them from a strong position as a successful football coach. Not a man reeling on the ropes. Not a man who had lost the confidence of the England dressing room and the nation as a whole. He had taken on the media and now the whole country was against him. It was his last mistake. The reaction was incredible. Everyone had a view, including the Prime Minister Tony Blair. Hoddle could not believe the anger against him. He asked Graham Kelly, now sacked by the FA, for advice and quickly apologised in a prepared statement. It was too late.

The FA, who had always been worried about Mrs Drewery's involvement, seized the chance to ask him again about her and the faith healer's involvement. Again, Hoddle was not responsive to their concerns. She had nothing to do with it, he said. But by now the FA felt enough was enough anyway. He was sacked. A majority of the media celebrated. Yes, it proved the power of the press. But newspapers reflect public feeling. Hoddle had to go.

The man who sacked Hoddle was Geoff Thompson, the then acting chairman and now confirmed chairman. Thompson had stepped up the ladder after the sacking of Kelly and Wiseman, and here the FA were again faced with another crisis. Thompson may not come over as a bubbly personality, a man for the new millennium, but he has his principles and is a strong character. As soon as he read Hoddle's comments that Saturday, he knew he had to go. Thompson picks up the story:

'My first reaction was that we needed a very quick meeting with Glenn because it was a very serious matter. Members of the International Committee spoke on the phone and held a meeting at White's Hotel in London at six pm on the Sunday evening. Members of the International sub committee, Dave Richards, Noel White, David Dein and David Davies were there. I knew we had to act quickly because with every hour the publicity was mounting. We had to make decisions, the way we had been so positive in the handling of Kelly and Wiseman.

'David Davies contacted Dennis Roach and Glenn and they came to London for a ten o'clock meeting on the Monday morning. We discussed the situation with them for about forty minutes and continued talking as a committee after they had gone. Glenn had been apologetic, to a certain extent. The one that we were unanimous on was that Mrs Drewery had to go. He was not happy. We also told him that he had to eat humble pie. How much? he asked, and we said loads, and loads, and loads, and again he was not happy. We told him that we wanted to call a press conference where he would apologise to the nation and again he was not convinced. We told him he had to go down on bended knees to the people. He could not cope with the thought of it.'

A second meeting with Hoddle was called, this time on the Tuesday morning. Thompson adds: 'Speculation and opinion was hardening all the time. The Prime Minister got involved and we also spoke with the chief executive of Nationwide (the England sponsors) although that was not a focal point.

'Maybe if Glenn had said sorry at a quickly arranged press conference, it might have saved him in some people's eyes. I have to say not mine. The moment I read the article I knew and thought he had to go. I never moved from that. I wanted to hear what he had to say about it. But there was not a shadow of doubt in my mind. In the end it was unanimous between us all. And in the end Glenn realised it too.'

The Tuesday was a day everyone involved with England will never forget. Lancaster Gate was dominated by gangs of media men, TV and radio control vans, people dashing about and waiting for the inevitable news. From early morning right way through to night time there was anticipation in the air. The anticipation of the sack. The anticipation of a huge story.

Thompson adds: 'Things moved quickly on that Tuesday. We kept going in and out of rooms, with messages and thoughts. In the end he and I had a one to one and he thanked me for being so honest with him. He said it was the only time that the FA had been honest with him. I told him that we had no option. It was left to Roach and myself to sort out the compensation and we did that quite amicably.'

What a roller-coaster ride of disaster there had been for the FA. After Bobby Robson's eight years there had been Graham Taylor, who had proved to be a genuinely nice man but not good enough for the job. Then came Terry Venables, the coach the players loved and respected but who fell out with the FA. There were just too many business venture skeletons in Terry's cupboard for them. The FA, after Venables, searched desperately for a clean-cut image and no skeletons please. They thought they had found him in Hoddle. He turned out to be the most controversial of them all. If they had looked deep enough into the cupboard they would have found Mrs Drewery. If only Venables had stuck to coaching ... if only Hoddle had stuck to football ... What next for England under Kevin Keegan?

'The results after the World Cup were not good,' says Thompson. 'We lost in Sweden and then had an absolute disaster at home to Bulgaria. I felt that Glenn was losing the plot. We heard that he was losing the confidence of the players and it was clear that the country too were raising question marks against him. Those results and all the other things that Hoddle had gone through during and since the World Cup had not helped, and then came his comments about invalid people. The comments were not the straw that broke the camel's back. It was worse than that. The collection of things did not help. But I believe he should have gone for those mistimed comments alone. We could not tolerate it. People are entitled to their opinions but when you are in public places you have to be careful. Glenn Hoddle wasn't. He was not someone the public related to, despite his apology. He never had the charisma of say, a Henry Cooper, Gary Lineker or, indeed, Kevin Keegan. As a public figure in the end he had no one on his side. Glenn was very intense. A very serious man.

'The book was a very big mistake. I don't mind anyone writing a book, indeed we can not stop them, but it should be done when their careers are over. Not during a major tournament. And it was the nature of the book that was so upsetting. It was like a doctor writing a book and revealing a personal discussion he had with a patient. It was written during the World Cup when I think he should have been concentrating the whole time on the football. I have said that to him and David Davies. It is embarrassing for David, and certainly embarrassing for the former Chief Executive who gave Glenn permission. All Graham [Kelly] had to say to Glenn was "No, wait to write your book." It did not take a lot of working out. I would love to know the reasons why Graham said yes to it.

'It was an unusual book. It went into far more detail about personal matters than an England coach has written before. No other England manager had done it. It gave me the impression that they were trying to find things to write to sell copies and make money. The stuff about Paul Gascoigne was wrong. It should never have been written. I have to stress that he was sacked, in my mind, for what he said about invalid people, and not for the other things. Those comments were serious enough on their own.'

After a day of cloak and dagger proportions, Tuesday, 2 February, David Davies finally appeared on the steps of Lancaster Gate at around 5.00 pm to announce, 'There will be a press conference at the Royal Lancaster at six o'clock.' One media man standing at the back of the pack of media men spilling out on to the street heard incorrectly and shouted down his phone, 'Blimey, it's Ron Atkinson at six o'clock.' The country would have accepted Big Ron. They had certainly had enough of Hoddle. We all had.

Noel White has been around for longer than he probably cares to remember. He is a wise old owl, one of those who has seen everything, or so he thought. He carries a lot of weight inside the FA when it comes to English football. He was completely involved in the sacking of Hoddle. Just as he had been with the controversial exit of Venables. There is a tinge of regret by White over the sacking of Venables and Hoddle.

He says: 'As soon as Glenn said what he said it was obvious how serious it was. The publicity it generated was extraordinary. The media came down on him like a ton of bricks. In the end it was the whole country, including the Prime Minister. All the other bits and pieces hanging over him, the book, Eileen Drewery, they all came out. In the end he had to go. I have to say that Glenn Hoddle's position was not under any threat before he made his comments about invalid people. Glenn Hoddle would still be coach today had he not made public those views.

'I do not think the that the PM should have got involved. The Government, they appear to want to be the guardian of everything. Football should be left to sort out its own problems even if, on this occasion, the end result would have been the same. What was on the go for the country at the time? But once Mr Blair got involved there was a new perspective to the publicity. I was not surprised by the weight of publicity. Some things should not be said, some things are twisted in the media and our first job as the FA was to make sure that Glenn had actually said what he was reported to have said.'

Liverpool had been playing at Coventry when the story broke and White, at Highfield Road as a club director, was asked before the match for his comments. Not completely aware of the detail of Hoddle's statement White said that any man was entitled to his opinion. But that he did not have to voice them in public, especially a high profile person. By the Saturday night White was involved in heavy telephone conversations with the International Committee and travelled to London for the series of meetings that resulted in Hoddle going. 'For the FA we moved quickly,' he jokes. While the FA met, Hoddle and his agent Roach were being told of developments by telephone communication from David Davies.

'I think Glenn knew pretty quickly that it was a *fait accompli*,' says White. 'Davies did not actually use the words, but we were basically asking him to resign.

'When we met Glenn for the first time since the story broke he was shocked and bitterly disappointed. He simply could not understand why something he believed in could generate such publicity and strong feeling. There was no jumping up or banging of the table at the meeting. Glenn was there with Roach and his lawyer. The amazing thing is that he was not under pressure, despite what had been written about his book and other things. There were concerns about Eileen Drewery but not enough to bring him down. He had just been given a rise when his contract was reviewed, as in the agreement between us.'

White is used to these situations. Venables believes he forced him out, something that White denies. The irony is that White thought Venables was good at his job. He wanted him to continue, just like Hoddle. He explains: 'I will always be known as the man who shot Liberty Valance. It used to upset and annoy me, not any more. When Terry was appointed he was number one choice. It was not that he was available that he got the job but because we thought he could do it, and do it well. He just pushed too early for a permanent contract. He was too pushy.

'I have taken stick and if that is notoriety, then so be it. We were heading for the European finals and he was in control of the job but went in and pushed us for a contract. If only he had waited, why did he push? Had he waited he would have got what he wanted. He asked us for an assistant after a couple of wins and we backed him. He would have got his contract had he not pushed. He just had to wait for the right time. Everything Terry wanted would have come to fruition, in those six months leading up to the finals he would have got what he wanted.

'We were not sure of his own commitments as far as court was concerned and his business details but what we did know is how well England had played during the European Championships. Especially after those finals, the International Committee would have given him what he wanted. I recall him saying that we only wanted to back the winner when it passed the winning post. That was unfair. He would not wait and that was the problem.

'What Terry forgets is that we gave him a damn good opportunity when we took him on. He had been really up against it. His appearance in court was not a good thing for the team but he was the manager, our manager, and we kept him in control. Had he not pushed so hard in the December, for his own situation to be sorted out, he would still be manager today. It is ironic, Terry could have stayed, so too could have Glenn.

'Once upon a time the senior England coach used to sign a contract and stick with it. At the end of that contract we, the FA, would sit down and decide what to do. Whether to keep the coach or change things. Now it is you lot, the media, who tell us that he has to go. What we desperately need is a period of stability for English football.'

Venables went, so too did Hoddle. There was time for one more moment of chaos under the Hoddle regime. At his final press conference he appeared, with agent Roach, at a packed conference hall at Lancaster Gate. The FA had given their own briefing and then in came Hoddle. Media cameras and radio reporters pushed to the front, despite a plea for calm. Police were in the room, as well as FA security staff. As Hoddle prepared to read out a planned statement one member of the public, who should not have been in the room, started shouting and abusing Hoddle and made to head towards him. He was pounced on by security men and dragged off. It materialised that his own sister was an invalid. Hoddle eventually left by a side door and was not seen in public again for weeks. It was an undistinguished and embarrassing end and not the kind of exit for a person who hated publicity. That night David Davies held an off the record briefing for the media in a different hotel in Lancaster Gate. We sipped drinks, finished our Hoddle stories and were pointed in the direction of a new era. Hoddle had gone and Davies, significantly, was in firm control.

The sub committee of the FA's International Committee were left with a similar problem. Who next? Who next for the biggest but hottest job in football? Someone strong enough to deal with the media and good enough to get results. Someone in this day and age of multi millionaire footballers to gain the respect of the players. That was critical. Hoddle had lost some of the dressing room. The cracks had started to appear before he put his foot in it, big time, and the cement to fill in those gaps had to come with the new man. There could be no papering over, it had to be a proper job.

On the Wednesday after Hoddle's sacking they met to discuss possible candidates. Howard Wilkinson had agreed to hold the job for one match, the home friendly against World Champions France, but something permanent had to be done quickly. To satisfy the thirst of the media, the confused fans and the players. The popular choice was Venables, the manager the players respected most, especially after Euro 96 when he got the team to the semi final and that agonising penalty shoot-out with Germany at Wembley. Kevin Keegan too was floated by all newspapers but he had said a firm 'no' in the *Sun*. He had been under contract to us and on the Wednesday morning following Hoddle's sacking Keegan's 'Sorry Not Me' story dominated the *Sun's* back page.

Keegan was the name on the top of the committee's list. All the men wanted Kevin and believed that he was the best man for the job as well as the depressing situation left behind by Hoddle. 'A number of names were mentioned,' recalls chairman Geoff Thompson. 'Alex Ferguson got a lot of support and discussion but the problem of Scotland did crop up. Would he have difficulty motivating England players and would there be a bias towards Scotland? Brian Kidd was another (now sacked by Blackburn) and so also Roy Hodgson. But by the time we met he had been ousted at Blackburn and that went against him. But he had been manager of Switzerland and had a good International pedigree. Dave Richards of Sheffield Wednesday put forward Trevor Francis. Terry Venables was discussed and so too was Bobby Robson. Clearly, after all the discussion, Keegan was the first choice. It left us with a big problem. Fulham.

'The Venables discussion was interesting. All the anti-Venables thing is unfair on Noel White. Venables was an option. We knew that he had been a very good International manager. But the great difficulty for us with him was the baggage he carried. For ethical reasons how could we sack Hoddle on non-football grounds and then bring back someone who had things surrounding him that had concerned us?

'We also did not want to go back to the Graham Taylor scenario. Go for someone who had had one decent club year, like he did with Aston Villa. Also to go for someone with no International experience would have been wrong, especially for the players. It is a great pity that Venables had to go in the first place. Also Bobby Robson. Here were two managers who achieved more than others. Who would have thought that Bobby, after leaving us in 1990, would still be discussed now? It is all credit to him. There was discussion of him holding the job for a younger man. But people on the committee felt that it would be turning the clock back too far.'

I find these comments extraordinary in so far as that Venables was allowed to leave when he, the players and now it seems the FA were so keen for him to continue. He wanted a new contract. He wanted security and they wanted him to wait for a few more months. Is that the grounds for the best man at the job to be allowed to quit? It could only happen in England. We shoot ourselves in the foot so many times. Venables is not blameless. I am sure there was method in his madness of pressing the FA so hard. Surely there should have been some compromise along the way. Why, why, why? Venables being allowed to drift away after the glory of Euro 96 will remain one of the great mysteries of the Football Association, in my 25-year involvement with them.

White, of course, was directly involved with the choice of a new manager: He adds: 'When Hoddle went we had to move quickly. It was not a matter of meetings, but there were phone calls all the time. Names were mentioned and moves were made to people. Does he have to be an Englishman? It would open the net and there was great interest in Fergie. We were looking for the best and he was the best. We did not think we would get Kevin away from Fulham. The more Keegan was discussed however the more it appeared that he was the best man for the job. He was the number one choice after all the talk and the meeting we eventually had. I said to the committee rather than chase our tails why don't we make the approach? There is no harm done. Let's ask him.'

It was David Davies who was told to ask the question. He was delighted to do it. Deep down Davies knew that he had made a mistake in writing the Hoddle book and here was the ultimate response from him, to deliver the man of the people for the country. He was determined – and, yes, excited. He had come a long way from working for the BBC and doing touchline interviews at the FA Cup Final. He had a huge situation on his hands. On that Sunday night, when he stood on the pavement talking to Keegan himself, Davies was convinced that he would get his man.

A few hours later, after a restless sleep, he was on a train heading for Keegan's home. He was to meet White and Wilkinson in the North before they all went to knock on Kevin Keegan's door. It was a loud knock. A positive knock. What would the response be from the little man who captained his country, had been double European Footballer of the Year with Hamburg in Germany, had wowed Liverpool, Southampton and Newcastle as a player, and taken Newcastle to the brink of glory? Before walking away from management. Now he was making a success of Fulham with the money and support of Mohammed Al Fayed. It was a daunting prospect for the FA trio as they parked their cars and approached Keegan's house.

CHAPTER 4

THE KNIVES COME OUT FOR KEEGAN

When Kevin Keegan was writing down all the pluses and minuses of taking the England job one thing would have been very much on his mind. The media. Was it worth the hassle, the aggravation, the pressure and, in the end, the public humiliation? Could he take it? Did he need it at this stage of his life? After all, he was a millionaire who did not have to work. He had been enticed back twice before, by Newcastle and Fulham, and now England were knocking on his door. In the end he said yes knowing that one day the knives would be sharpened and plunged into his back. He took the job bracing himself for it, expecting it but wanting to put it off for as long as possible. 'Bobby Robson did nine years,' he said soon into his new career. 'I want this to go on for as long as possible for me.'

Keegan said yes to England because he felt being coach of his country was bigger than anything. Bigger than any problems that would come his way. Anyway, he was good with the media. He was media friendly, someone who said the right things at the right time. The public would certainly be behind him. He knew that.

He had seen what the media had done to Robson, Graham Taylor and Hoddle and he did not much want the same treatment. Terry Venables was slightly different because of his off-pitch business puzzle and the unique headlines they produced. So Keegan said yes and went into the job with his eyes wide open as far as the newspapers were concerned. But not even he would have imagined that the knives would be produced the day after England had qualified for the European Championships, the job he had set out to do.

It was as if certain sections of the media had been waiting for him to make his first mistake. Instead of rejoicing at going to the finals in Holland and Belgium, Keegan was dismissed as a no-hoper, a coach who didn't know a tactic from a tic-tac and a manager who played players in the wrong positions and who could not change the direction of the game with a spontaneous decision. He was also accused of having no experience or expertise around him in the form of his backroom staff. It was the quickest character assassination in the history of England football coaches, but it didn't come from all national newspapers and a majority were behind Keegan. It was the *Daily Mail* that led the anti-Keegan campaign.

On the Friday following the second play-off game with Scotland the *Daily Mail* christened him Clueless Kevin and ordered that he had to go. Keegan read the reports and, despite the one hundred per cent backing of the FA's International Committee and, more significantly, the players, he was stung by the weight of the criticism. Yes, hurt too. He had been completely honest with us in the written press. He had said that the FA had taken him on knowing what he was like, that he was not a blackboard manager and that he did not yet know the best way of playing. They were honest comments that were rammed down his throat. Sections of the media took them and used them to try and destroy him. Some journalists who had not even thought about his tactical awareness, or lack of it, or other alleged non-strengths suddenly became experts, simply because Keegan had been open enough to admit his downfalls. Such treatment could only happen in England. Instead of encouraging and supporting a manager who had just qualified for a major Championship, we put the boot in. Other countries laugh at us as we self-destruct. It was certainly too early. At this point a campaign to oust him was utter nonsense.

I have been involved with all England managers since the days of the late Sir Alf Ramsey. Alf hated the media and would never have existed in today's commercial, sponsorship world. The spotlight has only intensified since the days of Robson. Bobby took enormous criticism but loved every minute of his reign. He would do it again if asked and, indeed, almost was as we have revealed earlier in the book. Taylor too would say yes again, despite the Turnip headlines in the *Sun*.

'To have the experience of what I went through, the knowledge of the job, yes I would do it again,' he says. He will, of course, never be asked. Venables would love a comeback but that, alas, is also out of the question. The clock will not tick back for Terry. Between them, Terry and the FA blew that particular period in English football. As a coach Venables should still be in control today, in which case there would have been no Hoddle, and certainly no Keegan. Hoddle was criticised, especially by me, simply because he lost his way, as a person and a coach. He carried too much baggage and created his own hole. He dug it, he fell into it and the media filled it in. With great big rocks. I take no satisfaction in saying that and comment is not made, conclusions drawn, for the sake of things. I hope that everything I write and say is constructive and in the end for the good of English football.

Keegan had done nothing wrong when the criticism came, other than admit his own failings. Yes, he lost at home to Scotland in his ninth game, and England were poor, very poor, but he led England to another major European Championship. He may well prove to be a disaster and deservedly take criticism, and yet at that point he was a success. It was an extraordinary situation that caught many people by surprise, particularly the FA and the players.

What led to the real abuse was a throw away comment by Paul Ince, the Middlesbrough captain who was recalled by Keegan and who enjoyed two successful play-off matches against Scotland. Love him or hate him, you can't ignore Ince. He is a swashbuckling player who lives on the edge of disciplinary action with his tackling and furious dispute of refereeing decisions. As one Scotland fan said at Hampden, 'I don't know about Ince, more like Mince', as Ince led from the front. He is not completely at home with the media but when he talks he is worth listening to. He carries weight.

After the Wembley match he started to walk through the mixed zone area which is just outside the dressing rooms in the Wembley tunnel and was asked by television and a group of reporters for a chat. He obliged and in the conversation about his joy of getting to another major finals he spoke of the players' respect for Keegan. He said that Keegan had become close to the players, closer than any other England manager he had known. 'He even stayed up with us on Saturday night, drinking, playing cards and watching the Lennox Lewis fight,' Ince explained. 'It was a good gesture and one we appreciated.'

That tribute was used to open up a huge debate about Keegan's style of management. Keegan in booze shame, screamed the headlines on the Friday morning and everyone began to ask: Is Keegan getting too close to his players? Is it getting all too chummy? The *Mail* went further and ordered Keegan to go. That was enough for Ince. By Friday afternoon he had spoken to Keegan to clear any air that needed pushing away (there wasn't because Keegan assured him that he knew what had gone on and for Ince not to worry about his place in the England squad) and now gives this public explanation of what happened on that Saturday night and Sunday morning after Hampden.

Ince says: 'We had had a good result, the players were pleased and so was the manager. When we got back to our hotel at Burnham Beeches the manager said that we could have Saturday night and some of Sunday off. Those who lived close to London went home and a few of us from the North stayed down. We had our meal and settled down in the lounge to watch television, play cards and have a few drinks. It was innocent stuff and no one got wrecked or anything like that.

'The gaffer joined us and the longer the chat went on I thought what a good bit of bonding it was between the players and the management. The gaffer has been fantastic to us and the whole of the dressing room is right behind him. We respect him, like him and want to play for him. The feeling for him is total. He treats us like adults and we all enjoy the set-up. I could not believe it when I read the criticism of him after we had qualified. OK, we did not play well at Wembley but we got to the finals. It was not long ago when no one thought we would make it. Now we have been slaughtered, I can't believe it.

'All it will do is close the ranks. It will make a "them and us" situation again, something that I know no one wanted. It happened in Euro 96 when we refused to allow any outside influences to get to us. We put up the barricades and got to the semi finals. It seems that is what we must do again. The most important thing is that the manager knows the players are with him.'

By the Saturday morning after Wembley the anti-Keegan feeling was running at full speed in some newspapers. The *Mail* led the way again with a back page headline of 'You Need Help, FA Tells Keegan' quoting an unnamed councillor saying that Keegan needed tactical assistance from an experienced coach alongside him. The story was later completely denied by the FA. Inside the *Mail* on that Saturday, 20 November, they also character assassinated the FA's technical director, Howard Wilkinson. One paragraph, from the unnamed councillor, cut deep into the heart of Wilkinson and Keegan. It read: 'If they were to string him up outside Lancaster Gate, there would be a few of us in the lynch party.'

Keegan, who had spent the weekend away celebrating his daughter's 21st birthday, only read the article on the Monday when he returned to London. On that Monday both Wilkinson and Keegan rang the reporter involved, Martin Lipton. Wilkinson asked, 'Is there a councillor and did he say it?' Lipton confirmed there was and answered in return, 'I hope you are not suggesting I made it up.' Keegan's call was more out of bemusement. 'Why?' he asked. He then vowed never to co-operate with the reporter again.

On Tuesday, 24 November 1999, Keegan attended an International Committee Meeting at Lancaster Gate where he was thanked for getting England to the European finals. FA chairman Geoff Thompson emerged from the meeting to repeat his support for Keegan and insists that there was absolutely no pressure on him to appoint a different number two. The treatment of the media, especially the *Daily Mail*, had also been discussed at committee. Thompson had asked the councillors at the meeting whether they had been talking behind the coach's back. When he got a unanimous no, one of them suggested that now the chairman had their support should he not find out about the others? Thompson immediately sent out a letter to all 92 councillors, reminding them of their responsibilities and asking them if they had been talking out of turn. He demanded a reply by return of post.

'It was time to flush out any anti-feeling,' he said. 'Call it a frightener if you like. I suspect that no one would own up to talking like that about Kevin and Howard. Kevin was thanked by the committee and no one of us can understand why he is not supported by the country one hundred per cent. He has got England to the European Championships. End of story. Now he can improve, now he can build. He has six months to get the team he wants, and the team playing how he wishes. Why on earth in this country do we not support the England football coach all the way down the line? Why do there have to be negatives?'

Thompson saw nothing wrong either in Keegan staying up with his players. 'It was a day off for heaven's sake,' he said. 'Had the players gone home and stayed up all night then no one would have known anything about it, not Keegan, the media, us.' He has a point. I would like to know what would have happened had Keegan invited journalists into the hotel with him and the players, to share a few drinks, jokes, play cards and watch the boxing. Would the story still have been written? I doubt it.

Keegan was hurt. But again honest. 'Most of the criticism has been acceptable. In fact 99 per cent of it has,' he said. 'It is just that little bit that goes over the top. I was particularly disappointed with the stuff about Howard Wilkinson because that was not necessary, and I have spoken to the journalist involved. The reality is we are there at the finals. The FA's travel man Brian Scott came in with a map of Holland and Belgium the other day and Derek Frazakerly and I looked at it, and it was the moment when it hit us that we had done it. If I could have a wish it is that the whole country supports the players now. This is not about me qualifying, it is the nation. England have got to a major tournament, where they should be, and we should be getting behind Alan Shearer, David Beckham and the others who receive so much stick.'

The one worry for the FA, and particularly Thompson, is Keegan's reputation to blow, and walk away. They knew when they took him on that if Keegan is pushed too far then it can lead to dangerous ground. Soon after he took over Thompson came out with his famous 'It will all end in tears' statement to the *Daily Telegraph*'s Football Correspondent Henry Winter and there was a nag in the back of his mind as he read the *Mail* and other papers which had come out firing at Keegan. 'My hope is that he does not doing anything on impulse,' said Thompson. 'I do worry that one day he will just walk away. My message to him is that he must be strong. He knew that the stick would come, we are that kind of country.'

Wilkinson, the former Sheffield Wednesday and Leeds manager, was deeply hurt by the *Mail*'s unnamed councillor. He did not know Keegan before he was appointed but the two men have got on, worked together, and become friends. He has an interesting insight into how

Keegan and future England coaches have to be protected from the perils of being a massive public figure.

'The pressure that the media brings with the job of England coach is enormous,' he says. 'It has a huge bearing on whether a man will take the job or not. For instance, had the publicity for Kevin been anti straight away, had there been a feeling from the papers that he was not wanted as England coach, then I do not believe that Kevin would have taken the job. He has a very strong family set-up and would have talked it over with his wife Jean. She would have expressed the natural misgivings, anyone would. And all those fears are confirmed when the press gets anti.

'The media thing and its pressures definitely puts managers off. People don't fancy it. It is a big issue that England faces because the pressure the criticism brings has got worse and more severe over the years. There are some people for whom the price is just too high. Men will look at what has happened to their colleagues and friends and say that they just do not fancy it. You can not blame them. I know of managers in their own club jobs who have suffered terrific stress. It never gets reported and they do get over them. Had the situations that we know about been in an industry then it would have reported as a stress-related injury and damages claimed. On the other side, the job of management is well paid and no one forces you to do it.

'Also, a lot of managers today are financially independent. They do not have to work. They do not have to enter a job with such stress attached to it. They can also walk away if they find that it is not for them when they step in. The financial independence also applies to the players. That makes it a different type of management that is needed today. Players are millionaires. They are not more intelligent but they are more independent. You can no longer tell them this and that or threaten them, so management has to be become more interesting for them, more enlightening. And respect is the key word. If football has become a massive communication thing, so too has management. Players have to respect the manager. In football you get the respect you deserve and the results you demand. You will not get the results without respect.

'Liking is a key. You can like different types of managers, the miserable sod, the father figure, the knowledgeable one, the shy one, the tough one ... these are just the layers on top of the respect. You do not generally like someone that you do not respect. When the manager drops the player there has to be respect for the decision. The player has to believe that decisions a manager makes are an honest football decision, and not based on other considerations. It is all part of the pressure. Those are pressures inside the dressing room, the club, then come the outside ones from media that are running out of control.

'I feel very strongly that the England manager should be protected in some way from anything negative that could affect his performance. With Kevin it is difficult because of who he is and the public figure he has become but I think football owes him help when it comes to the publicity machine. He does not need to be too busy or distracted. That is a danger.

'I have been in meetings with Bobby Robson, when I worked with him for England, and Bobby has nipped out for a pee. An hour and a half later we are still waiting for him to return. He has been cornered by someone and been unable to free himself. He should not be caught. It needs to become almost presidential. The England manager needs to be followed by two security men in gaberdine raincoats with speakers up their sleeves ushering him from meeting to meeting, telling the public and the media if you like, that he can not stop, that he has to go into another meeting. I have spoken to Craig Brown, the Scotland manager about this, and he does not have the same strain, although it increases when it comes to World Cups. When Bobby Gould was with Wales it went down another notch. But with England it is different. It is a non-stop spotlight and Kevin will need help in avoiding certain situations as he heads towards the finals.

'Kevin is an easy target because of his personality. He does not like to say no. He signs autographs, he talks to people, he likes people's company and if he is approached during a dinner he will stop what he is doing. Yes, he is public property and he is honest with everyone, but there has to be protection. If you have good people around you there is a lot more control over the media than we think. If nothing is done it is going to get worse.'

Interestingly, Wilkinson was not concerned about Keegan's reaction when the criticism, especially from the *Mail*, started to get heavy after the Scotland defeat at Wembley. 'When I read it I didn't think it would be a problem. I rang Kevin on the Friday on his mobile. I knew it would be switched off and I didn't really want to talk to him. I just wanted to let him know I was thinking about him. I just told him to make sure he took the weekend off and that I would come back to him on either the Sunday night or Monday morning. It was clear by that Friday which way the media were going and I thought that he would come back from the weekend stronger, that he would be able to deal with it.

'That is what happened and at a meeting on the Monday he was bright and bouncy. I think the only thing that would be a concern to him, and the only thing I would worry about concerning his desire to do the job, was as if the criticism became personal. Then we would have a problem.

'When he was aware of what had been written about me, the lynch mob thing in the *Mail*, his mood changed. In a second he became furious. You could feel the atmosphere change in the room.'

There is no question that the FA, Keegan and indeed Wilkinson have one eye on the newspapers. They are worried about the power of the press more than at any time in the history of English football. Especially when we are dealing with someone like Keegan, who is known to have a fragile resistance to criticism. Keegan's boss Geoff Thompson knows it is something that could blow at any time.

In the aftermath of Wembley, Scotland and qualifying for the

Championships Keegan invited the Sunday newspapers up to Darlington for a Thursday de-briefing. It did not stop the inquest into his strengths and mainly weaknesses raging on. The *Sunday Times* admitted that Keegan was a spellbinding talker but likened him to Stanley Unwin in being just as muddled. They quoted Keegan as saying: 'If you ask me "Do you know exactly how you want to play?", the answer is no.' Condemned out of his own mouth.

Keegan admitted that he had picked the right players in his nine matches but not the right team. He was playing into the hands of anyone who wanted to hammer him. Was he being careless, naïve or just plain stupid. There was more. 'I was surprised how Scotland played,' he added. That was a public mistake. No International coach should be surprised how an opponent plays, whatever the circumstances.

There was more honesty from him. 'I know I haven't solved the problem of the left side of the team. I have tried four times now and it has not worked.'

The *Observer* highlighted the English disease of optimism. They attacked Keegan for raising hopes. After the defeat by Scotland at Wembley Keegan said: 'I know you will laugh but I know that we have the players and quality to win the European Championships.' But the country were laughing. At him and the players. Sadly, they were also laughing at the things he said.

Personally, I don't believe there is anything wrong with optimism. I am a very optimistic person. There is some of the Mr Micawber in me. Don't worry, something will turn up. I carry the dream with me into most things I do. The *Observer* dismissed Keegan's ramblings and recalled the time that Keegan the player said that England would win the 1982 World Cup. It was not his fault, however, that he was injured throughout the tournament. They accused Keegan of not being able to help himself when he opened his mouth and said that the England fans take their lead from the manager.

Wilkinson does have a concern about the optimism of the English media. He says: 'I don't think it says a lot about us as a nation or our attitude to football. The comments made are not seriously analytical; they always seem to be made in retrospect. There is a "let us wait and see" attitude that I think is utterly and totally dangerous. The expectation that it creates within in the public is completely unrealistic. It does not give out an overall feeling of good public behaviour. It encourages the yobs. It is too nationalistic. There is a feeling that because "he" is England manager that there is a divine right to win football matches. That is rubbish. It builds up support in the England team that is too quickly and easily pitched at an unhealthy level. Where is the history to support the claims? Why is it that we expect to win all the time? There is no foundation to the assumption.'

Nothing will stop Keegan being optimistic or confident. He is that sort of person. He does not hide behind anything when it comes to patriotism and shouting the cause for his country. For the media he is brilliant, a walking interview. Before the build-up to the play-off games against Scotland he was his usual John Bullish self and took more time out than normal to discuss his relationship with the players and the media. By the time England had won in Scotland he, clearly, felt at home with the group. For the first time he believed that this was his England and his players. He said: 'I feel very much at home with these players now. I'm getting to know them. I don't mean Alan Shearer and Andy Cole, because I knew them before.

'There is not a strict regime here and the players are getting to know how we do things. There is a lot of respect for one another. It takes time. Don't forget that I only intended to do this job for four matches and then hand over to someone else. It was only when I walked out at Wembley for the Poland game did I realise how much I wanted it. It was then that I said to myself, "If you do not take this you will kick yourself forever." So I took it and now you people can have a kick at me. I think that maybe if you tell yourself that one day you are going to get slaughtered it prepares you. I will just have to wait and see how long it takes. I have discovered that it is a different job. On the outside I heard Terry Venables and Glenn Hoddle say that. But it is different. It is hard working with the players and then, suddenly, they are gone. That is why I work so hard on the team spirit, treating them like adults, involving them. The spirit here is good. We are a close bunch.

'The players enjoy the atmosphere, not the manager. Some say that I have become a father figure to them. Is that just because I have grey hair these days? I try to treat them like equals. I have not had to be a disciplinarian with them. They know the things that are important to me, like being there on time. When I took control of the Under 21 team years ago the players turned up at all sorts of times. I got them together the next morning and told them I didn't care what they did with other people, this is what you do for me. If you call that being a disciplinarian, then I am a disciplinarian. I don't think you should be late for anyone, let alone England.

'There has to be that trust because in a way my fate is in their hands. They also have their own fate in their own hands.

'I have my own way of dealing with them and I do not need massive coaching manuals for these players. I can do it a different way and the FA knew that when they employed me they were not getting a blackboard and chalk man. I am not going to be different just because I am England coach. People like Alan Shearer would not let me get away with that.

'You must have quality players and treat them well so they respond to you. I thought that the team Ron Greenwood built when he was England coach had everything. That is why some senior players asked him to stay when it was clear he was thinking of quitting. We asked him "why?" and told him that he would be missing out on the best days of his life.' Clearly, that is what Keegan believes. That this England job will give him more enjoyment and satisfaction than he has experienced before. Of course, he desperately wants to lead England to a major trophy.

Keegan added: 'I hope that I never have to resign. The trouble with this job is that you need instant success. I think I had one game as my honeymoon period, that first one with Poland. I accept the situation.'

It is no secret that David Beckham did not see eye to eye with former England manager Glenn Hoddle. There were too many incidents, particularly during the World Cup, which emphasised the gulf between them. Beckham and Manchester United manager Sir Alex Ferguson did not much like Hoddle revealing that Beckham was not focused enough to play in England's opening game. Perhaps the most damning incident was that of Hoddle's alleged attitude towards Beckham in the dressing room after Beckham had been sent off against Argentina. Beckham sat there with his head down when the other players came in after the extra time and penalty shoot-out heartbreak. Beckham was distraught and kept mumbling sorry to anyone who would listen. The manager is said to have ignored him and it was left to Arsenal skipper Tony Adams to put a consoling arm around the crestfallen Beckham. That is bad management and Beckham never forgot or forgave Hoddle.

It is an interesting insight into Hoddle. We have explained before that he is a very deep, almost lonely man. Is this emphasized by the fact that ten months after his sacking Hoddle had hardly spoken to anyone at the Football Association? Football people talk, see each other at games and call one another. Hoddle, for instance, had not spoken to Howard Wilkinson since two days after his controversial exit. Under Keegan, here was a change of atmosphere and before the Scotland matches Beckham went out of his way to explain how the mood had changed and improved for him under Keegan.

The Manchester United star, and the biggest name in English football, said: 'I think it is more relaxed before matches now. Even when we first meet up it is a lot more relaxed than what it was. You know, we are treated with a bit more sort of, I will not say too much, but as grown ups. You know, we can do more things. He is more lenient with us and that creates, you know, I think a better atmosphere. I think that if the players are more relaxed then you get better results on the pitch. He makes you want to play. There is a great atmosphere in the squad, even though there have been players coming in and out. There has been a great atmosphere since Kevin Keegan came in. He mixes the week up and makes life enjoyable. That is important.' Keegan responded by saying that he had no intention to change a single thing about Beckham as a player or person. No wonder the players love him.

It was that relationship Keegan had taken with him through the seven matches trying to get England to the European Championship Finals and then, finally, the two play-off matches against Scotland. It had been Sweden, the country who beat Hoddle's England in the opening group match, who had done us the favour by beating Poland in Stockholm and taking us to the play-offs. Keegan had watched the match on a big screen at Sunderland's Stadium of Light as he prepared for a friendly International against Belgium. Keegan sat in a high-backed chair, surrounded by only a few Football Association people.

They were people whom he didn't know particularly well, but who had become part of his professional life. People like press officer Steve Double, International secretary Michelle Farrer and executive director David Davies. It is an irony that they, people not exactly close to him, should share one of the big moments of his career. Keegan then went to Arken in Germany for the play-off draw and revealed that he had woken up hearing bagpipes playing before the draw paired his players with Scotland. 'I know my team for the matches already,' he said. 'Given full fitness I know the team I want and expect to win.' Confident? Yes. Exciting to work with? Certainly. Sincere? Of course. Foolhardy? Maybe. But who cares.

His squad for the two matches against Scotland saw him recall Andy Cole, the Manchester United star who had been critical of Alan Shearer in his autobiography. Cole said that Shearer was the golden boy and that he was contemplating quitting International football unless Shearer was selected on merit, like all the other players. Keegan rang Shearer to tell him that Cole was back in and the captain had no problem with the selection. Shearer said that it would make no sense not including Cole, especially in the form he was in. There was a first appearance for Steve Froggatt of Coventry, just to emphasise the problem England have on the left side of their team. Graeme Le Saux was injured, Michael Gray of Sunderland had been tried and dropped, Steve Guppy of Leicester made his debut against Belgium and now it was Froggatt's turn. Chelsea skipper Dennis Wise, overlooked by Hoddle and called up against Belgium, retained his place.

Everything went to plan at Hampden, despite the lopsided look to Keegan's team, with Sol Campbell of Spurs used as a makeshift right back and Jamie Redknapp of Liverpool asked to slot into the troublesome left-sided position. What we had not realised is that Scotland would be so poor. There had been real confidence before the kick off but it soon turned to relaxed pleasure as Scotland stumbled. Paul Scholes got two first-half goals to send Keegan and his team back to Wembley with one foot in the finals. 'It will be the biggest disaster to hit English football if we do not go through now,' Keegan said. Great copy. Again, did Keegan think before he spoke?

England did go through but only just. Their performance at Wembley was pathetic, the worst for years. It would have to be in the top five of low performances since I started covering the national side. There was no excuse for it. The same players who had won 2–0 at Hampden were a shadow of themselves. Keegan did not or could not motivate or reorganise them and he held up his hands after the match. 'The only good thing to come out of tonight,' he said, 'is that we have qualified. It is what I set out to do when I took on this job and we have done it. Now there is time to experiment and build.' He did add that he would like twenty friendlies, instead of the three in the year 2000, to help him prepare England for the test to come in June. 'There is a lot of work to be done,' he added.

There were some strange decisions made by Keegan that could lead to problems for him. At Hampden Park he sent on the in-form Cole for Michael Owen and yet at Wembley, with England struggling, he substituted Owen this time for Emile Heskey of Leicester. 'I am not sure what is happening to me at International level,' admitted Cole a few days later after scoring again for United. Clearly, it is going to take all of Keegan's motivation skills to turn Cole into a prolific England player, and scorer.

Also, at Hampden Keegan put Froggatt on the bench and not Guppy, who had played against Belgium. Guppy went to see him to ask where he stood and was told: 'You are in the England squad trying to force your way into the first team.' Guppy was duly placed back on the bench at Wembley and Froggatt disposed to the stand. In his de-briefing with the Sunday newspapers he indicated that Shearer and Owen might be rested in the friendlies in the search for a better up-front combination. Indeed Owen was tipped to go back to the under-21 side, something that he and Liverpool manager Gerard Houllier frowned upon.

Then came the criticism, the late-night drinks session that Keegan and the FA dismissed but some papers used beat him with, and for the first time the new England coach was on the ropes. He had prepared himself to get slaughtered, using his words, but he had not believed that it would come so soon. It allowed him time to think, regroup, talk to his staff, close friends and bosses up and down the country about the situation. He got unanimous support. It was a huge vote of confidence and England coaches don't usually get those, or need them, after just nine months. The biggest disappointment for Keegan is that he had to wait four months to see his players again, when Argentinia would arrive for a prestige friendly at Wembley. There was no guarantee of how many of his chosen squad he would get because England managers always suffer with dropouts for friendly matches.

So over Christmas and into the millennium Keegan did a lot of thinking and planning. Deep down he thought that England might just, might just, be able to pull off the biggest surprise of all by winning Euro 2000. Don't laugh, he said. It was hard not to. And the critics, some who already wanted him out, were lining up for him to fail.

CHAPTER 5

KEEGAN SAYS YES, NO, YES

Davies travelled alone from King's Cross Station in London to the North of England for the meeting with Keegan. It was an early start and he thought a lot as the train hurtled through the English countryside, stations and more built-up areas, and the coffee he drank began to taste of, well British Rail, really. Expensive and not top quality. It was a journey he wanted to take, indeed knew he had to, but it was also filled with apprehension. What if Keegan said no? What would the FA do then? One thing for sure, if Keegan did not want the job then English football would be in a mess. There was no other obvious candidate. Keegan was the top choice. The only choice.

Noel White and Howard Wilkinson made their own way by car and Davies was met at the station by one of the drivers that Keegan himself uses. Davies recalls: 'On the journey I thought about how the meeting would go. In fact, it was the only thing I could concentrate on. I believed that Kevin would want to be the coach and would find it difficult to turn down. But I was not taking anything for granted. I knew the commitment he had to Fulham and that Kevin was a man of his word, a loyal person. He would not want to let Fulham down in any way. Davies had arranged to meet the other two members of the FA party at a local hotel. It was important that we met to discuss any last-minute points or plan.' More coffee. More thoughts. More worries.

They eventually arrived at Keegan's home on Sir John Hall's estate at around twelve noon and were surprised that it was Keegan, and not they, who led the way as far as the England job was concerned. Within two or three minutes of their walking through the front door Keegan had offered to help, and he had his own plan. It was a plan that the FA had not really considered when they discussed going for Keegan. Davies explains:

'He said straight away that he was flattered that we should want to consider him for the job. He said quickly that if we wanted him to help us over the next few months he would, but quickly emphasised his contract and commitment to Fulham. He told us that he could not look beyond that with England. He said he knew that we had Poland at home in March and then a friendly before another couple of European ties in June. He said that he would hold the position for us as a caretaker manager, if that is what we wanted.' Then Keegan said very strongly, 'My doing that will give you more time to find someone else.'

Keegan's plan sent the FA trio into a huddle. It was a bizarre scene with the FA leaving to go into another room, while Keegan moved around his own home. He had Fulham Managing Director Neil Rodford with him and the two men, who had become friends and close working partners at Craven Cottage, had clearly hatched the plan between them before the FA arrived. Keegan, of course, had spoken to his wife about what he should do. But Keegan is his own man. This was his ultimate decision and it is what he thought best for both Fulham and England.

There were mobile phone calls from Davies, White and Wilkinson to other members of the International sub committee like Arsenal vice-chairman David Dein, Ipswich chairman David Sheepshanks and

Sheffield Wednesday chairman Dave Richards. The acting chairman, Geoff Thompson, was away on a family holiday in New Zealand. He had taken his mobile with him and contact was soon made and the message passed on. And the message was this. That Keegan will do it for four matches, and four matches only, what do you think?

After a two and a half hour stay, with the Keegans providing sandwiches and soft drinks, and more coffee, Davies, White and Wilkinson left and moved on to another meeting. 'We needed time to reflect on what he had said,' explained Davies. 'We had to make up our minds whether it was going to be a yes to him, a no, a thank you or that we had to go onto someone else for a permanent appointment.'

When the FA men finally said goodbye to one another Davies travelled to his Birmingham home, before returning to London. He knew that the clock was ticking, the public demanding, the media pushing and the Poland match approaching. 'We had agreed to have more conversations over the next few days,' says Davies. 'We had also promised to give Kevin an answer sooner than later. The more I thought about him the more I believed that Kevin was adamant. It was a view shared by some of the members, while others thought that he might swing around. I knew Kevin better than Terry or Glenn and knew that once Kevin makes up his mind it is set. He had thought about his response carefully and would not change that quickly. We had not offered him the job but we had said to him that if we could sort things out for him would he want to do it? He kept saying that he had a commitment to Fulham. I did feel that once he got into the job, if he did, then there was a chance that the position of England coach would grip him.'

Discussions, talks, phone calls, meetings and more talks went on through the week. The longer they talked the more the FA came down on the side of Keegan's idea. 'The enthusiasm for Kevin as the number one choice was such there was a unanimous call for us to take him up on his four-match offer,' says Davies. 'Some members thought that once he took the job that he would love it and others said that the public will love him. One committee member said that if he stuck to his word then it would give us time. I knew there was no danger of Keegan not sticking to his word.'

On 15 February Davies went to a football dinner at the Houses of Parliament and was bombarded with questions about Keegan and the FA's decision. Davies knew that a verdict had to be decided on and an announcement delivered to a waiting nation. It was huge newspaper headlines every day, back and front, and Keegan's name dominated every news bulletin on television and radio. By the next morning Davies was told that the committee wanted to press on and go ahead with Keegan's offer. A phone call Down Under to Thompson got the backing of the chairman and Davies, at last, could start to make official moves. It was not an ideal situation but the best in the circumstances. They wanted Keegan full time. He had agreed to four matches. The committee hoped and prayed that the job would grab him once he pulled the three lions over his head again, this time as England's tenth manager.

What the Football Association had not bargained for was how hard Fulham would pull in the other direction. They knew it was a no-win situation for them. If they had said no then the country would never have forgiven them for denying England the manager it wanted. If they were to say yes then the terms, the agreement and the handover was going to have to right, particularly financially.

The men who dealt directly with the FA were Rodford and Mark Griffiths, Fayed's right-hand man at Fulham. He was also close to Keegan. Mohammed Al Fayed did not get directly involved with negotiations or everyday discussion, but he was there in the background, being fed information by his people and either agreeing or pushing them in another direction. The bottom line was that Keegan worked for Fayed. Fulham had been adamant that nothing should come out until after that FA Cup tie at Manchester United. 'We felt strongly about that,' says Rodford. 'It would not have been fair on us if it had been disclosed that Fayed had agreed to allow the FA to talk to Kevin before that match. David Davies told us that he would honour our wishes and Kevin agreed. We were told of the outcome of the meeting by phone while we were in Manchester.'

After the match at Old Trafford Keegan went home to talk things over with his wife Jean. It had been the first time they had been together since the FA's official approach and Mohammed Al Fayed's agreement to let the FA talk to his manager. A lot had happened in the space of three days. Rodford adds: 'It was agreed that it was best for the FA to go North, rather than us turn up at Lancaster Gate in London. That would not have been discreet. When the FA arrived at Kevin's house I was there but I was not present when they discussed the job. They wanted to talk to him one to one. I spoke with Kevin after they had left and he explained that he had offered to help them see it through until the summer. He also offered to help them find a replacement. I knew they wanted him full time and they explained that further discussions had to take place with the rest of the committee. I knew there were some big decisions to be made and a lot of meetings to be arranged. If they said that they wanted him part-time it put pressure on us. Our season was at a critical stage and, here we were, about to share our manager with England.

'We had a lot of meetings with Kevin about what would be the right thing to do. The bottom line for us is that we believed in him. If he told us that he could do both jobs then we would support him. It was not ideal but we had seen what he had done for us over the two years we had been together. I had discovered that if Kevin says that he can do it it may not always be successful but he will give you 150 per cent.'

Fulham had a lot to lose. Keegan had been hand picked by Fayed who had trust in him. Rodford explains: 'It felt like a family thing. Kevin and I started the same day, September 24th, 1997. I will never forget it. I had been working for Mohammed in another part of his organisation and I was selected when Kevin explained that he wanted someone to work with at Craven Cottage on a daily basis. I helped him run his first press conference as Fulham manager and we got on like a house on fire from that day. I was not behind him coming to Fulham. That had been Mohammed Al Fayed. I know that Mohammed had met Kevin on a couple of occasions when Kevin was doing his soccer circus and their friendship had blossomed from there. What he saw in Kevin was the character who could ignite what he wanted to achieve at Fulham.

'He saw Kevin as the pied piper of Fulham. He had belief in him. What was needed was for Fulham to have belief in what Fayed saw for the club. That went through Kevin Keegan. They both believed in the future of the football club. That was the partnership.'

That attitude is not unlike the one the Football Association took into their talks with Keegan. They believed in him. There is just something about the man. It is like when Sir John Hall, then chairman and owner of Newcastle, went for this extraordinary little character. Hall said down a telephone line to Keegan: 'There are only two people who can save Newcastle United Football Club and we are talking to each other.'

It was exactly how Fayed felt about Keegan. And how the FA felt. They knew that the morale of the England side and the public was on the floor. It needed someone special. They wanted to reshape and transform English football (it was about time after years of talk about the same subject) and they saw Keegan as the starting point. The Newcastle call to him had come in March 1992. He left them in January 1997 and then took over at Fulham in September 1997. Now England were calling. A man of the nineties? It had been an amazing decade for him, a merry-go-round of highs and lows.

Keegan had a five-year plan for Fulham. To get the club from the Second Division to the Premiership. A few people laughed. He didn't. Nor did Mohammed Al Fayed. Rodford adds: 'There were a lot of cynics, there always had been at Fulham. But from day one Kevin had vision, belief and confidence. He did for Fulham what he did at Newcastle. He created excitement and expectation. He has this great knack of being able to make, not only the outside world, but people inside, believe that it will happen. It took him coming in to convince a lot of people that the Fulham revival was on. Mohammed was the catalyst and Kevin was the inspiration. You could see it happening before your eyes. The great thing about him is his belief. And he arrived having transformed Newcastle. He had done it.

'He has an aura around him that only a few people have. He is a leader, is charismatic, a man who does what he says. He is also incredibly down to earth. He will talk to the cleaner just like he does to the first team captain. He likes the involvement of others, especially the people he likes and trusts. He listens to other people's views but has the confidence himself to make the decisions. He is his own man. He has the ability to not get down about things, and insists that it can be done. He insisted that everyone at Fulham had to be confident about the future. He likes to win. I know that from the games of squash we had together.'

Keegan's transformation of Fulham can be judged by their attendances. When he took over the average home gate was 5,600. That quickly jumped to 8,100 and in the 1998–99 season, the winter when they won promotion to the First Division, the average attendance was 12,300. When he left it had risen to 15,000. 'We are the fastest growing club in the country as far as attendances are concerned,' says Rodford. Season ticket sales went from a few hundred to seven thousand. It was the love and respect for Keegan that Fulham took into their meetings with the FA.

On the other side the FA were just as determined. It was a fantastic position for Keegan to be in. On one side Fulham, owned by one of the richest men in the world, on the other our country. A tug of war with bells on. A tug of war with big money involved, although to be fair to Keegan that was not the issue. Chairman Geoff Thompson recalls the mood of the FA. He says: 'I was going away for three and a half weeks and left it to David Davies to make the approaches and the committee to discuss the situation. We had agreed on Keegan and I was happy with that. There were enough people in England and I was on the end of a telephone. Noel and Howard were also heavily involved and I was happy with that.

'What we liked about Keegan was that, among other things, he could rescue the dour position that Glenn had got us in. The England team were losing favour with the folk and it needed the right approach to win them back. We needed a man with charisma, of International experience and someone to lift the team and get results for us in the European Championships. The bonus was his patriotic nature. He loves England.'

Noel White was just as enthusiastic and the more he talked to his FA colleagues on the phone and face to face the more he grew to the liking and respecting of Keegan. He recalls: 'It did not disappoint me when Kevin said at the first meeting at his home that he would only help us out for four matches. When you make up your mind you want something you do not always get it at the first shake. We were prepared to accept his assistance for four matches and see how it developed. We were thinking about what happens in four matches? Or what would happen if we lost all four? Knowing Kevin he would have stood down and gone back to Fulham. There was no question of his being on probation. It was not like that. It was suck it and see for both of us.'

The third man involved in the early discussions with Keegan was Howard Wilkinson. He says: 'When Glenn Hoddle was sacked, and I have to say that Glenn's going was totally out of order, but in line with what happens today, it left us in a mess. The reasons for Glenn going, the circumstances, I was not happy with, but he had gone and the FA had to make decisions.

'There are two ways we could have gone. I told them that we were in the shite. We could stay in the shite but sort things out once and for all. It may have cost us two or three years, in other words the European Championships while someone held the job, me if you like or someone else, and worked with a younger coach while things were sorted properly. I said to the committee that we could let the dust settle and then tell the nation what we were doing. Or, try and rescue something from the ashes.

'That second option was a Herculean task. What we needed was for someone to come in and go ... whoosh ... I said that there isn't anyone out there who can do that, apart from Kevin. Who else has that impact, personality and charisma. When he came it was like John Wayne dropping in, the gunslinger in town. He was instantly recognisable, the popular brand. The FA had to tell the public whether they were going to go long term or go big. Rightly, they went big. We could not go in between, we either had to be black or white. Grey did not come into the equation. We needed Kevin's rapport with the public. Some people have an aura and reputation that is untouchable to the great English public, like Henry Copper, and Keegan has that. He is untouchable, the fans are behind him. He instantly gels everyone. We agreed that he would be the perfect person, if he was inclined to do it.

'If Kevin had said no then we would probably have had to go back to route one. It would not have been a problem in the long run but the immediate effect would have been dramatic. People would have been up in arms. Life is not simple any more and you can't ignore the demands. Everyone wants it now, there is no waiting, it is a fact of life and it is one of the problems the FA has had.'

The first meeting between the FA and Fulham was held on Tuesday, 16 February. David Davies had met Fayed and got permission to talk with Keegan, who had offered his services for four matches and now the loan had to be thrashed out and agreed. Davies, the FA's Company Secretary Nick Coward and financial director Michael Cunnah had all discussed the situation and were prepared for the Fulham party when they arrived just before 6.30 in the evening. For Fulham their negotiating team was led by Rodford, plus director Mike Griffiths and their legal expert Stuart Benson. The talks were long and hard. The FA say they ended at midnight, Fulham recall that they were still going strong at two in the morning. It doesn't matter. What was obvious was that Fulham were not about to roll over and pass Keegan on without a fight, even if it was for only a loan period.

'Mohammed Al Fayed had agreed for the FA to talk to Kevin, and Kevin had said that he would help them, it was up to us to make sure the loan deal was in the best interest of Fulham,' says Rodford. 'There were two negotiations taking place as the discussions went on. Our claim for compensation for the time that Kevin would be away from us on England duty. And his own salary while he was on England duty.' Rodford was completely hands on with both. Keegan had asked him to negotiate his own match to match fee with England. 'Yes, I acted as his agent if you like,' said Rodford.

'We wanted compensation and they had a different view,' he added. 'It was a question of what they wanted to pay and what we thought they should be offering for the loan.' It led to a series of phone calls as men disappeared in and out of different rooms inside Lancaster Gate. Davies rang other members of the committee to get their support to up the offer, and Rodford contacted Fayed by mobile phone to ask if he agreed with what was being discussed. Keegan, at home, was also rung by Rodford and Davies. He must have felt like an International sandwich.

Rodford adds: 'Mohammed likes to know. He is an interesting character. He is not hands on but demands to know what is going on. The stadium is his passion and does not influence the day to day running of the club. But this was serious for him because he had left the football side of his club completely to Keegan. He knew how valuable he was.'

The two teams took a break at midnight. Davies recalls how hungry he was because he had not eaten and went around the corner in Lancaster Gate to White's Hotel to grab a steak and chips. Rodford says: 'When the break in talks came we had reached the stage when we were preparing to walk away. The talks almost broke down. We did not want it to be seen as Fulham versus England but we were not going to be treated like Little Fulham. No way. We also did not want headlines saying Fulham say no because the media would have turned on Mohammed and that would not have been fair. He was in the background over this, certainly not in the front row of negotiations. It had to be right for both parties, that's all. We would have stayed there until six the following night to make sure we got what we wanted.

'Kevin Keegan was the most important person in our business, and they wanted him as their most important person. We had him, they wanted him. We would have walked away even though we were trying to be accommodating.'

When Davies went for his snack he picked up a couple of the next morning's first editions. He was not happy with the back-page headlines. 'Keegan to sign for three years', they screamed. Davies knew that to be completely wrong. It simply added to the pressure on the FA and a lot stuck in his throat as he chewed on his steak. The Fulham compensation still had to be resolved and the expectation of the public was growing. They wanted Keegan, the papers had virtually delivered him and he knew he had to produce. It eventually took two days to thrash out the deal with Fulham.

Davies says: 'When I went for that steak and chips my resolve was strong. My attitude was that I was determined to pull this thing through. I was not pleased with the first editions that night because I knew the stories not to be true. I know what I am responsible for and the leak could not have come from the FA because the people directly involved had been with me all night. I was not best pleased. I know now who talked to the media. It was not one of my people. Had it been I would have beaten them up.'

Davies called another meeting with Fulham the next day, Wednesday, 17 February, and this time the same men went to a different venue, a secret one. The All England club close to Fulham's training ground and near to the Wimbledon Tennis Courts. Davies chose to get away from the huge publicity that was building up around him. 'The previous night we had agreed the basis that a loan deal could work for Fulham and us,' said Davies. 'Before the meeting in the early afternoon I had put things into perspective with a radio interview but I knew we were under pressure.

'Fulham were concerned that their promotion challenge would suffer and had it gone pear-shaped there is no doubt where the blame would be placed.' Agreement was finally reached and Keegan, ironically, had travelled to London when both sides signed on the dotted line and shook hands. Davies adds: 'It was for four matches, that was the agreement and there had been no suggestion that it was anything else.'

On Thursday, 18 February 1999 the FA called a press conference at London's Metropole Hotel to announce that Kevin Keegan was to take over as the next England coach, but for four-matches only. Davies adds: 'I knew the reaction we would get. The expectation had been that Kevin would sign for three years and a four match loan was not what the public or the media wanted to hear. There was a huge turn out. We had held Terry Venables first press conference at Wembley, Glenn Hoddle's was called at the Royal Lancaster and now the Metropole was staging the start of the Keegan era.'

Keegan trained with his Fulham players on the morning of the 18th before travelling to central London for one of the big press conferences of his career. Davies describes his performance at that press conference as 'quite sensational. It was. Quite sensational. He was the star of the show and behaved like it. It was a master at work.'

It was Keegan at his best. Relaxed, confident, saying all the right things, smiling into the cameras and leaving behind the gloom of Hoddle's era. He was an open book. He talks a good game, does our Kevin. He spoke of the bulldog spirit needed by England, of passion and determination. Of pride and everything that has made up his character. He used Chelsea's World Cup defender Frank LeBoeuf to emphasise what has gone wrong with England. After the World Champions had eclipsed England 2–0 at Wembley in February LeBoeuf, never short of an opinion, said that England's famous fighting spirit was not evident at Wembley. Keegan, for ever the master motivator, pounced on that and told us that his England would not lack the fight that is needed to win matches and qualify for European and World Cup tournaments.

The FA were there. So was his new backroom staff, Arthur Cox and Derek Fazackerley, plus Howard Wilkinson, and Keegan left the door open for a return when his contract with Fulham ran out. He said: 'I really hope this job – and I think it is the biggest job in the world – becomes available again when I have finished at Craven Cottage. The only reason I have not taken it on full time is that it has become available at the wrong time for me and I will not break my promise to Fulham. I will not do that. Maybe I will get another chance but I am going to give this a real crack for four matches.'

It was exactly what the FA and the country needed. Keegan in full cry, the mighty mouse flying around the York Room in the basement of the Metropole as if guided by a spirit. In this mood Keegan is infectious. Forgotten was the prospect of the FA having to find someone else in four matches' time, or any shortcomings Keegan might have. They wanted a whirlwind and they had got one. He took everyone's breath away with the things he said and promised. It is almost difficult to describe him perfectly because here was a man, to use that famous football saying, on cloud nine. All what he said made sense. He was eloquent and, most importantly of all, he was persuasive. Had he been chatting up a girl she would have been swept off her feet and fallen madly in love with him. Just like the FA had.

It was a performance that offered hope. If you did not peer too deeply into the razzmatazz of Keegan's words and sayings, then you could only be impressed. There was hope for Paul Gascoigne, he said.

Hope for any player who proved at club level that he could produce on the big stage. Those England players in the squad Hoddle left behind and the ones with International ambition will have hung on his every word as they watched on television or listened on radio and then read him in the newspapers the following morning. If this was like one of his team talks, it is no wonder players want to play for KK.

Keegan had been called many things in his career. This was the messiah coming for English football.

Can't wait was a phrase he used a lot. I can't wait to get going, can't wait to pick my first squad, can't wait to meet all those quality players and can't wait for the first game against Poland. But he could wait for the job. He kept insisting that he was around for only four games, because of Fulham, and he had promised Mohamed Al Fayed that he would not desert what he had started in West London alongside the Thames. Significantly Keegan refused to discuss his relationship with Fayed, or the fact that he had been given permission to first talk to England, and then agreement to help them. 'He is a magnificent chairman, apart from saying that I do not want to talk about him,' he said moving quickly onto the next question.

The media, of course, were mentioned. After all, we had played a huge part in the downfall of Hoddle. Keegan said: 'I didn't and will not allow the media to put me off the job. All the words you write and things you say will not matter. We will write your stories for you.'

The FA went away happy, talking of the next four matches and thinking of what happens after Keegan. In a way they were still in limbo although David Davies quickly dismissed Keegan being a short-term appointment out of desperation. 'It is far from that,' he said. 'What we have is the best man for the job leading the country for the next four matches. That is not limbo. That is common sense.'

Everyone in the game, managers and players, were quoted as saying that Keegan was the best man for the job. Indeed the only man. No one voiced any disapproval or concern. Bobby Robson, the former England manager, perhaps got the nearest when he said that Keegan would have to keep control of a temperament that has sparked in the past. David Davies insisted that the search for a full time manager would go on, and that by the end of the season, after Keegan's short-term reign, significant possibilities would occur. All the usual names were put forward to replace Keegan when he left, sacked FA Chief Executive Graham Kelly said the only man for the job was Terry Venables (how strange when Kelly was in office when Venables was allowed to slip through the net following the European Championships in 1996). Keegan insisted that he would be going when the four matches were up. Definitely. No question, he said.

Deep down the FA did not believe him. David Davies held the opinion that the job would grab Keegan by the stomach and force him to take it full time, so too did Geoff Thompson and other members of the International Committee. There were worried thoughts too at Fulham. They had loaned out their manager. Would they ever get him back?

I will be back, Keegan had told them before dashing across London for his first press conference. And he ended the meeting with a comment that emphasised the concerns of Fulham, and hopes of England. 'My team against Notts County on Saturday will be ....' and he could not finish the sentence before the laughter exploded. But it did not sound right. The England coach talking about playing Notts County.

CHAPTER 6

I JUST COULD NOT SAY NO

Kevin Keegan had been in the home dressing room at Wembley many times before. As an England player he had felt the adrenalin, been inspired by the noise of the crowd tumbling down the sloping tunnel from the pitch and excited by the sound of the buzzer that sends the players into the last of their rituals before kick off. As captain of England he had listened to the late Sir Alf Ramsey and Don Revie and then Ron Greenwood giving their last instructions, encouraging and inspiring. As skipper he had done his own bit for the spirit, going round the other players, an arm around the shoulder here and a fist waved in front of their faces there. For a small man he has always been big on doing the right things.

He had also experienced the thrill of a Wembley cup final victory, the pure joy of the after-match celebration when the dressing room was transformed into a swirl of champagne, happy faces and songs.

This was different. This was Keegan the England coach, standing in front of his players, moving from one to another, listening to the crowd noise as it became louder when someone opened the dressing room door and closed it again quickly, watching individuals he had never managed before doing their own thing and standing back in awe as that same buzzer went and the players jumped into a huddle, encouraging and shouting instructions. It was then that Keegan wished he was still playing. The memories rolled back, of his first time in the famous dressing room, the thrill of pulling on the England shirt for the first time and the nerves that ran through his body as left the dressing room behind and blinked his way up the tunnel into the daylight.

'It is when that buzzer goes and the players are together that a manager can feel lonely,' he says. 'That is a special moment for the players. Their moment if you like. The manager's work has finished for the time being. In a way you are left behind.'

Keegan let his players go on that Saturday in March 1999 and stayed behind for a moment, gathering the bits and pieces he wanted to take with him up on to the pitch and that funny little bunch of seats that acts as the dugout at Wembley. He knew from experience that none of the players would hear his shouts and screams from the touchline. At Wembley the players are too far away from the coach. The dressing room was suddenly quiet. Keegan allowed himself one last look before he stepped outside. His players were already at the top going onto the pitch and he could hear the noise rumble around as the crowd realised the players were emerging. It was like thunder spreading. This was his first game of four as England coach, a European Championship tie against Poland, a match England had to win. He was confident of winning, he always is, just as he was sure that after four games he would hand over to someone else and go back permanently to Fulham. 'Whatever happens I am going to enjoy the next four games,' he said to himself as he too emerged into daylight.

Kevin Keegan's life and career were to change with the two-minute walk from the top of the tunnel around the pitch in front of the fans to his spot on the halfway line. It was a walk that he would never forget.

Keegan was soon spotted. Then he was lost in a sea of cameras, officials, security guards, substitutes and backroom staff. Somewhere in the huddle was the man who was going to save English football. When you could see him through the throng his smile spread from ear to ear and he waved continuously to the supporters who were cheering his every step, he stopped on three occasions to shake some hands and then waved high into the main stand as he searched for family and friends in the sea of expectant faces. Keegan did not need to look far. Everyone was his friend that Saturday afternoon. Everyone was smiling and laughing. It was a welcome fit for a Royal happening outside Buckingham Palace or the American President on his election walkabout. The two-minute walk took a little longer that day.

Poland were beaten before a ball was kicked. And Keegan had made up his mind about his future before the first of his four caretaker games had even started. He wanted this job. He fancied it. People power had influenced him more than anything he could have imagined. The Geordie folk up in Newcastle had been fantastic to him and he would always have a special relationship with them. But this was England. His country. And the message Keegan was getting was that he could not say no.

'It just took my breath away,' he says now. 'I hadn't thought about my reception. I wanted the team to be shouted to victory and for everyone at Wembley to enjoy themselves. The crowd, the players and the staff. It was their day, not mine. But when I walked out I felt their warmth and kindness. I felt they wanted something special and felt responsible for that. I definitely felt that I just could not turn it down, turn the people down. It is difficult to describe because until you have been England coach and walked out at Wembley for the first time no one can explain what emotions happen to you. It is a moment I will never forget. It was the moment that made up my mind for me that, somehow, I wanted to take the job.'

Saturday 27 March, as the emotions engulfed him, was certainly not the time for Keegan to worry about the complications that would come with him changing his mind.

Apart from the expectancy of the crowd, there was some hope and glory being played in the directors' box too. David Davies sat at kick-off time thinking back at the events of the last couple of weeks. It had been a roller-coaster ride of emotions, meetings and press conferences. The FA had the man they wanted, the people's champion, but he knew defeat against Poland would blow the whole things sky-high. No European Championships, no forward planning, certainly no Keegan.

He recalls: 'The atmosphere of the match had changed dramatically. For the good. Everyone seemed happy. In the build-up I deliberately did not go anywhere near the training ground at Bisham Abbey, or the team hotel at Burnham Beeches, as I had done every day under Venables and Hoddle, because I wanted to let the new set-up just be, well, new. I did not want to cramp anyone's style. I wanted to hear from others what the new set-up was like. From the reports I got it was clear that it went brilliantly.'

Just before kick-off Mohammed Al Fayed had rushed up to Davies and wrapped an enormous scarf around his neck. 'This is my lucky Fulham scarf, wear it and Kevin and England will win, Fayed said to me,' recalls Davies. 'I was just about to go on to the pitch for the presentations when he came over. He said I had to wear it. I eventually sat on it as it would have seemed odd, me sitting in the directors' box with a huge Fulham scarf on.'

Fulham Managing Director Neil Rodford watched and feared the worst. 'Glenn Hoddle had become media and people unfriendly. Keegan was the perfect choice to lift the nation. We knew that. He was sexy for the country. He is a fantastic communicator and I feared, deep down, that the call would be too great. You could see as he walked around the pitch that he was enjoying himself. He felt at home, that was obvious. He had insisted that he could do both matches and when he made his decision to us all the coaching staff were involved and told what was going on. While he had been on England duty Paul Bracewell, Frank Sibley and I rang him all the time to ask him questions about the club and the forthcoming match. The plan was that he would come back to us after the matches but we had to keep in touch in the days building up to them. Keegan has tremendous mental energy, he is a dynamo, someone who can easily cope with more things in his life than the normal guy. He is inspirational. We would not be where we are today without him.'

Noel White liked what he saw as he waited for the game to kick off. The talk in the banqueting hall before the game was that the International Committee had done well that they had got the right man. There were pats on the back all round. White says: 'The starting point for Keegan was that the whole country liked him. He was an inspiration after the "down" of Hoddle. There was no risk on that count. Everyone was relaxed and it felt right. But all that does not get results and what had all those other qualities about him got to do with management?' The FA were about to find out.

There had been one or two surprises in Keegan's first squad. Chris Sutton, of Blackburn, who had fallen out with Hoddle and completely ignored after refusing to play for the Under 21 side, was quickly whisked back. There was a place for Arsenal's midfield star Ray Parlour, who had not made the World Cup squad despite having a superb season, and Andy Cole, the player Keegan signed from Bristol City, turned into a goal-scoring sensation and then sold to Manchester United, was also in. The mood in the build-up to the game was extraordinary. It was completely positive with not a doubt coming from Keegan. Typical of Keegan's comments came when he examined the first injuries he was to suffer as England coach. 'Whatever side I send out, it will be fantastic,' he said. 'I have two fit strikers, Alan Shearer and Andy Cole, not bad bare bones, are they.' Every word was positive, every word used by an adoring media.

What a marvellous relief to cover this England after the secrets and whispers of the Hoddle era, was typical of the comments made by journalists after Keegan's first couple of press conferences. He talked of the agony of 1973 when he was on the bench when Poland got a 1–1 draw at Wembley and knocked Sir Alf Ramsey's England out to qualify themselves for the 1974 World Cup, and the newspapers responded with 'Revenge' headlines. Anyone unhappy with Keegan's appointment, any doubters, were washed aside by a football public, and media, in overdrive for the man everyone hailed as the saviour of English football. Dangerous stuff? Perhaps. But it is what the country wanted and most of the newspapers got completely behind Keegan. You could tell he enjoyed the build-up. He smiled all the way through the conferences, offering bits of information that would make even more headlines and talking in glowing terms about the players.

He volunteered one bit of information that did backfire on him. Keegan revealed during the week that he had invited a 'motivator' into the camp, an eccentric Scotsman called Watt Nicol, one night to entertain the players. It is nothing spooky or weird he quickly explained as we groaned in anticipation of more Eileen Drewery-type goings on. It wasn't that bad although the motivator turned out to be someone who eventually milked the situation and his moment of glory. He even called a press conference when he had gone home to reveal what he had done and said to the players. Keegan didn't reveal his name but Nicol soon did and could not resist the temptation of much needed publicity and even offered exclusive interviews, through a business agent, to anyone who wanted to listen. It was someone whom Keegan did not invite back into the camp. It was a mistake because it was something the media pounced on as a vulnerability but the coach argued that the players were entertained and enjoyed the evening. No harm done. Although I suspect that the coach will put it down as one of few off-pitch mistakes.

The morning of the match was greeted with huge headlines, pages and pages of 'come on Kev' material and pictures of Keegan holding the England flag proudly aloft. He was rightly proud to be there and we, the media, were delighted to have him. Victory was vital. Defeat unthinkable. The result, as they say, was never in doubt. You just get feelings about certain matches and this was one of them. I recall Graham Taylor having to play Poland, again, in a vital match and bumping into him in the grounds at the training headquarters in Bisham. 'You will definitely win,' I told him and that is how I felt about Keegan's first match. It was a foregone conclusion as far as I was concerned.

Walking up to Wembley on match day the feeling only got stronger. I know this is easy to say in hindsight but you will just have to take my word for it. And so it proved. Keegan's first team for the convincing 3–1 victory was: David Seaman (Arsenal), Gary Neville (Manchester United), Graeme Le Saux (Chelsea), Tim Sherwood (Spurs), Martin Keown (Arsenal), Sol Campbell (Spurs), David Beckham (Manchester United), Paul Scholes (Manchester United), Alan Shearer (Newcastle), Andy Cole (Manchester United), Steve McManaman (Real Madrid). Ray Parlour (Arsenal), Philip Neville (Manchester United) and Jamie Redknapp (Liverpool) came on for McManaman, Beckham and Scholes respectively.

Paul Scholes of Manchester United was the star of the show with a hat trick, two goals coming in the first half and a third shortly before the end. Scholes is an interesting character. Shy and quiet off the pitch, he changes character on it. He is fiercely competitive, tackles like a man possessed and has this wonderful quality of being in the right place at the right time. He also never swaps his shirt at the end of the game. While teammates exchange their colours with opponents, Scholes always politely says no. 'It is just something I have promised myself,' he says. 'I have never done it and never will. I keep all my England and United shirts.'

Keegan would not have swapped Scholes for anyone or anything that day, nor could he have wished for more. He raised his arms aloft at the arrival of every goal and spent most of the match standing just alongside the England bench. He felt at home and the walk back to the dressing room only cemented his thoughts that, yes, this was the job for him. He did not go around the old greyhound track this time, striding out instead across the pitch itself and heading for the tunnel. He stopped to hug and thank each one of his players and staff for their help and by the time he got to the entrance to the tunnel the crowd were on their feet. Smiling faces, an explosion of cheers, just like when Keegan had emerged two hours previously, the people had a big effect on him. He loved every minute of it.

The England dressing room was a happy place. Noise, players laughing, staff moving around making jokes and enjoying an after-match beer. After a quick 'well done' speech Keegan was led by FA Press Officer Steve Double to the many interviews the England coach has to face after an International, television, radio and written press. His message to them all was that he had enjoyed it but give all the credit, he insisted, to the players. He was tempted to say, but didn't, that he had already made up his mind to take the job full time.

While Keegan gave his interviews the FA's top brass were enjoying their after-match meal and drinks. While chairman Geoff Thompson wined and dined Polish officials, offering commiserations, he thought about Keegan. 'I wondered if the pendulum had swung further in our favour,' he recalls. David Davies knew it had the moment he first saw Keegan after the victory. 'We met in the banqueting hall and I offered my hand and congratulations, and then I looked into his eyes,' says Davies. 'I thought to myself, "He is thrilled." It was obvious. After all, he is a human being before anything else. He had been asked to do two things, win the game and lift the morale of the players and the nation. He had done that with bells on. He had also lifted the Football Association, there is no question about that. Yes, we were relieved, because victory had been the bottom line and let us not forget that we, as an organisation, had been through a lot. There was strain. Keegan had lifted it.'

Keegan, after all the press conferences, chats, hugs and kisses from well-wishers, eventually went home to Newcastle. It was a job done. The job he wanted. As yet, there had been no indication to anyone that he had already told himself 'yes.' Davies appeared on Sir David Frost's television chat programme the next morning. 'You look knackered,' Frost said to him. 'Knackered but elated,' said Davies. 'I was excited because "it" had come off. Davies adds: 'Later in the day I spoke with Kevin on the phone and knew how excited he was.'

Another man who discovered just how excited Keegan had become was Neil Rodford of Fulham. 'I knew him well and when we spoke on the Sunday I knew that it had started to go towards England. I talked with him on the phone and he said how much he had enjoyed it. He used the word fantastic. I knew in our conversation that part of Kevin had already gone to England. Yes, I knew we had probably lost him. The pull of the Poland thing had been too great for him. He loved Fulham, there was no question about that but, deep down, he loved England more. I said well done and we hung up. Shit, I thought.'

Keegan went back to masterminding Fulham's progress towards promotion from the Nationwide Second Division to the First. It was a seamless change back, just as he had assured Fulham that it would be. Inside him, however, the feeling was not the same. He still insisted that he would not walk out on Fulham. No way. He was adamant about that and here is an interesting chink in his makeup. Keegan has always been portrayed as a man of his word and yet he kept assuring the Fulham supporters and chairman Mohammed Al Fayed that he was committed to the cause and the five-year plan they had together.

This is perhaps one of the most interesting periods in this particular Keegan story. He loved Fulham but clearly loved England more. A big part of him wanted to keep working for Fulham and take them to the Premiership. He knew he could do it. But a bigger part of him wanted to take the England job. Yet he still kept saying in public that he would not desert Fulham. At that stage, and it was delicate with the Fulham fans wondering what would happen, he should not have been so insistent that he would not switch. After all, they were paying him £750,000 a year, more than £400,000 a year more than Glenn Hoddle had received as England coach.

After Fulham had clinched promotion with a Craven Cottage victory over Gillingham in April 1999 he held court in the club's tiny offices upstairs in the famous old Cottage and said: 'I came to Fulham to do a job. It is in my hands, it is my decision and I am staying. Fulham are in my blood, it has been like that since day one. I have to have that feeling. I have to wake up in the morning excited about what I am doing. It is a gut feeling. I do not think you can have the same feeling with England. England comes and goes.

'Managers miss the day by day involvement because you get just twelve games a year. I would be no different. I would miss the day by day thing too much.

'I believe I am a winner. Mohammed Al Fayed has put some trust in me and he wants me to do here what I did with Newcastle. That is what I intend to do. People trust me at Fulham and I will not let them down. I can guarantee that I will still be here at the start of next season in the First Division.' The Fulham fans, the directors and Fayed read those comments with a great deal of interest.

The next twist, a major development, came later in the month when England went to play Hungary in Budapest. It was a friendly that Hoddle had wanted but not many others. There were also concerns about the safety surrounding the match with Hungary being close to the border of the war raging in Yugoslavia. There were weekly talks between the Football Association and the Foreign Office and at one stage it looked as though the match would be called off. A number of players, including Tottenham skipper Sol Campbell, voiced their concerns. Keegan, as always, remained upbeat. He wanted to go, even if his squad was eventually decimated by injury and withdrawals. It was. Manchester United's young defender Wes Brown was called up, and played in the game, as did Kevin Phillips, the scoring sensation at Sunderland, who partnered Alan Shearer up front.

One man who wanted the game on was David Davies, the FA's acting Chief Executive who had done all the negotiating for Keegan and who knew that going away with the FA and the players would be a good carrot for Keegan. Davies explains: 'There was a lot of discussion about the match. Should we go or not? Glenn had wanted it but the closer the game came there were reservations. I wanted the game on because I wanted Kevin to go. I wanted him to enjoy the experience, of travelling and being part of the family atmosphere and talking to other managers about players, availability and, yes, drop-outs.

'I warned Kevin before we left that we would get questions about his England future. That we were coming to a head. I knew he would remain positive and I thought that perhaps he might say that he was still thinking about things.'

Keegan did more than that. Out of the blue after the 1–1 draw he announced that he definitely would be taking the job, and that he wanted to become the full-time England manager. It took everyone by surprise, certainly the media and the FA committee, the players (skipper Alan Shearer was told of the news at his after-match press conference) but not perhaps Davies. He had been working cleverly for this moment. And certainly not Neil Rodford of Fulham, who had sat at home watching the game and then the drama unfold. He knew that the decision he listened to had been inevitable.

The journalists who sat in the conference room at the Nep Stadium in Budapest had no idea what was going on in other parts of the ground. We had no information that Keegan had been talking positively about the job to radio and television. He had apparently indicated strongly that he was ready to take the job. It was only when Keegan arrived at the press conference with us alongside the FA's Steve Double that the story really unfolded. As Keegan was talking and answering questions about the game Double passed me a small slip of paper.

On it was written 'Ask him about the job.' Double had heard what Keegan had said to TV and radio and didn't want us, the written media, to miss out. I did, and Keegan said that he had made up his mind and that he wanted to become the full-time manager of England. The story had hardened up and it was rapidly relayed back to London. England and Fulham fans, indeed all football fans, woke up the next morning to headlines saying just that. 'Kev Says Yes' was a typical banner headline. Confused? The Fulham fans were.

Davies recalls: 'I thought he would say that he was loving the job when he was asked the question. He didn't. He said that he wanted it. By the time he got to the written press conference he had hardened up his thoughts and was even more enthusiastic. There had been no meeting between the FA and Kevin in Hungary. There had been certainly no indication from him that he was going to reveal all. But he decided that, having been with the players for three days abroad, it was make your mind up time. He was asked the question and answered it in the best possible way for us. It was an amazing night.'

Keegan said: 'I have taken the job, that is my decision. The FA have offered it to me full time and I have said yes, but please give me time to finalise what comes next. The bottom line is that I have made up my mind. What has convinced me to say yes now? The reaction of the players. They have been magnificent. I want to do this job and be with them. It is time to stop playing games. Sometimes you want your cake and to eat it too. A decision had to be made. I have just made it.'

The decision had been such a surprise that the FA Committee, sitting on the coach waiting for the players to finish showering and changing so that they could be whisked back the airport by police motorbike outriders, had no idea what was happening. Noel White remembers the moment Davies got onto the coach like it was yesterday. White says: 'David stepped on and said to me, "You will never believe this, Kevin wants the job." I said, "He has got it," and David added, "No, he wants it full time." We had no idea that a decision like that was coming. As we travelled home I did a lot of thinking and was pleased with what had happened because it is the way we wanted to go. It wasn't "Thank God, we have got him." But we were pleased that he had made up his mind.'

Geoff Thompson recalls: 'I always felt that once he had got the feel of the job he would like it. Him walking out against Poland was a huge turning point for us. That is when the pendulum swung. He is an emotional man and when the crowd took the roof off for him it made a huge impact on him. But the plan was always four matches and then, suddenly, in Hungary he said that he wanted it. There had been no meeting with him in Budapest although I had told David Davies that it would be impossible to get to the end of the four match period without knowing a decision. I said that we were in a major competition qualifying group and we needed to know. I said to Davies "You know him, you talk to him." But there had been no pressure placed on Kevin in Hungary to prompt his public acceptance. David had the confidence to talk to him and I am great believer in delegation. I believe that if you have someone on your staff better equipped than you to do the job, then get him to do it. David always had the responsibility, with our blessing, to do the talking and negotiating with Keegan and Fulham. I did not interfere, only kept in touch. David had the confidence.'

After Keegan had given all of his press conferences and was walking out of the Nep Stadium he turned to Davies and said: 'It is up to you now.' Davies knew what that meant. More negotiations with Fulham, more talks into the night, more press conferences. Davies says: 'I talked to Kevin all the way home on the flight. I knew that Fulham would have been caught by surprise by his statements. They would not have known he was going to come out that strong.'

The next step for Davies was to contact Mohammed Al Fayed again. The England party had got home in the early hours of the Thursday morning and by lunchtime Davies was on the phone again to his friend at Harrods, Laurie Mayer.

It was hugely ironic that at the very time Keegan was admitting he wanted the job that Sir Alf Ramsey, the only man to win the World Cup for England, should die in a Suffolk nursing home. Ramsey was never treated properly by the FA. They kicked him out without thought, respect or real gratitude for what he had done, but that is another story. Keegan said he wanted to go full time with the same feelings and passion for the job as Alf, even if he could show those emotions much more than Ramsey was able to bring himself to do. But winning the World Cup is the ultimate for any England coach, not just qualifying for it. And Keegan was no different. He had said yes, desperate to become the second man in our history to hold aloft the World Cup.

He explained later in more detail what had been running through his mind. 'I thought the players needed a signal from me. We had vital games against Sweden and Bulgaria coming up and getting to the European Championships together is the vital step we must take. I didn't want doubts in their minds. I think we can take it forward a pace if we dig in together and know where we are heading, and that, ultimately, has to be the World Cup. The players and I know that we should be right at the top of the league, not floundering around in a poor place in the world ranking. England belongs and should be at the top.' We had heard all the tub-thump before, of course, but no one talks a better game than Keegan. The FA, for instance, believed him and were delighted with his comments in Hungary. The only people not deeply surprised that this was it, were Davies, Mohammed Al Fayed and Rodford.

It emerged later that Keegan had spoken to his chairman a week before Hungary, a few days before leaving for Budapest. The England job had been bugging Keegan and he opened his heart to the Harrods owner. Keegan admits: 'Had he said you are not going anywhere and I am going to sue the FA then I would have stayed. He told me that he did not want me to stay if I was going to be unhappy. But I was never unhappy at Fulham, so it was just difficult to make the break. In the end it was my heart that told me. I followed my heart.'

David Davies – and I have to emphasise that he was the key figure in the whole getting, signing and securing of Keegan – knew that he had to contact Fayed and the new contact was made on the Thursday following England's return from their 1–1 draw. After Keegan's statement the scoreline seemed almost irrelevant.

Davies says: 'Mohammed Al Fayed's latest attempt to secure a British passport had been turned down that morning so it was not the best of timings, but I knew that it could not wait. I rang in the morning and asked if I could return perhaps the next day.' Once again Fayed acted quickly, inviting Davies over there and then and, once more, Davies slipped down the side road and in through door ten and up the same escalators. This time it was slightly different. Before the FA had wanted Keegan on loan, this time Keegan had wanted the FA. Davies recalls:

'I went past a group of ITV people and their camera crews, who were waiting for some reaction from him after the passport thing. They did not react to me and I am not sure what they thought I was doing.' Fayed kept Davies waiting longer than before. 'When we did see each other I insisted on seeing him on my own,' Davies says. 'The FA had to be seen to be doing things in the right way and I wanted to explain to him every detail. I told him that Kevin wanted to come and that he had said that it was always up to Kevin.' The two men chatted for fifteen minutes only before Fayed told Davies that Keegan was his gift to the nation. Not exactly a gift, of course, because there was compensation for the two years left on Keegan's contract.

'It was Mohammed Al Fayed's present with a price tag,' said Davies. 'He told me about his passport before the meeting ended.' Davies then went into the dining room where the Fulham delegation was waiting. There was a brief chat and the two parties agreed to start negotiating for compensation in a couple of days' time. 'Then I left and slipped away back to the FA,' said Davies. But the job was done. When Davies eventually sat at his own desk and sifted through the letters and messages he thought about Kevin Keegan a lot. 'I realised that at no stage had we said to him, "Here is the job, do you want it?" It had just been progress and a situation where we always wanted him and eventually he wanted us. It was a coming together.'

Fulham asked for £2 million compensation for Kevin Keegan and eventually got £500,000. Mohammed Al Fayed explains: 'What is £500,000? It is nothing, peanuts. It does not buy you a player. I said to the FA, you take Kevin Keegan from me and give me £500,000 in return. How can I replace him? Tell me, please?' The fact that Fayed let Keegan go in the first place, and then for so little money, indicates that he knew that he had no choice. The criticism he would have faced, and the media received, was not worth it. But there was still a lot of haggling done between Fulham and the FA. And the half a million took a lot of squeezing out of Lancaster Gate.

Fulham Managing Director Neil Rodford explains the traumas that his club went through. 'Kevin is his own man and speaks from the heart. We did not expect the Hungary thing but when he said it I knew that he meant it. There was no going back. We had lost our man. When he returned to us from Budapest he explained that he asked the FA to come forward with a proposal for us as well as him. We had been considering all our options before this. Would we lose him, should he go upstairs and like any other business we were looking for the alternatives. Mohammed kept saying to us, "Relax, let Kevin make his own decision." He was adamant that it had to be decided by Kevin and not us. If Kevin stayed, great, and if he decided that he wanted to go we would shake his hand and say thanks because he had done a great job for Fulham. A fantastic job.'

Fulham and the FA say the negotiations for Keegan were smooth. However, Fulham reveal that there were long and complicated issues surrounding the finances. As with most negotiations there were different objectives. Indeed, Fulham even considered the prospect of taking the Football Association to court over the money they believed Keegan was worth. They were advised that by going to court they would get more compensation than the Football Association were prepared to hand over.

Neil Rodford, the Fulham Managing Director, explains: 'They were long and complicated negotiations. Basically, we could not agree. Mohammed said that the people he wanted to negotiate for him were myself, Mark, Tim and Stuart. Bill and Andy Muddyman, the previous owners who still own 25 per cent of the club, were also involved. Our attitude was that even though Kevin was going the thing had to be done properly. We were definitely hardball. We had lost our man. We were no longer loaning, we were losing our man. The sum of our financial risk was £30 million, that is how much Mohammed Al Fayed had invested in the club since he took over. Kevin had been at the helm of that investment and now someone was taking it out. That was a serious risk and we wanted compensating for it.'

The Football Association team was led by David Davies. 'We were a long way apart at one stage,' said Rodford. 'There was a serious difference between what we wanted and what they were offering. We agreed to not agree.' Meetings broke up, phone calls were made mid-meetings to Fayed and the FA International Committee members, and it went on for weeks rather than days. All this talk with the public believing that the Keegan deal was done and dusted.

Rodford explains the possibility of Fulham taking the Football Association to court like this: 'We discussed many times what might happen if there was no agreement. We took advice from a guy called Stuart Benson, who is an expert on sporting legal situations, and he told us that we would get more compensation in the courts than the Football Association were prepared to offer. We thought about that hard. It was a possibility at one stage. I suppose deep down we knew there had to be an agreement because a court case would have been absolute turmoil for English football, Mohammed Al Fayed, Fulham and the Football Association. We knew we had a strong case.' It is interesting that Mohammed Al Fayed did not want to go to court with Keegan. He too thought it would have been too messy.

Rodford adds: 'It was an interesting situation because England had made a statement that they were going to appoint Kevin Keegan and here we were trying to find a way to release him properly and legally. It was Mohammed's money at risk, his future if you like. Would his ambitions be fulfilled without Keegan? We had to take everything into consideration. It was a stressful period and the FA were very much aware that we were thinking of going to court. It was not just Kevin's salary that we were taking into account, but the risk element for us. They were taking away our lead player. We were also running a football club while all this went on.

'Every newspaper, television station and radio channel ran the story all day every day. But they had no idea of the drama behind the scenes.' Keegan himself was not involved in any of the talks, well, not directly. Rodford kept him in touch with daily bulletins. Keegan also spoke to Davies. 'Kevin and I are friends and had been through a lot,' says Rodford. 'It was only right that he should know how the talks were going. We trust each other. He was always professional with me and gave me credit and I am grateful for his attitude. There were times when it did become fraught and emotions ran high. That was obvious because there was an extraordinary tug of war going on behind the scenes.'

Fulham at this stage were unable to say anything official to their supporters or players, and there was no compensation from the Football Association, and therefore no statement for the waiting country. Rodford adds: 'I felt sorry for Kevin because everyone was asking him and it was not resolved. I remember Mohammed saying to Kevin once: 'This is your spiritual home, it is where you belong.'

But Keegan, of course, thought he now belonged to England. He felt part of the FA set up and wanted the job desperately. It was a huge relief to him when there was finally agreement between Fulham and the FA. There was no sudden decision, or climb down by one party, they simply realised that, somehow, somewhere, they had to resolve the saga. A figure of £500,000 was settled on, which, in fact, was not really satisfactory to either side. Rodford says: 'In the end we made recommendations, we discussed it with Mohammed and they agreed it with their people. It was a one-off payment with no spin-offs. We did discuss extra money if England qualified for the European Championships, but that was not the point for us.

'The final break, the handover, came with the termination of

Kevin's contract, and he started work with the FA the next day.' Rodford, who had negotiated Keegan's fee for the on-loan period, had nothing to do with the salary that was eventually paid to the new England coach. Keegan and his own business advisers did that and it was agreed that he should receive £1 million a year, £250,000 more than he was getting at Fulham and considerably more than Glenn Hoddle received.

Keegan was later to make an interesting observation. He said: 'Had there been other candidates, then Fulham would not have been paid compensation by the FA.' Noel White, chairman of the International Committee, answers that. He says: 'It is a fair point, but a hypothetical one. At the time Kevin Keegan was the number one choice.'

There had been another twist, another difficult time for Fulham in the Keegan saga. It led to a temporary fall out between Rodford and Keegan. Fulham's last game of the season was at home to Preston and, as Division Two Champions, there was to be, quite rightly, a celebration. Fulham were worried that Keegan's presence at the game might anger some of the fans. They were concerned that a section of the Craven Cottage crowd who had come to enjoy themselves, and had also heard Keegan say he would never desert them, and then change his mind, might look upon him as something of a traitor. Rodford says:

'Since the England thing started Kevin had surprised us with some public statements we had not been expecting, like in Hungary. Then just before the official break he went on television and spoke about the England job. He was only being honest and when he was asked the question at a forum he simply told the truth. Yes he had been asked, yes he wanted it and yes, he would be going.'

On the Friday before the Preston game Rodford and Mohammed Al Fayed visited Fulham's training ground to discuss the situation with Keegan. Rodford said: 'We knew that some of our fans were disappointed and I told Kevin that, on a public safety point of view, I thought that it was best that he did not attend the game. Kevin did not like that. He thought I had communicated it wrongly. He said that we had been together for two years and that I had not handled the situation well. Yes, we had an argument. He said that I was wrong to say it was a risk if he went to the game, I said that it was a risk if he did, and I was thinking only of the safety of supporters.

'But Kevin was adamant. He said he was big enough to take any flak and wanted to attend. He related it to Newcastle. He said that he felt the parting with Newcastle was wrong because he had never gone back to say goodbye. He was determined to say goodbye to the Fulham people.' The dispute continued back at Craven Cottage in Rodford's office. 'Eventually Kevin got his way,' says Rodford. 'Mohammed agreed after I had spoken to him.' It proved to be the right decision. The party was not ruined, Keegan ran the team and the crowd gave him a great send-off. Keegan and Fayed went on to the pitch at the end of the game for a lap of honour, linking arms and Fayed draped in that 'lucky' Fulham scarf. 'It was one of the best decisions we made because the Keegan era ended as it should have done. With a warmth from the people who had enjoyed having him. There were a few who were bitter that he had not seen through what he said he would do, but it did not spoil things in any way,' said Rodford.

Mohammed Al Fayed also enjoyed it. Rodford again: 'In a way he had been more mature about it than any of us. He had told Kevin, 'Come on, let's show that we are together.'

Keegan waved goodbye, the fans waved back and when he finally disappeared down the tunnel with one last look over his shoulder another era in this extraordinary little man's life had ended. The biggest one was about to start. There was still the compensation to resolve between Fulham and the FA but Keegan knew that he had managed his last game for a club he had fallen in love with. He enjoyed it down by the Thames and honestly believed that he would see though his five-year plan with them. All the things he said about

Fulham, before and after the England thing began, he had said with honesty. When he said that he would never quit on Fulham while under contract he meant it. It is just that not even the passions of Keegan realised how big the pull of his country would be.

The irony is that Fulham were just about to negotiate a new contract with him when the England situation broke. Rodford confirms. 'Yes, Kevin was happy to extend his contract with us and talks were about to open. We knew how important Kevin Keegan was to the future and dream of this football club. Then along came the England thing.' As one Fulham official said: 'If Hoddle had not opened his big mouth then this would never have happened. Keegan would still be with us.' That, undoubtedly, is true.

Fulham were inundated with agents asking about the job as Keegan's replacement. 'I was staggered by the number of high-profile men who said they would be interested. I did not think that they would be available but they made it known that they would love the job,' said Rodford. Who next was discussed by the Fulham board and they considered another high-profile name. 'But Ruud Gullit was never on, as was written many times,' says Rodford. 'We asked the players what they thought and in the end we went for continuity. We thought that had we gone high profile then it might have rocked the boat. Paul Bracewell had been learning under Kevin and in the end he was the unanimous choice. We knew that in Paul we had someone with managerial pedigree. Only time will tell if we have made the right decision. At the time it was the right decision. We had achieved massive growth and we needed to keep building.'

Keegan, at last, was freed to do his own thing with England. Two matches down, many more to go before he could call himself a successful England manager. You have to qualify for European Championships and World Cups, and be successful at the tournaments, to have that alongside your name. But he was confident. Oh boy, was he confident. And looking forward to it more than anything in his life. One interesting thing. There was never any serious talking done by the Football Association to Keegan about his strengths as a manager. Strengths as a man, yes, but not strengths, or weaknesses for that matter, as a manager. They had employed Kevin Keegan the Messiah for £1 million a year, and nothing else. He had been the perfect man in the perfect place when Hoddle put his mouth in it. For instance, not once was Keegan asked about tactics or how he likes to play the game. New FA Chairman Geoff Thompson confirms: 'Tactics and me do not go together. They were never discussed and it would have been difficult for me.'

It was those tactics, or alleged lack of them, that were to soon haunt Keegan and the FA.

CHAPTER 7

THE SEDUCTION OF KEVIN KEEGAN, FAYED STYLE

There was one man who could have ruined the England and Kevin Keegan dream. One man who could have made the whole thing impossible. Mohammed Al Fayed is not a football man. He has grown to love Fulham without, I am sure, knowing a great deal about the sport. He sits proudly in his directors' box seat at Craven Cottage, he never misses a home game, and has huge ambitions for the club. Keegan told him that it was possible for Fulham to be in the Premiership within five years and he believed him and will continue to chase the dream.

He would have preferred Keegan to have stayed with him. He trusted him, liked him and respected him. More, importantly, he let him do as he wanted with his football club. Fayed bought it and, as in all his business interests, he delegated. Keegan was his appointment and very definitely his man.

Why then did he not fight harder to keep him? Why did this ruthless businessman not take on the Football Association? It would have been messy and generated huge anti publicity for him, but Fayed has proved in the past that he is not worried about a scrap, in public or private. Had Mohammed Al Fayed said to Keegan, 'You are under contract and going nowhere' Keegan would have stayed put. Either that or he would have had to walk out. The England coach does not often talk about Fayed and only says things like: 'He is a damn good chairman and apart from that I'm not getting involved.'

Around the time that the FA were pushing for Keegan, Fayed was once more appealing to the Government for a British passport. He has tried, appealed and fought for one and each time been turned down. There were many cynics who suggested that releasing Keegan to the country without fuss was his direct attempt at a swap deal. I will give you Keegan, you give me the passport I want. Fayed strongly denies such thoughts and the FA, interestingly, are split on the idea.

Chairman Geoff Thompson says: 'I was not surprised Fayed said yes when we asked for Keegan full time. He is a political animal. He must have thought, 'I will give Kevin Keegan to the country, and perhaps I will get my passport.' There was probably something in that. But I do believe that he would have found it difficult to stand in Kevin's way once he had made it clear that he wanted the job.'

But Noel White, chairman of the FA's International Committee, denies any suggestion of a passport-for-Keegan swap. He says: 'When we were negotiating with Fulham for Kevin Keegan and compensation figures were bandied about, it was suggested that Fayed might let him go for nothing because it could lead to a passport for him. As far as I am concerned that never came into it. No mention of it was ever made to us, it was simply not an issue. It was a straight forward settlement.'

There was only one thing for it as far as I was concerned. Go and ask the man himself. So, like David Davies, I rang Laurie Mayer and arranged an appointment with Mohammed Al Fayed. Like Davies I slipped down the side street, into door ten and up the stairs to the fifth floor. At the top of the escalators, like Davies, I doubled back on myself to find the big impressive wooden doors that house Fayed's offices and the pulse of the empire that is Harrods in London's Knightsbridge. A couple of firm knocks brought a secretary to the door and I was shown to a large room with a table in the middle. 'The Chairman will be with you shortly,' she said, but it was Mayer who arrived next and we chatted about Keegan, Fayed, Harrods, Davies, the BBC (where he and Davies once worked), before in bustled Mohammed Al Fayed.

It had been his bright waistcoat that had caught the eye of Davies, but it was the smile that was the first thing I noticed. A big, bright smile that had welcome written all over it. 'Why does your Editor hate me?' he asked, a reference to the *Sun*'s anti-publicity for this larger than life figure. Fayed was also smaller than I had expected.

Mayer had told me that Fayed would talk about anything connected with Keegan, England and Fulham. What about the passport?, I had inquired. Try him, was the answer. So I did. 'Ridiculous and unfair to suggest that I would do a trade,' he said, his mood changing slightly. And now the words came thick and fast, delivered with a clipped accent but with the impact of someone firing a machine gun when trapped down a one-way alley by the enemy.

'I believe my passport should be a matter of formality, as an appreciation for all the things I have done for this country,' he said hardly taking breath.' I have built so much for industry here, put so many people in jobs, eight thousand people work for me and over the years I have brought millions of pounds into this country for business. Do you know how much I pay in taxes? One hundred and eighteen million pounds. Do you think that is fair?'

Fayed was now in full flow about the subject he likes to talk about most and feels so strongly about. England. And I don't mean football, although it was why I was sitting in front of Fayed with my tape running. There is a common link with Keegan, as you will discover, and there is no question that Fayed identified with the England coach who admits that he is a self-made success story. Keegan was not a great player when he started with Scunthorpe yet with sheer determination he turned himself into a superb forward. With hours of sweat, training, advice and will power he forced himself up the ladder. From no one he made himself Double European Footballer of the Year. He forced himself to become an outstanding footballer, and, I suspect, is still learning to become a great manager. There is no question that when he was given the England job he was better at man-management and inspiration than he was at tactics. But you would not bet against him turning it around again. Fayed says that, like Keegan, he started with nothing. There is no doubt that he liked Keegan for his simple background and his relationship with real people.

Fayed says: 'What I discovered about Keegan was that there was jealousy and envy towards him. Not from everyone, but some parties reacted to him because he had created his own success from nothing. I suffer from that. Envy is a wicked thing. He created Newcastle and yet there were always rumours to bring him down.

'You must live for what you create out of your life. Ask the real England fans what they feel about Kevin Keegan and you will get admiration. Ask Fulham fans what they think about me and there will be a strong feeling of support. Without me there would be no Fulham Football Club.'

He proceeded to talk about his hatred of the establishment, his views on the Royal family and, inevitably, Diana's death, but it was easy to bring him back to talking football because he has a passion for it and, yes, a passion for Keegan. He added: 'The Diana situation is so much like Keegan. He is a person of the people. He says what he thinks and has a great touch with the public. He is a leader. Like me. I own Harrods but I am also the doorman tipping his cap, and the man in the kitchen helping to clean up. Leadership is a gift, like a singer can sing and a painter can paint, God has helped me with what I have done. Keegan has this gift and that is why I had to give him to England. It was nothing about passports or anything like that. That is an insult, to him and me.'

The two men first met when Keegan approached Fayed to ask him if he would support a football circus for kids that he was organising. Like David Davies and myself, Keegan made the phone call and got a favourable response. The two men met, talked, liked each other and the rest, as they say, is history. Back in football as Fulham's Chief Operations Officer, then a switch to management again after the sacking of Ray Wilkins and on to England. Fayed brought him back, paid him handsomely and then gave him away.

Fayed adds: 'Our relationship began when Kevin approached me to help him with the football circus that he had planned. It was by chance really and we just got talking. The circus was for youngsters and I said fine, it was something that appealed to me. I thought it could be fantastic and in the back of my mind thought that I might be able to involve Fulham with recreation, games and youth development. Kevin and I discussed this.'

The more Fayed talked to Keegan the more he liked him. He identified with him and soon realised that here was a man from his own heart, someone who had come from nowhere and built his own empire and reputation through hard work. It was not long before Fayed was considering Keegan as the perfect man to run Fulham Football Club. And it was not long before he was agreeing to his returning to running the team as manager.

'I knew that Kevin had said many times that he did not want to return to management or football. One day I just took my chance. He knew what I was involved with at Fulham and I asked whether he might be interested. I said that what he had done for Newcastle, he could do for Fulham.' Fayed had laid down his own mental ambitions for the club and here was someone he knew who could fulfil those plans. He would provide the money and Keegan could provide the inspiration, know-how and leadership. It would, he thought, be the perfect partnership. 'The first reaction I got from Kevin was that he was happy doing what he was doing, enjoying his family and horses. I said fine.' But Fayed was never going to take no for an answer. He never does.

'I knew I had to wait for the right moment to ask him again,' said Fayed. 'You could say I wooed him and then seduced him. I knew that I could convince him but it was a question of how. I told him that he was still young and that this was a great opportunity. At last he said that he would think about it. He said that he wanted to talk it over with his wife and family. I waited. When he came back he said that the job and the challenge appealed to him. 'I like the sound of it' were his words and we were a partnership from that moment. We only talked for about two hours. I asked him what his fee would be, he told me, I agreed and that was it. We shook hands.

'Looking back it was easy. It was easy because football is Kevin Keegan's life. It is in his blood. He loves it. Something like this perhaps was in the back of his mind. I ignited the feeling again, the will to return to the game. It was just instinct from me. I am not like these big-shot chairmen with expensive shoes and ties, I have ordinary shoes and ordinary ties. I am an ordinary bloke. A simple guy.'

It was then that Mohammed Al Fayed suddenly asked me if I liked the tie he was wearing? Very nice, I said. 'Would you like one?' he asked. That would be nice, I added. Fayed then flicked his tie off at the neck. It was a tie that did not go around the neck but instead simply clipped on at the top of the shirt. 'I will get you one,' he said. In fact, he got me two and they arrived in a Harrods bag before I left his office.

Extraordinary man, Mr Fayed. I have mentioned these ties to my family and one or two friends and someone suggested that they are used so that the wearer can not be strangled if gripped by the tie. The tie simply comes off in the hand of the aggressor. I have no idea about that but maybe I should wear one when I visit certain football grounds whose supporters I have upset with comments about their team! Another friend asked whether it was unwise to accept gifts from Fayed following the gifts for votes court case with the Hamiltons, which Fayed won. I don't think so. I found Fayed an interesting and stimulating person, someone who, if he likes and trusts you, will offer support and help. He bats against authority but there is nothing wrong with that. He upsets people because he opens his mouth and says what he feels. There is nothing wrong with that, either. Sure, he is ruthless. But show me a millionaire who has not been ruthless, and I will show you flying pigs.

He certainly liked and trusted Keegan. 'He was in charge of everything at Fulham,' added Fayed. 'I left it to him. I gave him the whole club to look after. Trust is important to me. When you feel that in a person you must give trust a chance. I trusted Kevin straight away. I told him to take the ball and run with it, and he ran like mad from the first day.

'He is a good-tempered man, someone who knows what he is doing and, more importantly, believes in what he is doing. Nothing fazes him and he gives one hundred per cent. Once I had made up my mind I knew that Kevin Keegan had what I wanted for Fulham.'

Keegan, in fact, did not start as team manager. Fayed appointed him as Chief Operations Manager – in other words the boss – and former England star Ray Wilkins, who had been manager of QPR, was elected team manager to work with Frank Sibley, another former QPR man, on the playing side. Keegan ran every aspect of the club, was Wilkins boss and there was soon the unhealthy situation of both men being on the touchline at matches. Many critics began to ask whether it was Wilkins or Keegan running the team. Who selected the side was another point raised as the Fayed and Keegan show ran into its early months.

It wasn't long before Wilkins was sacked and Keegan took over full control of the side, as well as running the club. It was a massive job for him but, as we have discovered, this is an extraordinary man with a capacity to do more than one job at the same time. When Keegan told Fayed what he wanted to do and that Wilkins would have to go, Fayed supported him one hundred per cent. 'He was in charge. I had made the decision to give him total control and backed the decisions he made,' added Fayed. 'It is what you call delegation.'

Fayed added: 'Under Kevin Fulham grew and grew, just as I had expected. But it was a joint effort because without me there would be no Fulham. I did know that without Kevin there would not have been the success we enjoyed. It was a joint effort, a team game. I left the decisions to him. It was his club. I had my people there and they obviously talked. I did not and do not interfere.

'I wanted Kevin to deliver and he had no excuses. He told me what he wanted and I gave it to him. He made the signings, he made the decisions. And he did fulfil, he did achieve, there is no question about that.'

Under Keegan the Fulham story accelerated away. For the first time since the days of Johnny Haynes, and then the period when George Best and Rodney Marsh entertained, followed by Bobby Moore and Alan Mullery taking the club to the FA Cup Final in 1975, there was hope and anticipation in the air. Real excitement. The crowd grew, as did the expectancy. New signings arrived, like Paul Bracewell from Sunderland for £75,000 (the first capture and Keegan's successor), Ian Selley from Arsenal for £500,000 (who has twice broken his leg and at the time of writing was attempting another comeback), Oaul Peschisolido from West Brom for £1.1 million, Maik Taylor, a great signing for £75,000 from Southampton and then Chris Coleman, £2 million from Blackburn. They were all masterminded by Keegan and financed by Fayed. Keegan told him who he wanted to sign and how much the deal would cost, and Fayed rubber stamped it. In his first season Fulham got to the play-offs but failed to win promotion from Division Two. But the supporters had been seduced, to use Fayed's own expression, and they knew that the new season would bring more signings, and the real chance of promotion. It did. Fulham went up as Champions.

Then came England. Fayed listened to the speculation surrounding his manager when Glenn Hoddle was sacked, and noted with interest when Keegan let it be known that he did not want that England job and would never walk out on Fulham. Fayed, interestingly, does not believe that Hoddle should ever have been sacked for passing public comment on his thoughts and inner beliefs. He says: 'Hoddle should not have been sacked by the FA. It was a man's opinion, for heaven's sake. We are human, we make mistakes. We are not machines and to destroy a guy like that ... he was doing a good job. I thought he was a great guy and a great leader. Everyone makes mistakes, everyone's tongue slips. The FA should have forgiven him for saying something that was not intentional. It had nothing to do with his professional job as England coach. His job was to create success, nothing else. You just can't ruin the lives of other people.'

It is exactly what Fayed told David Davies of the FA when the two men met at Harrods. The plea from Davies to Fayed was amazing. Fayed recalls: 'Davies said to me "Please, we have no one else. There is no other man for us to turn to."'

That Davies admission perhaps sums up exactly why the FA pushed so hard to get Keegan. Yes, he was the number one choice with all the International Sub Committee but they had no one else. Had Fayed or indeed Keegan said no they would have been in serious trouble. An England side without a manager. When they sacked Hoddle, and I agreed with the decision, they had no one in mind. They came out of the Hoddle débâcle hoping for Keegan. It was a huge gamble to take. Who else was there for them? We have already learned the names they discussed, from Fergie to Brian Kidd. Who knows who they would have ended up with had the Keegan appointment not taken place?

Fayed was surprised by the admission from Davies, especially with negotiation to be done. He adds: 'I told him that he had a lot of trouble. I said that they had got themselves into it, and were asking me to help them. But it was their trouble not mine, their game. Kevin Keegan had proved himself at my club and now you want him, is what I said to Davies. He said yes, that is right. I told him that I would not interfere. I told him, the FA, to go ahead. I gave them permission. It was up to them and Kevin.

'It was a very difficult decision to sacrifice Kevin Keegan. He had done so much for me and Fulham. The players loved him. The fans too. I simply could not stand in his way. He wanted to try the job and I gave him my blessing. It was the glory of his country and I can understand that. How could I say no when the whole nation wanted him? I said to Kevin when we spoke, "The decision is yours, whatever makes you happy, If this is your dream, then you must go."'

The FA are also lucky that Fayed did not fight them hard for compensation. The talks may have been long and gruelling for the people involved but had Fayed put his foot down then it could have got messy. He did not want that. 'The FA took Keegan from me and they gave me £500,000. Peanuts,' he says. 'I asked for £2 million. But he left me with a great guy in Paul Bracewell. Kevin put a little bit of himself into Paul.' Had Fayed stuck out for £2 million, or indeed demanded more, there would have been no deal, no Keegan as England coach. The FA have made it clear that they did not want to pay much compensation at all, let alone £2 million or more.

'I wish Kevin all the best. He did a great job for me, he did his best and that is all I ask from people,' adds Fayed. 'I could have said no to the FA but always knew I couldn't. He may have been pulled between the two parties but when he saw I was relaxed about it, his decision was easier for him. Then came that first game with Poland and it was all over. The reaction of the people was the final pull. The public are very strong with Kevin and me. They mean a lot.'

The last time that Fayed and Keegan really spoke was at the final game of the 1998–99 season when Fulham played Preston at Craven Cottage as Division Two Champions. 'We joined in the party together,' he adds. 'Kevin Keegan can work for me again whenever he likes and he is always welcome at Fulham. I was going to make him a director of the club and he had already turned that down.

'I wish him all the best with England. He can do it, he can be a success. He is a maestro. He has motivation, energy and determination. He is someone who knows what he wants and what he is doing. Like me, he does not get hurt by criticism. He is a strong man mentally and that is important.

'And there is always criticism. I know that. All the bastards who attack me will no doubt give Keegan shit too. It is the society we live in and you have to be strong. He left Fulham happy and I thank him for what he did for us.' Fayed then fell silent for a while before delivering his last thought about the Keegan and FA affair. 'England fucked up,' he said eventually. 'So I had to help them out.'

Only time will tell whether Fulham will continue to live the Fayed dream. The publicity for them is not so great, which is only to be expected, and Paul Bracewell, the new manager, certainly does not have the same charisma. The Fulham crowd respect Bracewell but they could never love him in the same way as they did Keegan. Neil Rodford says: 'We are credible now. We are an organization that people believe in. The objective here is to build on what Kevin Keegan started. Newcastle didn't, we must.

'Will Kevin ever return to us, will he come back to Fulham? I don't think so although it is not a complete no no. He and I speak regularly, we have a great relationship and are friends. It was good that the Fulham experience ended well for him. Mohammed held a huge party after the Preston game, opening up one of the suites at Harrods for the Fulham people. Any wounds that had been opened were healed that night.

'It was a very emotional night. Kevin spoke and explained to everyone that, having played for England many times, he had now been asked by his country to become manager. "It is the only reason I am leaving. To manage my country," he told us.

'The interesting thing is that football is just a tiny part of Fayed's life,' says Rodford. 'Fulham is only a dot in his business empire. Harrods turns over billions of pounds and he has so many other things and interests. He is a people's champion and has so many ideas to develop his interests. We relate to Chelsea here and what they have achieved so quickly. These are important times for Fulham and it is a big season for us. Kevin started all this and we are grateful. But you can not look backwards and life must go on.'

In the many discussions that Rodford and Keegan had one phrase was used a lot. Rodford says: 'Kevin was always saying to me "Football is the only profession where you are judged every day." How right he is. Keegan at Fulham was judged by the people he worked with and by the results he achieved.

As England coach he is public property. Kevin Keegan is judged by everyone. The whole nation has an opinion about him and that is something that he has to live with through the intense scrutiny of the European Champions Finals. How he emerges the other end of those finals will probably decide how long he stays as England coach.

CHAPTER 8

KEEGAN: THE MAN AND THE MANAGER

This Kevin Keegan story, indeed every Keegan story, is dominated by one thing. His personality. The sheer drive and determination of the man. When Keegan wants something, he goes for it in a big way. Any faults are covered by hard work and the ability to make himself better. Very rarely have we seen another side of Keegan, especially in public. But no man is perfect. There is another side of his public perception, of course there is. But, very rarely, do you get anyone who wants to talk about it. Criticism of Keegan is almost unheard of.

Mohammed Al Fayed was bitterly disappointed with Keegan for repeatedly saying that he would never walk out on Fulham for England and then quitting. He was even more annoyed when he heard about it officially on television. Yet Fayed never tore into Keegan. Although the Harrods owner is happy to point the finger of blame at the establishment for various shortcomings, there is only praise for Keegan, when there has to be a tiny bit of him that feels let down.

Geoff Thompson, the chairman of the Football Association, stands by his 'Keegan's reign will end in tears not trophies' comment. He says: 'I do not regret saying that, and certainly do not retract it. His record suggests that sometimes it ends in tears, like at Newcastle.' Thompson is referring to the end of Keegan's reign at Newcastle when he asked to quit over differences with the board and then finally walked out. Thompson adds: 'I said it before I went to New Zealand, before we appointed him. There are people who do not have to work, who are financially secure, who can be affected by things. Things can influence their desire. I am not necessarily saying this about Keegan only, but people like him. I hope that Kevin is not like that. It is certainly a different ball game now. I want him to be successful and to see out his contract, and beyond it.'

There is no question that Keegan has a short fuse, a fierce temper and the ability to bring down the red mist when something, or someone, stands in his way. It is known that he does not like criticism and a rare glimpse of what he can be like was seen on Sky Television after Newcastle had lost another match as they had a huge lead at the top of the Premiership cut and were overtaken by rivals Manchester United. Keegan's now famous outburst 'I'd just love it if we could beat United' was aimed at United manager Alex Ferguson just as much as his critics. Fergie had been playing his usual mind games in the media and Keegan fell for it. For those few minutes on live national television he lost it. His face was contorted, his eyes cold and for a few moments we were allowed a glimpse behind the mask that Keegan rarely drops. Sure there was passion. But this was anger the public had not seen before. I wonder if we will again. Turning into the year 2000 the media had not seen it either, not since he took over, but I suspect that we will.

He hates losing and there is nothing wrong with that. Failure and criticism is a different ball game. Noel White, chairman of the FA's International Committee, admits: 'Kevin has a lot of strengths but one of them is not standing up to failure.' That statement sums Keegan up perfectly. I can recall in the 1982 World Cup in Spain when he refused to talk to the media for the entire tournament because question marks had been raised about the captain's fitness and ability to play. Keegan eventually slipped off in the middle of the night and drove himself back to Germany where he was seen by a specialist in whom he had confidence from his career in Hamburg. He returned to make a short sub appearance in our final game against Spain. We drew 0–0 and England went home, out and yet unbeaten in the tournament.

There are many people, and some inside Lancaster Gate, who fear that Keegan will walk away from the England job if England fail miserably in the European Championship Finals and the exit is followed by media criticism of his ability to do the job. 'I don't need this' is a saying that follows him around. It is denied by Keegan but he knows, and so do we, that the test has yet to come. The test when you feel isolated by failure and the feeling that the country is against you. You have to be strong to survive it. Bobby Robson did and became a hero. Graham Taylor wanted to and was sacked while Glenn Hoddle could not withstand the tidal wave that is media coverage these days. You look over your shoulder and it is like running up a beach with the wave behind you, it engulfs you before you reach safety. It is a fact of life in football journalism today. There is no grey, it is black or white.

I have lived through many stages of popular sports coverage and I have to say that at times it is nothing to be proud of. The problem is that too many people now making decisions have no concept of what it takes to do this job of journalism. There are many reporters, yes, some covering England, who have no idea what a story is, let alone how to get one. There are also too many of us, all fighting over the flesh that is a story or a good interview. In a way many of the clueless ones have been helped by today's system with England. There is hardly any digging needed, no need for real personal relationships with the players, no access for a night out or meal with players who become friends. The FA wheel in the players, security guards stand around waiting for the interviews to stop, before the players are whisked off.

No longer do the media travel now with the official England party on trips. It was Glenn Hoddle who banned the media from flights and Keegan has maintained that. It is a shame but probably there are too many journalists now who want to be part of the England scene. It is also the era of comment. Everyone has an opinion, about Keegan, his tactics, players, motivation, knowledge and success chances. Eventually Keegan will inevitably ask himself: how much do I want this?

The Keegan we don't know publicly definitely came into focus in his first year at Fulham. Changes were made behind the scenes that suggest that Keegan has a ruthless streak. No one gets to the top without having some kind of 'Me or them' attitude inside them and Keegan is no different. It is how those steps are taken and decisions made that are important. For the first time in this particular story, Keegan's heralded man-management skills raise questions.

He was employed by Mohammed Al Fayed to be the Chief Operations Officer at Craven Cottage. A funny title for a football man but, as we know, it gave Keegan the power to run the whole show. Any decision taken at the club had to go through him. It was complete power. Strangely, the position did not involve Keegan directly with the football side of things, and the running of the first team. He had the power to hire and fire and was the overlord but did not involve himself in the day by day running of the team, certainly not the coaching or selecting of the side. It wasn't long, however, before he found the temptation too great. It was not a surprise because after all, he had been a football man all his life. It must have been difficult for him to see Ray Wilkins down on the touchline, doing all the things that he had enjoyed at Newcastle. Ask any manager, it is the day by day involvement that brings the most satisfaction. Winning is the climax.

The first big decision the club took was to sack the club's manager Micky Adams and employ an old friend, former England star Wilkins, who had been manager at West London neighbours Queen's Park Rangers. Frank Sibley, another QPR man, was Wilkins' number two. The sacking of Adams was not popular at first because he had been liked by the supporters and they had accepted that he had done a good job in difficult circumstances. The change however was an eventual success and the Wilkins and Sibley partnership took Fulham from fifth from bottom of Division Two when they arrived too close to the top. They did not make it into the automatic spot and instead qualified for the play offs, and a two-leg contest with Grimsby to get to the Play Off Finals at Wembley.

Keegan had attended team meetings, even stood alongside Wilkins in the dugout at times, especially when promotion became close, and it was his right to do as he liked, but shortly before the play offs the Chief Operations Officer started to act like Team Manager. It became a problem for Wilkins. He found Keegan's interference difficult, especially when Kevin started to advise him on tactics and selections. It came to a head when Wilkins wanted to play one side and use certain tactics in the first play off match, at home to Grimsby, and Keegan preferred a different way.

At the start of May 1998 Keegan and Wilkins had a meeting to discuss the situation and it was soon clear to Wilkins that his future at Fulham was heading in the wrong direction. Keegan's views and his determination for more involvement with tactics and selection were never going to work. Wilkins, a proud man and someone who has complete faith in his ability, is not weak, or stupid. He felt that it had come down to a 'me or him' situation.

Three hours after their meeting Wilkins received a phone call from Neil Rodford, the club's Managing Director, telling him that his services were no longer required. Wilkins has never forgiven Keegan for not telling him face to face that he was out. The two men have not spoken to this day. Wilkins, it is claimed, would have made the effort to put out the hand of friendship if Keegan had not seemingly got Rodford to do the sacking. Wilkins, at the time of writing, has still not been paid for the three years left on his contract. There have been counter claims from the club that he walked out and was not sacked. Wilkins is adamant. He believes he was sacked by Keegan.

Keegan's arrival saw other changes behind the scenes, including

Press Officer Ian Gibbs' departure. What does this tell us of Keegan? A tough man? Well, you have to be when you are running a business, and he would not be the first man to sack a manager. Most disturbing for me was Wilkins' assertion that Keegan did not tell him face to face that he was out. If the allegations are true then they reveal a different Kevin Keegan. Not the lovable Mighty Mouse, everyone's friend, or the Messiah, as he was known with Newcastle and now England.

None of the above will damage the public's view of 'Our Kev'. He is right up there, for the time being anyway, as one of the nation's much beloved. He is an untouchable in the eyes of the supporters and the Football Association. They want him, he wants them. It is a marriage made in heaven, just as long as things go his way. The test has yet to come. Maybe it won't. Maybe he will always be a success. 'I have always been taught that if you give your best, if you give everything and never look back and so "if only" then the conscience can be clear,' says Keegan. 'I like to think that is me from the day I could walk until now. I have always gone for it. I knew I had limitations and tried and tried to make myself better. I wanted the best and worked for it. I don't see anything wrong with that. It is something I am proud of.'

Kevin Keegan was born into a poor Yorkshire mining family in Doncaster, living in a house he himself describes as a slum. He earned his first money cleaning cars for the rich at a local racecourse, hence his love today for the Sport of Kings. He wanted to be a footballer, a goalkeeper in fact even if his height, 5ft 8in, was against him. But his sports master told him 'Thee will never make a footballer as long as thee lives. Go and do something else.'

Keegan did, although still determined to prove his master wrong. He took a £25 a week job in a foundry and spent time plate-laying on the railway lines around his home. He played football for his works side and was spotted by Scunthorpe United. He joined them on a wage cut of £15 a week, such was his determination to make it. They soon told him to run up and down the terracing with weights on his shoulders to build up his strength and muscles. It was the start of the Keegan success story. He ran up and down that Scunthorpe terracing until he could feel himself getting stronger. In 1971 the late great Bill Shankly spotted a little lad playing for Scunthorpe and persuaded them to part company with Keegan for £35,000. Shankly has admitted many times that it was daylight robbery.

The phenomenon that is Kevin Keegan had started to roll. The permanently permed hairstyle appeared in all the newspapers and he was soon scoring goals and winning prizes. He became the King of the Kop and the rest, as they say, is history. He spent six years at Anfield, formed a stunning partnership with John Toshack, before quitting at his peak to go to Germany with Hamburg. Keegan knew that it was the right time for a move and it was just another challenge. The Germans didn't respect him at first. He made them. All through his career he has proved people wrong. The master at school, those who said he would never play for England, the Germans, and he is determined to show his critics who now say that he does not have the tactical ability to pitch himself in with the best coaches in the world. If hard work is the essence of success, then Keegan will win the European Championship and World Cup.

He staggered the football world again by returning to England from Germany to join unfashionable Southampton. Then he returned North to go to Newcastle before hanging up his famous boots. He had won the lot, made his money and insisted that he had absolutely no interest in football management. 'It is not for me' he said and headed off to the Costa del Sol with his childhood sweetheart Jean, playing golf and relaxing. In 1992 he saw a business opportunity in developing the Newcastle United ground, St James Park, and was persuaded to become a manager after all by Sir John Hall. Hall is no fool. An astute business man, he knew the potential of Newcastle. What it needed was stirring up with passion and desire. Newcastle needed setting alight. It needed Keegan.

They were made for each other and his first match was billed as 'The Second Coming'. Keeganmania swept through the area like a tornado and the results improved from day one. 'Walking in a Keegan wonderland' his public chanted and Keegan's enthusiasm, his brand of attacking football, the Geordie faithful and the black and white of Newcastle was a heady combination. He spent £60 million in trying to win the Championship for them and his notable signing was England skipper Alan Shearer from Blackburn from under the nose of Manchester United. Alex Ferguson thought he had got Shearer when along came Keegan with his powers of persuasion. 'Come home' he told Shearer and Shearer followed the Messiah.

The bigger and more successful Newcastle became the more ambitious the club got, especially off the pitch. Keegan didn't always like what he saw happening or heard from the boardroom. He didn't like Hall's plan to turn the club into a European sporting club and he caused controversy by ditching the club's reserve side. The king eventually turned into something of a recluse and he eventually quit just as Newcastle went public in 1997. For all the excitement, attacking flair, big signings and promises, there were no trophies. Not the ones he wanted. How Keegan wanted to give the fans the Premiership! He couldn't do it and had to watch his arch-rival Alex Ferguson win the lot time and time again. It will bug him for the rest of his life, even if Keegan does say that he never looks back.

The Newcastle public loved Keegan. They identified with him and followed him just like the Pied Piper. His dreams were theirs and when it was going well Newcastle was a heady place to be. The Geordies never had the same relationship with Kenny Dalglish, they could not understand Ruud Gullit but are happy now with Bobby Robson. He is one of them. Robson has got the job he always wanted and the Newcastle people may have just forgotten Kevin Keegan.

Kevin Keegan will always be known as the man who rescued Newcastle. He was quickly called the Messiah when he swept back into football on 5 February 1992. He had vowed that management didn't interest him and he was happy out of the game. That changed with the phone call from new club owner, millionaire Sir John Hall. 'There are only two people who can save Newcastle,' he said. 'And they are talking to each other.' Keegan found the pull of the club he loved too much to turn down. It was just like the feeling he would experience with England years later. The Geordies loved him and Keegan took his club to the brink of greatness.

The support went through the roof, season ticket sales brought in millions, St James Park was improved, Keegan spent heavily and there was a wild anticipation around the club. Keegan was mobbed everywhere he went and the man could do nothing wrong. He was like a whirlwind and Newcastle became the force they should be. Interestingly, his base for success was the support. He is a man of the people and he and the Geordies soon had a relationship that would never be broken. He was idolised. The same thing happened when he took over England and, clearly, it is part of Keegan's management plan. Win over the fans and you are half-way there. He said and did the right things at Newcastle, just like he did with England.

The first signing that turned people's heads was Andy Cole from Bristol City. Cole had been rejected by then Arsenal manager George Graham and had something to prove. Cole cost £1.7 million on 3 March 1993, Keegan turned him into a star and Cole, like the manager, was idolised. He helped Keegan gain promotion from the First Division and continued to score goals in the Premiership. Newcastle fans were stunned when Keegan sold him to Manchester United for £7 million. It brought the famous confrontation on the steps of St James Park between Keegan and supporters. 'Why?' they asked him. Keegan explained that he did it for the best interest of the club and development of the team. There is still controversy surrounding that transfer, and also over Cole being picked, then dropped by England under Keegan and his subsequent absence from Euro 2000.

Other signings came, like David Ginola from Paris St Germain, Les Ferdinand from QPR, Wimbledon's Warren Barton and in all Keegan spent a staggering £59.8 million in search of the one thing he wanted most of all, the Premiership title. His two most controversial signings were the £7.5 million arrival of Tino Asprilla in a bid to win that title and Alan Shearer, in a then British record £15 million from Blackburn. The gamble on Asprilla failed and even Shearer couldn't take Keegan and Newcastle to the very top. Which is where Keegan has always loved to be. The football was often breathtaking. The failure to win something took the breath away.

At one stage a 12-point gap was thrown away and his main rival, Manchester United manager Alex Ferguson, grabbed the Premiership. It is when Keegan appeared to crack in front of the television cameras and produced his famous 'I'd love it, I'd really love it, if we could beat Manchester United.' Ferguson had teased and prodded him with a war of words and the pressure seemed to have told.

There had also been pressure growing behind the scenes on Keegan. He considered his own position many times and decided that he wanted to spend more time with his wife Jean and family. On more than one occasion he told the board that he wanted to go. That put pressure on Newcastle who were soon to go public. They knew that they could not float and inform the Stock Exchange without a manager. On 8 January 1997 Keegan did resign, in a blaze of publicity and stunned disbelief from the Geordies.

He went without winning the one prize that he had spent so much time and money on trying to collect. The Premiership. It will always bug him. That is why, when questioned about Newcastle in a Euro 2000 press conference he asked one reporter 'Was Newcastle not a success under me?' and when the answer was 'No, it was failure', you could see the hurt in his eyes.

Keegan has never been a failure. He does not look upon himself in that manner. He views Newcastle as a huge success. And Fulham. Yet when it comes to winning things Keegan, as a manager, has only won

First Division promotion with Newcastle, and Second Division promotion with Fulham. It is not a lot for a man with a massive reputation. Will he ever win anything with England?

As he has said many times: the jury is out.

CHAPTER 9

KEEGAN: A MAN OF HIS WORD

One man who knows Keegan well and who worked close at hand with him is Lawrie McMenemy, the former Southampton manager, Graham Taylor's assistant with England, and the man who produced one of the stories of his decade by wooing Keegan back to English football from Hamburg. McMenemy has only praise for Keegan and the job that he did for him and the English game. McMenemy was as surprised as anyone that Keegan actually agreed to join unfashionable Saints in the footballing outpost of Hampshire. How this came about tells us a lot about Keegan the man. A man who knows what he wants and where he is going.

McMenemy recalls: 'I was ambitious, the club were and we had had some success. Peter Osgood had been the first signing that had surprised a lot of people, including my colleagues at the club. He was a big superstar at Chelsea and I persuaded him to sign for us. I recall Terry Paine saying to me that he never thought that he would see the day when a player like Osgood joined Southampton.

'Osgood lifted the standard and the expectation. Without him we would never have won the FA Cup as a Second Division club. The more success we got the more bigger names I wanted to attract. The better the player the more beneficial it was for the younger players at the club, like Mark Wright, Nicky Holmes, Steve Williams and Steve Moran. Times and things were changing at Southampton. We were promoted back to the First Division and there was real expectancy in the air. I knew that to get Southampton right to the top – and it would have been a miracle – I had to get real quality.' McMenemy was still searching and thinking of the right players when he read an article by Keegan in a magazine. It got his mind racing. Maybe, just maybe.

'The article was interesting; it was all about Kevin's lifestyle and Hamburg and then he said that he might just be ready to move on. It set my mind ticking, and eventually racing. Keegan had been one of the first players to go abroad and he had made a huge impact in Germany. He did not have to go because he had been flying high with Liverpool but wanted the new challenge. That said a lot to me. I knew that he had twice been voted European Footballer Of The Year and another challenge, another club, was the kind of situation he had been involved with.' Maybe, just maybe.

'I also knew that if he was thinking of returning to England then he could take his pick from any clubs. Something nagged me and I knew that I had to ring him, even if the answer was a quick thanks, but no thanks. You have to try, have to make that call, otherwise you regret it for the rest of your life. I got his number in Hamburg from somewhere but then thought to myself 'I can't just ring up the captain of England and say do you fancy playing for Southampton?'

So McMenemy hatched a plan. A cunning plan. At that time McMenemy and his wife were having a new house built, on the outskirts of Southampton, in Chandlers Ford. The architect designing the house was a big football fan and loved talking the sport with McMenemy. One day the two men were chatting about a wall that was being erected under the stairs and the architect told McMenemy that he needed a light and showed him the kind of design that would be best suited. 'The trouble is,' he said. 'These particular lights come from Germany.' McMenemy's interest shot up. 'Whereabouts?' he asked. 'Let me have a look,' said the architect. 'Oh yes, here you are, Hamburg.' The plot was hatched.

McMenemy chose his moment to ring Keegan at home. They chatted about football, Hamburg, England and McMenemy then mentioned the light. 'I explained that the light I wanted only came from Hamburg and if I was to order it would he possibly bring it back to England for me the next time he popped over for a visit? Kevin, of course, agreed, because he has always been a gentleman.' Just before their first conversation finished McMenemy held his breath and mentioned the fact that he had read that Keegan might perhaps be considering leaving Germany. 'I mentioned Italy and Spain and he hesitated,' recalls McMenemy. 'So I took the plunge and inquired whether he was even considering returning to English football. Kevin said "perhaps" without being definite and I kind of joked about Southampton and the leafy lanes of Hampshire. I did tell Kevin that in Hampshire he could walk around without being pestered. I just dropped it in.'

McMenemy had made his first move. The cunning plan had been started and he left Keegan alone for a period while he started to do some homework of his own, not least on the financial package that would be needed if Keegan ever agreed to what was one of the sensational transfers of the modern day.

McMenemy adds: 'I can be quite persistent and once I made contact with Kevin I did not want to let the relationship go. I had other conversations with him and it got to the stage when he was beginning to become interested in Southampton. With every phone call and contact I felt that a deal was getting closer.

'My next job was to talk money with Southampton. I had to establish whether we could afford him. It was no good me going right down the line with Kevin if the club turned around and said no.' McMenemy held a meeting with the club's then financial director, Guy Haskill, who later became chairman. 'I swore him to silence and complete secrecy,' added Mcmenemy. 'I knew that if it ever came out that Southampton were trying to sign the England captain, and that Kevin Keegan was thinking of coming home, then every club in the country would be interested.'

McMenemy, of course, was bursting to tell someone, but bit his lip many times in conversations with others at the club and friends. That is the impact Keegan had as a player, and still does to as certain degree as a man and a manager. With Keegan involved things happen, and McMenemy knew that if he got his man then Southampton would never be the same, certainly not under his control.

McMenemy established that Southampton were willing and able to finance the deal and a secret meeting was arranged between Keegan, McMenemy and Askill. 'There was a lot of small talk before we got down to the nitty-gritty of deals and money,' says McMenemy. 'I am one of those managers who lock the door, throw away the key and don't let the player out until he has agreed.' The more the men talked the more Keegan grew to like the idea. In the end he said, 'OK, let's do it.' McMenemy's heart jumped an extra beat and he adds: 'Kevin actually signed a blank piece of paper which acted as a contract between us.' As the men shook hands on their 'gentleman's agreement' Keegan told McMenemy that he had to sign and keep him happy because he had forgotten to bring the damn light over with him.

McMenemy left the meeting on cloud nine. He was overjoyed, excited even if his adrenalin was tinged with worries if the story was to break. Only a handful of people knew. Keegan, his family, McMenemy and his wife and Guy Askill at Southampton. The chairman was also told and somehow the biggest secret of that time was kept from the media, other players and club officials. 'How we did it I will never know,' says McMenemy now. 'It was a miracle and could never happen today with the media focus and agents running about all over the place. Our meeting and agreement was in the February and Keegan was not unveiled until the summer. Keegan proved to me then that he is a man of his word. He saw out his contract with

◀ The boy in his prime: Kevin Keegan celebrates a goal against Scotland, May 1979

▼ Man and boy: Responsible for England's footballing hopes, Keegan, England Manager, Feb. 2000

▲ Kevin Keegan, Alan Shearer and Prince Andrew in a photocall for the NSPCC, March '99

◄ Kevin Keegan signs a young fan's shirt during a training session at Wembley, June '99

◄ Keegan congratulates David Beckham on his performance in a Euro 2000 qualifier, March '99

▼ Talking tactics: Keegan with assistants Arthur Cox and Howard Wilkinson, April '99

► Keegan in confident mood, June '99

▼ A brief moment of glory: The Group A coaches get their hands on the European Championship trophy, Dec '99

► Euro 2000. Keegan instructs his players during training before the crucial first game, 11th June 2000

▼ Euro 2000, Portugal v England. The England bench look on in disbelief as Portugal come from behind to win 3-2, 12th June 2000

▲ Euro 2000, England v Germany. The agony & the ecstasy: Kevin Keegan leaps in the air as Alan Shearer puts England 1-0 in front of Germany, 17th June 2000

► Euro 2000 England v Romania. Looking to the quarterfinals an ebullient Keegan gives the thumbs up before the game against Romania, 20th June 2000

▲ Euro 2000. England v Romania.
Alan Shearer gets a hug from
manager Kevin Keegan as he walks
off the pitch having played his last
game for his country, 20th June 2000

▶ Keegan holds his head in despair

Kevin Keegan, England's manager looks to the future

Hamburg without telling a soul or allowing his news to affect his performances.'

That unveiling ceremony was also masterminded by McMenemy. It was planned for a Monday morning and Southampton had released a press statement on the Sunday night, instructing journalists to attend a press conference at The Dell to announce a major new development. No one got a sniff that the development was Kevin Keegan.

McMenemy almost let his guard down on the Sunday evening when he and his wife went out to dinner with good friends, the author Leslie Thomas and his wife. 'There were no mobile phones in those days and before we sat down to dinner I told the restaurant owner that I had given their number to some people just in case anyone wanted to get hold of me. Leslie guessed straight away that something was up and quizzed me all night. I told him that I was trying to sign someone and hoped to complete in the morning. 'Is it a big name?' Thomas asked. 'You could say that,' replied McMenemy. It was gone midnight when the friends said goodnight and McMenemy decided to put Thomas out of his misery. He walked back over to the Thomas car and said: 'Look, it's KK.' Thomas looked at McMenemy with his eyes wide open.

McMenemy had asked Keegan whether he wanted to involve Harry Swales, a business adviser Keegan had used, and Swales had also been involved with the England team. 'Kevin was not fussed but I insisted that he told Swales. It was better to tell him than Harry find out in the media as soon as the story broke. Kevin had said to me, 'It is your day, do what you think is best,' and that was so typical of Keegan. There are not many other players who would have stood back and allowed someone else to do the arranging. This was a big transfer and there was a lot of money involved.'

But Keegan did stand back and on that Monday morning was collected from a private airfield in Hampshire by Swales. On board was also Gunter Netzer, the famous German player who was at that time Hamburg's managing director. 'Netzer's involvement was also incredible,' says McMenemy. 'He did not want Kevin to leave and had become a friend of the Keegans. But he went along with Kevin's wishes and also did not tell anyone about the transfer. Like Keegan, Netzer kept it from everyone else for five months. That again shows the quality of Keegan. A Hamburg official not only flies with him to make sure the deal is OK, he keeps it a secret.'

When McMenemy told the packed room of media men that Monday morning that it was a historic day for the club and that he had called everyone together to make a major announcement, the atmosphere in the room was electric. When Keegan appeared from behind a curtain there was a roar of excitement, of surprise and the realisation that the journalists involved were central to a major story. The news hit every television and radio station across the world. Kevin Keegan signs for Southampton, the headlines screamed. And in every picture there was McMenemy's smiling face. 'It was a very proud moment for me and the club,' he says.

'It was a scoop, a coup and the icing on the cake for Southampton. Peter Osgood was the first signing and Keegan the ultimate one.'

There had been a clause in Keegan's contract that Liverpool had first option to buy him back but he never swayed from his promise, made at the first meetings with McMenemy. Keegan gave his word and signed on the dotted line. 'I still don't know how we kept the secret,' says McMenemy. 'It was like when I appeared on *This Is Your Life* and my wife kept the secret from me.'

One of the first calls McMenemy received after the news broke was from Leslie Thomas. 'He told me that he had been kept awake all night thinking about KK,' says McMenemy with a smile. 'Eventually Leslie decided that it had to be Kevin Keelan, the Norwich goalkeeper. But then he asked himself why we would want another goalkeeper? He was delighted, as the whole of Southampton were.' McMenemy also got his light and it still swings happily in the same spot in his home today. The light that helped sign Kevin Keegan and every time

McMenemy switches it on he thinks of the transfer that caused the biggest shock for years. And he smiles to himself every time.

Keegan's impact on Southampton was dramatic. They loved him. Everything went up. Gates, season ticket sales, expectations, atmosphere, league placing and the little Dell ground on the south coast was at bursting point. 'Every player I signed had a purpose and Keegan was the biggest,' says McMenemy. 'We were not just signing a footballer, we were getting a major star, a big personality. With all my signings I had to think if they could fit into what I was trying to achieve.

'I recall getting the police to stop Mick Mills on the motorway when he was on the way to sign for someone else and they persuaded him to ring me. He thought they were booking him for speeding. I managed to get Mick to turn back. There were so many, Dave Watson, Ted MacDougall, Phil Boyer, Frank Worthington, Charlie George, Alan Ball, it was a fantastic time. They did not all play together at the same time (it would have been one hell of a piss up if they had) and they all played their part in the Southampton story. But it was Keegan who changed our lives.'

Keegan cost Southampton £400,000. 'I thought it was £100,000 and he certainly had a fixed price in his contract,' recalls McMenemy. 'Whatever the price it was a bargain. And what would a player like that cost today, at a similar stage of his career? He made an immediate impact with the community. There were people pestering him for guest appearances, trying to sell him houses and asking him to put his name to everything and anything. He handles that side of his life so well and it never affected him as a Southampton player. He got us into the top six in the First Division.

'He was a great example to all the players, young and experienced. He never missed training and was always on time [this is an interesting insight as Keegan stresses to all his England players that he must have punctuality] and never gave me any headaches. We had a helicopter arriving at the training ground a couple of times to whisk him off somewhere but I never asked questions because he was so reliable. As long as he did the business for us it was fine by me. Football always came first.

'I always think there are two kinds of player. The naturally gifted, fantastic talents, like George Best or Matt Le Tissier. When Le Tissier is continually asked why he always tries the hard things he answers "Because I find them easy." Then comes the Balls and Keegans, who had to work at their game skills. They were never as gifted but made themselves go to a different level. They were kids from humble backgrounds who fought and fought to get to the top.

'When Kevin first went to Hamburg the other players would not even pass the ball to him. They did not respect him or want him in their side. Kevin's attitude was "I will show you." Rather than hide he puffed out his chest and won them over. Two European Footballer of the Year awards followed. People admire that. The average person likes to see someone with nothing battle to the top through pure hard work. Keegan has determination at everything he does. He never looks at something and says "I can't do that," instead he looks at it and says 'Yes, I can" or "Let's have a go." Effort, passion and determination go into everything he does. He is a man of his word. There are huge demands on him but he puts even more demands on himself.'

McMenemy knows all about the pressure of managing England, having been Graham Taylor's right-hand man. He lived the pressure, the highs and lows, the wins, the defeats and the intense media coverage. He also experienced the warmth you feel when you walk out of Wembley for the first time. McMenemy was not manager but he can still sense the shivers down his neck when he thinks back to the Wembley days and the roar of the crowd that greets you. That is why he knew that Keegan would take the England job when the 'will he, won't he?' speculation started.

He adds: 'I knew that he would want it. He could have carried on doing both jobs with Fulham and England but the moment you walk out at Wembley in front of your country you know you have to say yes, know that you must do everything you can to bring success. Graham Taylor was the same. I will tell you how you feel. You feel wanted. Wanted by England.'

McMenemy just hopes the media will give Keegan the chance to bring the success that everyone wants. He says that we shouldn't be surprised if we see a flare-up along the way, but that it is just part and parcel of being in the biggest job of all. 'There is more pressure on managers these days than ever before. TV cameras follow you everywhere, your every move is scrutinised and you can not make a comment, pick a side without what you are doing being up for debate. If there is the odd crack, the odd flare-up, so what? Managers are human and we all react differently.

'Kevin Keegan has been used to expectation. It has followed him around since he was a young player at Liverpool. He will be aware of the responsibilities surrounding him and has the passion for it. I will ask the media this question. If they start to criticise and put the boot in if the first couple of results go wrong, who else is there? Who do we get? The Archangel is not available. This fella is the closest you are going to get. He has the passion and feel for it. He looks comfortable being England coach.

'Press comment can be hurtful and don't believe anyone who says they do not read the papers. We do and criticism is read. The personal stuff that goes over the top is completely out of order. It is how you react to that criticism and comment that holds the key. I don't see Kevin walking away from the job. I believe he has the quality to cope if things do go wrong.

'Every England manager has been the logical choice. The media wanted Taylor, and this time they wanted Keegan. The great thing about Kevin is that people judge him from what they see. There is nothing hidden. There is an admiration there for him and it does not matter where he goes, into a pub, Wembley or down Doncaster High Street, it will always be "Good Old Kev." There will be a pat on the back for our lad, the lad who has done good.

'He has the same qualities as someone like Jack Charlton. There is respect. A bit of England inside him. He is as comfortable with kids as he is with the Prime Minister. Jack was surprised when he visited the Pope and the Pope knew who he was. Jack treated him just like anyone else. That is a rare quality to have. I have the feeling that everyone wants Kevin to do well.'

McMenemy does see a problem looming for Keegan. Not the media or the demands of the job, because Keegan takes those in his stride. But the players themselves. McMenemy says: 'I defend professional football but I am not sure the players have the same desire today.

'They are millionaires. When Kevin looks around the England dressing room he will he see a group of men who are delighted to be there, really wanting it. The players are top of the tree financially. So the manager has to have their respect. Without it he is dead. I am sure Kevin has that. Managers, especially club managers, no longer have complete control over them. Players now tell us how they will be treated and agents certainly don't help the situation. If some of the England players today showed the same determination and passion as their manager then we would be successful.

'He is a great example to follow. When someone says that Kevin Keegan looks knackered that is when the determination comes out. He has done everything that these England players are trying to achieve (apart from win a European Championship or World Cup) and if the current group of players won half what their manager has won then, again, England would be successful.'

McMenemy's point about the attitude of today's players is a hugely valid one. The money is going through the roof and, I don't care what anyone says, it has to affect them, especially the young ones. An 18 year old with talent can be plucked from a humble background and, overnight, pocket £20,000 a week. Keegan had to sweat and work for his rewards and the luxuries he now has did not come easily for him.

He admits: 'It took me 18 games to become a really established England International. It also took me that long to be happy with myself.

'I knew that I did not have the talent of some of the other players but I desperately wanted to be successful. That was my dream, my target and I worked and worked for it. I was brought up to believe that there is nothing wrong with hard work. And that hard work brings rewards.'

Keegan is surrounded in the England dressing room by millionaires. He can't shout and scream at them, fine them or threaten them. They would laugh in his face. What he must do is hold their respect. He treats them like adults and expects them to act like adults. Going into 2000 no one had let him down, certainly not off the pitch.'

McMenemy is also concerned about the expectation that comes with the job and the hype that is pushed higher and higher as England head towards a major Championship. He says: 'What right do England have to be so expectant? We have only won one thing since 1966 and yet, as a nation, we believe we can beat the best. Where does the confidence come from? The media must take a huge slice of the responsibility. They build it up and when it crashes they turn the other way. Kevin must cope with that swing and he will. I know he is strong enough to.'

McMenemy can see Keegan building for the future away from the glare of the job. 'He is the first England manager to go into the schools and work with the boys at that level,' he adds. 'That is the future, he knows that, and he tours the country coaching and inspiring. I don't think the public understand how much an England manager does away from the cameras.

'It reminds me of how much charity work Kevin and Alan Ball used to do when they were at Southampton. I can still see them playing with the handicapped kids, throwing themselves around in the mud on the training pitch to give the kids a day to remember. Make no mistake, Kevin will be aware of all his responsibilities.'

Keegan and McMenemy have remained close friends. 'Our wives are also close and we have seen our daughters grow into young ladies.' The friendship was emphasised by an incident at an England press conference early in Keegan's career. Press conferences are a no-go area for mobile phones. 'Mobiles off' growled David Davies when he was in control of press affairs and it became a catch phrase for him. On this occasion Keegan's phone rang and it was McMenemy. Instead of telling him that he would ring him back Keegan chatted for a couple of minutes. It is unheard but showed the friendship and respect.

The character of Keegan that emerges as his story unfolds is inspirational, determined, single-minded and passionate. But others have told me that if you fall out with Keegan you fall out for good. He is not particularly forgiving. He also does not like criticism. How will he handle it when the going gets hot, as it will? McMenemy, who knows him better than me, believes that he will ride all storms. I am not so sure.

He gave a little glimpse of his unforgiving attitude at the height of the *Daily Mail*'s campaign against him. He attended a press conference to help an old friend, Kelvin McKenzie, re-launch Talk Radio into Talk Sport. There was not a senior *Mail* reporter there and covering it for them was David McDonnell, one of their young football men. Keegan could not help himself and had a pop at McDonnell. 'Who is here from the *Mail*? They have sent a boy, have they? I don't trust the others, why should I trust you?' he said. It was unnecessary, not because the *Mail* were right, but it showed them that they had caught a nerve in the England manager. It might just have inspired the paper to go even heavier on him.

The only hint of criticism from football came quite early in Keegan's reign as England coach. Ian Stott, the Oldham chairman and an FA Councillor for many years, was voted vice-chairman behind Geoff Thompson at the 1999 FA Annual Meeting. No sooner had he been appointed than Stott said that he thought that Keegan's appointment had been too hasty. 'Have the FA jumped too soon?' asked Stott.

It was a strange question considering the positive atmosphere surrounding the appointment and Stott quickly got his knuckles rapped by Noel White, the chairman of the International Committee. He said: 'I think Ian was flexing his muscles after getting appointed. It was his opinion and a little unreasonable and odd, and maybe he had not understood the facts and certain situations surrounding Kevin's appointment. We wanted Kevin. It was not a question of pleading with him but then there he was, telling us he was ready, and what were we supposed to say – "Sorry Kev, you've got to wait"? Stott was not re-elected vice-chairman.

White added: 'I liked Kevin's inspiration after the down of Hoddle. The whole country liked him and there was certainly no risk as far as popularity was concerned. I know results count but he gets people relaxed and feeling confident.' White reveals that Keegan has introduced a first to the England set-up. 'In seventeen years on the International Committee I have never been introduced to a new cap brought into the squad. Under Keegan that has changed,

'Kevin Phillips for instance was brought across to be introduced to the committee. Big deal, you may say, but it is common sense and just part of Kevin's man management. It is all about getting the best out of people and I think little things like that say everything about the man. The little things are often neglected. I believe there is a now a different atmosphere among the players and I hope we get success for their sake, Kevin's and the country's.'

One thing is crystal clear. Kevin Keegan can do no wrong as far as the Football Association are concerned. They are committed and hope that he is the England coach long after the World Cup in 2002. They desperately want stability and are banking on Keegan giving it to them. A tantrum or walk-out would be a disaster for the FA and, indeed, English football. The entire International Committee kept their fingers crossed as England moved towards the European Championships.

Noel White, the International Committee Chairman, is typical of the FA thinking. He says: 'We are behind him. Are you? He has to be given stability and support and another upheaval would be no good to anyone. Let us not destroy the man and the manager as we have done in previous years. We have appointed a manager, paid him well and want him to succeed. He can with support from across the country. That is from the media, supporters, players, everyone in England who cares about the game we all love.'

Geoff Thompson, the FA Chairman, is just as supportive and says: 'I believe that England will win the World Cup again in my lifetime. But we will need co-operation from everyone in the game. I know that Kevin Keegan is extremely proud to be the coach of England. I hope the players feel the same way. I just wonder if today they have that deep feeling. One thing is sure, they will need to have it if we are to win the World Cup. There is a greater strain on them. There is a greater strain on everyone as ideals change. I do worry that that they play too many matches. We ask them to lift and raise themselves for England when it is often impossible. I do believe that the players are in good hands with Kevin.'

David Davies, the man responsible for bringing Keegan to the FA, says. 'No, winning the World Cup is not an impossible dream. They tell me that the England dressing room is a happier place today. If Kevin Keegan can maximise the potential of the players then we have a chance of winning anything, and he can. People have faith in him. Everywhere.'

There has never been support like it before for an England coach. Keegan has got everything at his finger tips. Power, players, the complete backing of his bosses. It is, as they say, down to him. There is no question that football in England is changing. The FA are streamlining, decisions are being made to alter thinking and as Thompson says: 'We are in the twenty-first century and simply can't stand still.'

Keegan is lucky to be the manager at a time when the FA

themselves are altering their own image. If he wants to, if he rides any storm that is around the corner, Kevin Keegan can be England coach for a very long time. He is in the fantastic position of having the biggest job around in his own hands.

CHAPTER 10

THE TIMES THEY ARE A-CHANGIN'

The one thing that the Football Association had never been good at was public relations. Ask any fan from across the country and his perception of the most powerful sporting body in the country was of old men in blazers, out of touch cronies sitting around a polished table at Lancaster Gate and making decisions. Men nodding off in meetings, clueless about the game today, the players or what supporters want. David Beckham? It could have been Tom Finney, so far behind the times were the men directing the game in this country.

The late, great Bobby Moore once told a story about introducing the England team to the Guest of Honour and VIPs before an England game at Wembley. He deliberately muddled the names up to the then chairman of the Football Association, so George Cohen became Alan Ball, Gordon Banks, Nobby Stiles, Geoff Hurst, Martin Peters and so on. The chairman, bless him, didn't have a clue. He said 'Great goal the other day' to Ray Wilson thinking he was Bobby Charlton. Oh well! I recall going down to breakfast at my hotel on the morning that England played Germany in the World Cup semi-final. The FA had invited over all the councillors to Italy to watch what was one of the biggest matches in our history. The breakfast room was like a meeting of the Darby and Joan club. I am sure I saw a zimmerframe.

It was not only supporters and the media who had such a contemptuous view of the FA, but players too. Kevin Keegan was no different. When he was a player and captain of England he peered inside the running of the International scene and wasn't particularly impressed. He knew that changes should have been made. So, when they asked him to be manager, he understandably had reservations about life inside Lancaster Gate.

Whenever there has been a crisis, or indeed a mini crisis for the game, the call has been the same. Not enough quality players, no young ones coming through, what about the schools, how is the standard at grass roots level, we play too much at the top, the demands on players is too great and, yes, you guessed it, they don't have a clue at the FA. It is an institution still run by duffers. Well, times are changing.

Keegan peered in again before saying yes to the coaches job and this time he was encouraged with what he found. He discovered a new era being formed inside Lancaster Gate, of younger-thinking men and women, fresh ideas, forward planning and a real mood that at last FA did not stand for Fuck All happening, but Forward All Together. He talked with Howard Wilkinson, the Technical Director, about his own blueprint for the playing side future, and he knew, of course, David Davies from the negotiations he had with England. There were also men like Adam Crozier emerging, the FA's new Chief Executive. Keegan was delighted with the new wave of thinking and it helped him make his decision. He knew that he was taking the biggest job of all at a really exciting time for English football.

There is no hiding the role of David Davies in the new FA. From the moment he walked into Lancaster Gate in 1994 he realised that, to use his own words, 'There was a major job on.' From his seat in the media office he could see why the organisation had received such criticism in the past. It was caught in a time warp. Long before he was made acting Chief Executive and then Executive Director he hatched a plan in his own mind. Yes, he is ambitious, but he has driven through some new ideals in his short reign that would have taken years to decide in years gone by.

Geoff Thompson has been there, done it and worn the blazer. Now chairman, he is aware of the new image being created and says: 'If the public is asked about the FA then they all say the same, load of old duffers. OK, let's get rid of the blazers, that would be a start. But I do ask you to examine the facts behind some of these so called old farts. People who start a career in local football are usually close to retirement age when they reach the top. They have a wealth of experience and there is work for them to do.

'A lot of the councillors are over 60 but there is still a contribution for them to make. We do need to get younger administrators and, I agree, we have to try and find a way of pushing decisions through without having to rely on a series of committees to do it. Streamlined is as good a word as any for the future of the association. But, having said that, there are still decisions that have to be made by all 91 councillors, like voting for a new chairman for instance!

'We need to get the Football League more involved with us and get rid of the old argument of the split between the professional and amateur game. Let's get young blood, let us have a smaller board of directors ... and all this leads to one thing in my mind, a stronger England team. Kevin Keegan's success with the England side encourages so much else. If the England team is winning there are so many positive spin-offs.

'I would like to make the FA's public image more higher-profile. The FA needs to talk to the public, the players and get a better understanding of what we are about and trying to achieve. We have to listen because I dare say that they will have better ideas than us. There are a lot of people who do a lot of damn hard work inside Lancaster Gate. We all want a better game. For the first time I think that the public can see that we are heading in the right direction.'

Thompson is an interesting character inside the FA. He is small in stature but extremely strong in principles and he does not like being crossed. He trusts people and delegation is a key word for him. He will make decisions and sit on committees and allow others to go public because he knows that they are better than him at doing it. He trusted Davies, for instance, with most of the discussions with Keegan. 'There has to be trust,' he says. 'Without trust how can anyone operate?' He felt let down badly by former chairman Keith Wiseman and Chief Executive Graham Kelly in the summer of 1998 and has never got on with either man again. He explains:

'In 1997 we said, as an association, that we would support Lennart Johansson as the next FIFA Presdient. We went to Helsinki, Keith, Graham and myself, and signed a document stating that we would support him. There was only one country who did not, Denmark, and they had their reasons. The English FA were behind Lennart Johansson and the councillors approved it.

'Then two or three days before the congress in 1998 that was to decide the next President, Keith rang me and said that "we" had changed our minds and that the FA support was for Sepp Blatter. I was in France for the congress and I asked Keith who had decided and he explained that there had been a meeting in London. Wiseman said that he thought that Blatter would help England get the vote for the 2006 World Cup. I said, "Come on Keith, are we really selling ourselves for the 2006 vote?" They had been told, apparently, that we did not have a chance unless we had someone on the FIFA Executive Committee. They were concerned that Johansson had argued that UEFA should vote for Germany. I asked them to reconsider but Wiseman and Kelly said that, even after another meeting, they were adamant that it had to be Blatter.

'It brought huge distrust in Europe and inside UEFA for us. I have been on the UEFA Committee for years and it was a very uncomfortable period when so many of the other countries realised that we had gone back on our word. The Russians said to me: 'We thought the Englishman's word was his bond.' I went to see Johansson in Stockholm and he was miserable. He said he felt sorry for me but had no pity for the other two. He believes that our late change influenced others and Blatter, it was, who won the vote. In the end there were twenty votes in it and I am sure had Wiseman and Kelly not had a change of heart then Johansson would have won. He is a good friend of English football.'

Wiseman and Kelly, of course, parted company with the FA in January (technically they were sacked although the FA prefer to use 'left the building') over the votes for cash scandal. Thompson took over as acting chairman and at the annual meeting of the FA in June 1999, was voted the new chairman. 'I don't look back at that passage with any satisfaction,' he says. 'It did not do our image any good. It took me and others a long time to repair the damage inside UEFA and FIFA that our change of decision caused. Thankfully, the repair has been done but it was an uncomfortable period.

'There is a new mood now. Kevin Keegan also helps this new image. He is such a world figure and everyone wants to know him. He is asked for his autograph wherever he goes. He is brilliant at public relations, so much better than Glenn.'

It was the new mood, new progressive thinking, that so influenced Keegan. So, who are these new men inside Lancaster Gate who are going to help put the world to rights? Streamline the running of the game and polish the old rusty image. Let's start with Howard Wilkinson, the FA's Technical Director who was in place when Keegan arrived. It was a big decision for Wilkinson to take up a job at the FA after a career in management and coaching.

He explains: 'Anyone who knows me knows that my interests and strengths are coaching and working with people on the training ground. I am an ideas person. I get turned on by ideas, they are my thing. I love to make progress.

'When I left Leeds I had time to do a lot of thinking, about my own future and the game in general. I started to run again, play golf and do a lot of reading. One day I had an interesting conversation with a man called John Camkin, a friend who I had known for many years and who I had worked with, with me being chairman of the Managers Association and John being Chief Executive. He said something to me that really stuck. He said: "Between the rut and the grave is a matter of degree."

'It got me thinking. I thought back to Leeds and my last few months in charge and I recalled how I used to be in the dugout five minutes before half time and think to myself "I have got to be angry again for five minutes." As I walked to the dressing room I was mentally searching for something original to say. Everything that came up in a game I had covered with the players, in some form or other.'

'It was around that time that something Roy Hodgson once said came back into my thinking. Roy had told me, "A man who knows a lot about little has done everything there is to know about nothing at all." These things were haunting me as I thought about the future and the FA kept pestering me about joining them. They said that the FA was changing, they wanted me to help them with the reconstructing of the coaching side of the game. It was something different for me but was I being daft? I was, after all, a manager and a coach.

'It was like talking to Les Silver all over again. Les was my old chairman at Leeds. He had said to me, 'Tell us what we need to do and within reason we will do it,' and here were the FA giving me the same question.' Wilkinson agreed to travel to London and talk with the men who ran the game and the England team. He was fascinated as well as interested in the job. He eventually sat round a highly polished table with a group of men he hardly knew or recognised. He did recognise, of course, the then chairman, Keith Wiseman and his Chief Executive friend Graham Kelly. Wilkinson adds: 'My stereotype for the FA was like most other people's. Grey suits, people pushing paper around and hiring and firing.

'I found Wiseman good but could never understand how he could do the job most effectively with the time he left himself to fit everything in. One day he was in Southampton with his own club, then up in Newcastle on FA business, then off to Europe, talking at a boys' club the next night and surviving on three hours' sleep a night. Kelly was always with him. I thought "How can you do the job in a lifestyle like this?" There was not enough time to consider the major issues.'

What made Wilkinson say yes to the FA? 'I once did a newspaper article years ago with a reporter called David Walker, who was then working for the *Daily Mail*. We were on a trip and out on a boat together. We started talking about International football and I said to him that the state of the International game drives me crazy. I told him that I didn't think it would ever change.

'I said that on the one hand we had the media and the public and their perception and the need for instant success. But we are nowhere near as good as we think we are. People blame coaches but I said to Walker that it was a whole lot of things ... that in England we do not have a coaching culture, not even a preparation culture. Football is changing, kids are changing and I just don't see it getting any better. I just wish that people would have a real objective package to football.' After the article in the *Mail* appeared Kelly wrote to Wilkinson and said that he liked his ideas and that what he had said fitted into where the FA were trying to go.

'So eventually I joined the FA,' adds Wilkinson. 'I can now do what I preached all those years ago in that boat. I am doing something different in my mid fifties, making my brain use parts of me that have never been used before. I am doing what I said had to be done. My job is to raise the quality of the playing standards in this country, right across the board. The more people I talked to once I had started the more the message came back to me. That there is no plan. In England we go from competition to competition, tournament to tournament, season to season, crisis to crisis, without anyone really knowing where we are heading. And we are talking about a fleet here, not just the odd ship.

'I discovered that so much needed doing and that became obvious to me very quickly. It was scary for me. At a football club at least you can go out onto the training pitch, talk to the players, work with them and sort it out. When I walked into Lancaster Gate I didn't even know where the paper clips were, let alone the problems. I soon found out.

'It was and has been a great new challenge. It is so different to management and I am coming to terms with it. In management sometimes you survive, sometimes you don't, and when you don't you just bob around in a port waiting for the next ship to come in.'

Wilkinson, unfairly and unjustly, received a lot of criticism when he first took over as Technical Director. He was greeted as boring and not the man to rekindle the new spirit of English football. The criticism hurt him. 'The FA had thought about this job for some time and could not find someone to fit the bill. Then I came and the first thing the critics said about me was what is an ex-teacher doing at the helm of our football? That was unfair because I was a teacher for just two years, long before I went into football. Teacher? I was a teacher of sorts. Football is me. I played a bit and managed a long time. I had also gone through the whole spectrum of coaching. I got an invitation the other day from Whitehawk Boys' Club in Brighton, where it all started for me. It was their 50th dinner. I have done my time and always supported the FA coaching scheme.' He was Jimmy Sirrell's number two at Notts County before making a name for himself at Sheffield Wednesday and then Leeds.

Wilkinson adds: 'People have always looked upon me as a miserable sod. I am certainly very different to Kevin. We have different personalities. If I make a decision I like to think I give it complete consideration, almost overkill if you like. If I don't do that, then I am not happy with myself. I was not easily available on the phone as a manager and if I said to the missus "I need an hour to do some work" she knew to leave me alone. There had to be the right preparation if I was to go out on the training pitch with the players. Sometimes at the end of a session I was not happy because I had not given myself enough time to prepare properly.

'Kevin is different. He needs people and it is finding the balance. He copes with people easily. I believe that we, the FA, have to find a balance for the right way to help Kevin cope best with the pressures of the job. That is going to be vital.

'My ultimate target is to help England win the World Cup. To give this country the best possible chance of doing that. The genuine target is 2006, the more realistic one is 2010. But it is not unreasonable to think that we could win the European Championship and then the World Cup in four or five years' time. We are going to need help and I can not do this on my own. There is no magic wand. It is not simply a question of having the best players in the world, which we do not have. We are also not going to find a crop of world-beaters naturally, nor is there a manager who is the combination of a superb coach and a magician, a man who can suddenly transform 24 players into the very best. That is not going to happen, it takes time, planning, hard work, co-operation.

'I look at the players in 2000 who would be ready for 2006. David Beckham, Robbie Fowler, Michael Owen, Jonathan Woodgate, Alan Smith. You write down the names like me and it is an impressive list, a group to work with. Alan Shearer, Tony Adams and David Seaman will be gone but a genuine development of the players I have mentioned and others can take place with the right methods and the right circumstances. We have only reached the tip of the iceberg in the time I have spent at the FA. England must have a system from the 15-year-old boys upwards. So what you get when the batch of Under 21 players moves up, a team coming through playing the same way, using the same system and learning the same tricks. Wearing the same numbers. Look how Paul Scholes, David Beckham and Nicky Butt play together, these are lessons that must be learned. It is important that our boys all know how we play the game at every level. We are trying to make England a big club at the top of the iceberg. I coined the phrase Club England and that is what we are aiming for.'

It was no surprise, then, that the FA asked Wilkinson to hold the reins after the sacking of Hoddle. He was the experienced man, the former manager and was available, sitting on the doorstep. What no one would believe was that Wilkinson did not want the job for no more than just the one match. More criticism started and it was said that Wilkinson would love to be the new England coach, and that he and Hoddle had never got on. There were even suggestions that Howard had helped push Hoddle over the edge. All the stories were unfounded and, again, they hurt Wilko.

We have heard how inspiring Keegan felt in the dressing room before his first game in charge. How the walk from the room to the dugout, past the celebrating nation, helped him decide that he wanted to take the job permanently. There was no such feeling for Wilkinson just before the match against World Champions France at Wembley. 'I felt embarrassed, like a house sitter, an impostor,' he says. 'I was Monty's Double.

'I just could not get anyone to take the reality of the situation seriously. Only my family believed me that I was doing the job for just one game. Not even my friends accepted it. All the talk was of long term and that was never the case. Never what I wanted. I agreed to stand in for one match while the dust settled after Glenn and the FA looked for a new manager. It was simple to me but not to others.

'Someone had to sign the team sheet. Before the game the FA said to me "What about the squad?" I asked, "When is it due out?" and they said, "Tomorrow morning." I told them to put it out and we went with the squad that Glenn had already selected. I just said to the FA, "Put it out and we will get on with the game."

'Of course it was a good experience. On the Monday night I only had eleven players in the team hotel, having sent the others home with injuries. Then there was the call-ups. Tuesday was freezing and in the afternoon I strolled down the lane to the training pitch to do some set pieces. Incey was there in his woollen hat. I found the whole experience interesting and it was something I will never forget. The media were there in strength and I have always said that, with the right people around you, there is a lot more control over the media than we think.'

France beat England 2–0 at Wembley with two Nicolas Anelka goals and the result was almost inevitable. It left the country asking: 'OK, who next?' It was never going to be Wilkinson. He didn't want it.

It was no surprise either when the FA went to Wilkinson to ask him about Keegan. They are on record as saying that if Wilko had not fancied Keegan, or there had been bad history between the two men in the past, then Kevin would never have become England coach. Yes, Wilkinson is that powerful inside Lancaster Gate. Fortunately for David Davies and the International Committee, Wilkinson had no objection. He encouraged the appointment.

'Initially, we worked closely together,' explains Wilkinson. 'I told Kevin that I would show him around the shop and then he was on his own to pick the teams, decide the tactics. My job is to make sure that Kevin, and whoever is the England manager, gets the best possible players for International football, and to have the system in place, and the backup team ready, to give him the chance to be successful.

'Respect is the key word in management these days and Kevin has that. The manager has to have the respect of the players. You get the respect you deserve and the results you demand. But you get no results without respect. Like is also a quality that comes into it. But players don't have to like just as long as they respect. You can not like someone you do not respect. If the manager gives the player respect, then most players deal with that. And that is whether the manager is outgoing, a miserable sod, the one who goes out with the players or who is shy and reserved, the father figure or the fun type, the knowledgeable one. These are all the layers on top. The bottom line is respect. When he drops you, the player must understand and appreciate the decision. It has to be an honest football decision and not based on anything else.'

The one big blow and problem for Wilkinson since he took over as Technical Director came over the Under 21 side, and the subsequent exit of the successful and popular Peter Taylor, the former Spurs and England player whom Hoddle had brought in to run the Under 21 team. 'The situation with the Under 21 team is simple and clear and the criticism I have received, and the things said since Peter left, have not been accurate,' says Wilkinson.

'Before I took the job I explained what was needed, and in my opinion, what was needed to make a success of the whole thing. From the Under 21 team down there had to be a development strategy, as part of the overall picture. I told them that the Technical Director should be in charge of that because the Technical Director should be here for more than two years. It is highly unlikely that any manager would be but you can't have quick changes of Technical Director. It would destroy all the basework that had gone on.' Graham Kelly, then the Chief Executive, agreed to the Wilkinson plan. One problem. He did not tell Glenn Hoddle.

Wilkinson adds: 'Soon after I took over I spoke to Glenn and told him what the situation was. I told him that I had an agreement that I would take over the running of the Under 21 team when he left, or sooner with his approval. I said that I hoped he saw the sense in it. It was not a question of taking over as manager but the Under 21 side falling into the development scheme. Glenn didn't agree and had not been told. He went and saw Kelly, who confirmed that I had an agreement. It was certainly not the right way to do things but too late by then. I assumed that Glenn would have been told. I assumed wrongly.'

What was Kelly doing? In my opinion it was either a terrible oversight or just a plain bottle job, that Kelly did not have the courage to tell Hoddle what was going on because he knew that he would not be happy. But how can you say yes to a major change like this for the Technical Director without explaining it to the England coach? The mind boggles. And how come Kelly had so much power? I thought the FA did everything by committee. On this occasion someone else should have been told, if only to kick Kelly's backside and order him to discuss it first with Hoddle. It is easy to understand why Hoddle was unhappy, why he smelt a rat and why, after his sacking, his entire backroom staff lined up to confront Wilkinson. I have to say that I find it worrying, and slightly odd, that the England coach does not have overall power of all the England sides. If you are England coach you are top man and other members of your staff should do as you want.

'Within 36 hours of the French game John (Gorman) Ray (Clemence) and Peter (Taylor) came to see me, as did Michelle (the International secretary) and they came collectively and then individually,' explains Wilkinson.

'John said straight away that under no circumstances could he stay as he was Glenn's man and would be leaving. Fair enough. I was not going to fight that. Peter and Ray both wanted to know what their futures held. All this was unfair on me. I was the Technical Director, they had worked for Glenn and should have been talking to the Chief Executive. I just told them that they would have to be patient because there were a lot of balls in the air and that a lot of things were happening.

'I eventually spoke to Ray first. I told him that there was definitely a job for him in the technical department and explained that a lot of big things were happening on the restructuring side. Bigger things were on the move. Ray asked if it would still mean him working with the senior England team and I said "yes" just as long as the new coach wanted him. I said that I would be disappointed if, whoever took over, did not want a goalkeeping coach. I did say that I could not promise him anything because who was I to make those promises?

'I said the same things to Peter when I saw him. He also asked, "Will I be manager of the Under 21 team?" and I said that I could not promise that. The job for him was is in the technical department with coaching responsibilities. He would certainly have been manager until the end of the season and then, who knows? I wanted the freedom to move people within teams. But I am not daft, I know the Under 15 coach can't work with the Under 21s. Peter repeated, "I want to be the Under 21 manager," and I repeated, "I can't guarantee that." I explained to him that here was a job for life and again he said no and asked me to help him negotiate a get out package. Peter was saying that he did not want the job that was on offer. Listen, they, the FA, could have been saying, you can Fuck Off.

'Everything was hunky dory and a package was negotiated when, right at the eleventh hour, history starts to be rewritten and I am supposed to have sacked Peter Taylor. The Under 21 side had just had a great result at Southampton and Peter, I am sure, started to have a change of mind. Maybe he thought to himself "Have I made a mistake here?" Had he stayed he would have been manager, he would probably have been manager of the next lot, but I could not guarantee it under the new regime.

'When Peter left I took over the Under 21 side against my will and without support from the FA. They kept asking me, "Why are you doing this job when you have got so much else on your plate?" and I answered, "Because there is going to be a lot of shite thrown." It would have been unfair to put one of the staff in charge after what had happened, or take someone else from a club. So I borrowed Sammy Lee from Liverpool to help me and Peter Reid also came in, but Reidy had a look and found it too time-consuming. He kept having to rush back for board meetings and, after all, he is running a successful Premiership club at Sunderland. Peter was never given a permanent job with the FA and never had responsibilities.

'I like to get people on board who might work for England one day. For them to see that the job is not as frightening as they think, nor is it as attractive.

'It is not a bad job, is it? One thing for sure, we can't keep having these witch hunts with skeletons emerging from the cupboards. We desperately need a period of stability with the Technical Director preparing players all the way through for International football. That's my job. That's what I do.'

Wilkinson and Keegan have grown to like and respect each other. They talk often and discuss players although the final decision over squads, teams and tactics – for the senior team – is always Keegan's. The buck stops with him. Wilkinson was fiercely protective towards him when the first wave of media criticism came down on Kevin. 'Helping him means protecting him too,' says Wilkinson.

Wilkinson's role is just part of the new FA. There is definitely a new broom sweeping through the corridors of Lancaster Gate. As one staff member said after the quick exit of Wiseman, Kelly and Hoddle, 'The times they are a changing.' The backroom boys, headed by David Davies and Adam Crozier, are building a new empire, and there are others supporting the walls and doing everything to make Keegan's life easier. One of those men is Phil Carling, the FA's Commercial Director.

Carling's job is simple. To make money. He explains: 'Like everything connected with the Football Association, the bottom line is this: The more successful an England team, the easier it is to operate.'

'What I have discovered with Kevin is that he is interested in us, and not only the other way around. When he first came in he wanted to know all about the Commercial Department and how we worked, the mechanics of it. It was the first time, in my experience, that an England manager had done that and I found it an interesting insight to the man.

'Kevin said that he wanted to meet representatives of CSS, the company who control the players on International duty. He wanted to see if they were giving value for the 20 per cent they take from the players' pool.

'Kevin also asked me to go to the team's hotel and explain to the players how the commercial side of the International scene worked. He said that he was not quite sure, so how could the players, particularly the younger ones, be? He wanted them to hear it from me first hand and to encourage a question and answer session.

'I went through how the FA makes money, and what we spend it on. I explained what the income was and the expenditure set against it. We are certainly not a profit-making organisation and every penny of profit that is earned goes back into the progression of the sport at every level. The more money we make, the better the sport should be. Kevin was very keen that that particular point was communicated to the players. It is not something that is generally known or given publicity. But a fact. That all the FA's profit is ploughed back into football in this country. The players were perceptive and I took questions from Alan Shearer, Michael Owen and Graeme Le Saux.

'Kevin has a lot of input, often knocking on the door for a chat. When I was at Arsenal George Graham, Bruce Rioch and Arsene Wenger were the managers and they were never as interested as Kevin is in the commercial department and the image of the game. His enthusiasm is heartfelt and genuine and I find it refreshing and very enterprising.

'When we went to the European Championship Play Off draw in Arken we got talking on the plane and coach journey and he was full of ideas. He said that he knew a guy in Disney World and perhaps there could be a link-up commercially. It was stimulating to have someone who cared about the things going on behind the scenes. He makes it clear that he is interested and that is only right because as a department we interact with the players and their agency.'

The changes at the FA coincided with the departure of chairman Keith Wiseman, chief executive Graham Kelly and manager Glenn Hoddle within the space of a few months, culminating in Hoddle's exit in February 1999. It allowed the people left behind to realise that here was the best possible opportunity to change, and march forward into a new century with fresh ideas and new directions. Were there people inside Lancaster Gate pleased to see the back of Kelly and Wiseman? Nothing has been proven. But I expect that the answer is yes. Wiseman and Kelly were felt to be too old in their thinking. They were once called the ugly sisters of the FA and, for some inside the corridors of power, I believe that the money for votes scandal was just the excuse the hatchet men were looking for. Off with their heads.

The same applies to Hoddle. I agreed with his sacking but had England got to the final of the World Cup in France, and then opened up about his religious beliefs, then he certainly would not have been kicked out. He was in a vulnerable position because of the bad publicity stacked against him and the FA seized on his comments about invalid people, plus the power of the papers, and made the decision to replace him.

The men who moved into the seats vacated by Wiseman and Kelly were more pro-active men, rather than older reactive types. The line in the sand was drawn, it was time to change. No looking back. No more being left behind. The product that the Football Association sit on, the national game, is bigger than big. It is massive. Times are a-changin' and, at last, we seem to being led, rather than other countries and organisations around the world, leading us by the hand, and telling us what we should be doing.

It is only right. The product up for grabs, that the FA have in their fingers, is what the whole world wants. English football. How it has taken this long to realise our power and significance heaven only knows. But, as I say, we must not look back.

Carling knows exactly what he is sitting on. The commercial world is greater and more exciting than ever before. The forming of the Premier League in August 1992, a TV deal that shot the money through the roof and the commercial opportunities make being involved with football going into the twenty-first century undoubtedly the place to be.

When you think that in 1989 the rights for the old First Division were sold to ITV for eleven million pounds and two years later, with the arrival of BSKYB, the going figure was £88 million – and it has gone up ever since – why was there an 800 per cent increase? Simple. Competition. 'The arrival of Sky drove the competition,' says Carling. 'Rupert Murdoch used football as his battering ram. And [at the time of writing this] he has achieved 42 per cent penetration for pay TVs in homes. And he knows that football helps him drive that business deeper into the public.' And there is no doubt that the public can not get enough of football. It has never been more in demand.

Murdoch initially said that he would not pay one billion pounds for the next deal (negotiated in the summer of 2000 for the season starting 2001–2). Carling adds: 'I think it was a negotiating tactic. My view is that if he did not have football in his portfolio then he would lose half of his subscribers. For instance, I would not have Sky without its football. If you have got seven million homes paying around £30 a month, that is a shed load of money. It will certainly be a different type of package that football gets this time. Short-term deals, multiple deals, multiple formats.'

The FA hired a special team of lawyers and negotiators to discuss their own deal for the England games, the FA Cup, Charity Shield and Women's Football. 'We needed clever people for a complex deal. There is huge money at stake,' added Carling.

Huge money indeed. The Nationwide Building Society pay £11 over four years for the privilege of sponsoring the England team. Axa, who sponsor the FA Cup, pay £26 million over four years. There are ten companies in total who also put their name to the England team. They are Nationwide, Axa, Umbro, Carlsberg, Sainsbury's, Walkers, Coca Cola, One to One, Eidos and Burtons and they all pay £500,000 a year as an entrance to being able to work alongside the England team. On top of their initial fee, companies can upgrade if they want to do more and, of course, Nationwide and Axa are the big spenders. In all the contract with the ten companies brings in an incredible £60 million over a four-year period.

Within their contract they get 40 tickets for England games, 40 for the FA Cup Final, hospitality facilities, perimeter board advertising and other rights. Carling adds: 'Part of the deal includes a certain amount of public appearances for the players and the ability to use their images as promotions. They get a certain amount of signed items, an exclusive use of their products (no rival company can use the product) and that means they are basically paying to keep their competitors away from England.'

The telephone company One to One sponsor the FA Charity Shield and companies like Sainsbury's and Burtons just buy the core package of being able to link with England, and they pay £500,000 a year. They also have access to the England players.'

If you are an England player you can print your own money. It is huge business. There is a player' committee and the squad is represented by CSS, who specialise in sport sponsorship and who are part of the Stella Management Group, whose chairman is Barry Gill, who is also involved with Formula One motor racing. Gill is at the helm. The system is simple. The FA enter into a contract with CSS to use the players commercially. They may play for England but the FA still have to get permission to use them for commercial deals. Carling adds: 'We basically enter into a contract with CSS to purchase from the players a number of public appearances and the sum of money that is paid goes into the players' pool. Then we put the rights that we have acquired into the contracts that we have entered into with our sponsors.

'Take Coca Cola as an example. They have signed for ten PA appearances a year. It is up for them to decide when to use them. They may want them for their mini soccer scheme. They say to us, "We would like some players" and we contact CSS. They in turn contact the player or players Coca Cola wants and they make sure that it fits in with their diary.'

The biggest requests are for Alan Shearer, David Beckham and Michael Owen. 'They are at the top of the sponsors' minds,' admits Carling. 'But in the contract we have there has to be a spread of players and we have the right to say which player does what, or not at all. Kevin is heavily involved and he can say, "Hold on a minute, I don't want him doing that or not at that time." That is the deal. Kevin has made it clear that we, the commercial department of the FA, interact with the players and their agency. He makes sure that it does not react against what he wants to do. He does not want distraction and you can not blame him for that.'

The players' committee heading towards the European Championships was Shearer, Tony Adams, David Seaman and Sol Campbell. It used to be Stuart Pearce, and Campbell is the latest addition. It was interesting that Keegan made sure that all the commercial network was explained to the younger players. It is just part of Keegan's hands-on involvement in every aspect of the job.

Carling adds: 'It is also important that we don't tread on the club's toes. We work closely with Kevin and produce a running schedule of events. It might say that on the Monday Nationwide will arrive with twelve customers to watch training, on Tuesday there will be a photo session with David Seaman and another photo shoot on Thursday. Kevin has the right to say no, as do the players if it clashes with something they are doing with their clubs. It would be easy for me to flood the whole thing because the demand is so great. It is my job to filter the requests and personal appearances and I have a team that works with me. We have to ask ourselves, "What is reasonable for the team and the manager before a big game?" The demand from them for the European Championship Play Off game against Scotland at Wembley was huge. It was the biggest demand since we played Argentina in the World Cup. You have to keep the sponsors feeling warm and wanted without going over the top.'

The victory over Scotland in the two-match play-off, putting England into the finals, was hugely significant for Carling and his team. The biggest benefit is for football as a whole in this country but, commercially, it is just another licence to print money. Carling explains.

'You can measure it in tens of millions. Gate receipts are a huge revenue. That is one side. The contracts we have with sponsors are nailed down and do not include clauses whether we qualify, or indeed don't qualify for Championships. The same rules apply. We do not own the television rights to our games, UEFA do, and so they market those. Where it will affect us is in licensing. The number of companies who come along and want to use our product, The Three Lions. As the interest soars so does the earning capacity of the companies. In the France World Cup Sainsbury's produced collector coins of the England players. A company called TCC produced 19 million as the first order and the final order was close to 65 million. That type of thing is huge and you only get such interest at a major Championship.' Carling had companies just waiting for the outcome of the Scotland game, willing England to get through. Once our place was confirmed the offers flooded in. It is quite extraordinary the interest in the England team. And England have not won anything since 1966!

It is not only the players who are in demand. The England coach has always been attractive to sponsors and companies. Remember the Weetabix advertisment that Glenn Hoddle did that was dropped when he split from his wife? Carling again. 'I go to Kevin and explain who wants him and for what and advise that the company is "family" or not and that it is up to him to negotiate his own deal. My only desire is to protect the commercial programme that I have put together for the Football Association. It is the same with players. We do not want them doing deals that conflict with what we are doing. If a player is advised badly we would have a word and, hopefully, the problem would go away.'

There is no question that Keegan's impact on the Football Association has been massive. Maybe more as a person than a manager. 'He is great news for everyone,' says Carling. Typical of Keegan's commercial thinking surrounded the marquee that the FA erected, on Keegan's instruction, in the grounds of the Burnham Beeches Hotel, their base for all home Internationals. It is a temporary structure that stands for about a week and it is where Keegan and the FA do their press conferences every day in the build-up to Internationals. Keegan immediately saw another outlet for it.

Carling explains: 'Kevin asked me whether the sponsors would be interested in the marquee. He wondered if he brought in a few players one lunchtime would it be helpful for me to entertain sponsors. I thought to myself, "This is a dream." Here is an England coach who is so switched on commercially it is untrue. He says, "Do you think it is a good idea?" and I want to take him by the arm and say "yes, yes" it is a great idea.

'Then I worry that we could be making a rod for our own back. When the wheels come off (if) would we still need to deliver something for the sponsors? And will I still get Kevin's co-operation? But there is no question that never before has there been an England coach with so much to offer all aspects of the Football Association. He is ideal for the new mood that is sweeping through the place. Take the Disney thing and his contact. He wants me to meet him because he knows that Disney and the FA have the same audience.

'Whenever I meet Kevin I find him stimulating. He is interested in what I am doing. In three years' time there will be doubtless countless more times for us to make use of his ideas, drive and enthusiasm. Plus, of course, his contacts.'

Keegan's ability to spot an idea that is good for the FA came with a letter he received from a school in the London area. It asked whether he might find time to visit the school and even talk to the boys. Keegan did more than that. He set up a coaching scheme within schools throughout the country. 'He thought it was a fantastic idea,' says Carling. 'He told us that it is what the FA should be about. Getting in at the very grass roots.' The upshot was that, with the help of coach Les Reed, there is now a schools coaching programme, sponsored by Walkers, and it involves Keegan visiting at least six schools a year. 'Players will also go along and, as Kevin says, everyone gets an input. The one thing that he did stipulate was that he did not want the school project to be sponsor-driven.

'He was strong on that. He said it was not about a commercial deal or the media, it was about him and the kids he was visiting. He did not want the media there so that he was pulled aside and distracted and the children were pushed to the background. "It is their day, their time," he said and we agreed. It came from the heart.

'There is no doubt that other ideas will follow from him. He is not someone whose mind stays in neutral.'

Remarkable man, Kevin Keegan. You can dig all you like but you rarely find anyone with anything bad to say about him. He will have enemies somewhere, but not the type that come hurtling out of the cupboards like the skeletons that helped chase Terry Venables and Glenn Hoddle out of Lancaster Gate. If they do emerge it will be a major surprise to the FA. In my research it was only Ray Wilkins at Fulham who fell out with him. There was no one, certainly no one in the game, who wanted to criticise him as a player, manager or person.

He quickly made friends inside the FA. He liked the fact that all the men in authority were on his wavelength and one of those, new Chief Executive Adam Crozier, quickly formed a good relationship with the England coach. Crozier says: 'You can do what you like inside the FA, work all hours God gave you, but the bottom line is that everything runs much more smoothly if there is a successful England side as the flagship.

'It is vital therefore that Kevin is given every opportunity to do the job properly, and to the best of his ability. We, the FA, must give him that opportunity. In a very short space of time it is obvious to me that Kevin has a better relationship with the clubs than has been seen or enjoyed for many years. That relationship is important. Kevin needs the players and there has to be give and take. He knew, for instance, that it would not be possible in April to put out the players he would have liked and we decided not to stage an International then. There will be no picking up of the date even for a training get-together.

'It is significant that the friendlies he chose as his build up to the European Finals, Argentina, Brazil and the Ukraine at Wembley, are all top-flight opposition. Kevin decided that it was better to have quality opposition rather than meaningless friendlies just for the sake of having a game.

'In the little time that I have known him, it is clear that Kevin takes a big interest in what is going on behind the scenes, and what we are trying to achieve. I want all people to think that this organisation is open, accountable, challenging and responsive, and all those qualities apply to Kevin. That is the way he is and it comes naturally and I certainly see him as the vision of the future. He knows exactly the kind of place I would like to be with England and the FA in years to come.'

I know what you are saying, I can hear it as I write this. Yes, yes, we have heard all this before from the FA. All talk and trousers but no action. We are not interested in the old duffers down at Lancaster Gate. It is only the England side that makes us tick, that gets us motivated. There is something in that, of course, and I have sympathy with the view. Indeed, I have been the biggest critic of the FA over the years. But things are really changing. David Davies saw the need for streamlining when he first walked into Lancaster Gate and has worked hard behind the scenes to achieve it. Adam Crozier also represents hope for a new era.

He adds: 'My own perception of the FA before I walked through the door for the first time was of an old-fashioned organisation, of a cumbersome outfit, and I probably wondered just how passionate they were about the game. I am pleased to say that everyone here is very passionate about football, and cares what happens to it. And that includes the 91 councillors, who get such bad publicity. These men give their whole lives to football and they have a lot to give to the sport. The stick they get is unfair.

'I can assure you that the decision-makers at the FA are young people, and young-thinking people. Myself, Nick Coward, Michael Cunnah and David Davies, who tells us that he is still a spring chicken. I do feel a frustration to get on faster with what is needed to be done. I have a clear vision of what is needed and I think the biggest breakthrough is that there is a willingness to change, by everyone, bar none, at this level. Once you get the will, then the rest is easy.'

There is no doubt that the biggest turning point in the FA's history was the sacking of Wiseman, Kelly and Hoddle. Out with the old duffers, in with the clear thinking. Out with Them Boys, in with more intelligent, better presented, progressive thinkers and even the councillors agreed. They saw the light. They realised that the FA had drawn a line in the sand and there was no stepping back. The image, direction and style had to be right.

Crozier adds: 'What is progress, what is streamlining that everyone talks about? Changes have already taken place and some of them will not be obvious to the public, the man in the street. For a start we have a new streamlined board in place, made up of the national game and professional people and for the first time I believe there is the right balance between all areas of the sport.' It was incredible how quickly that changed. After years of tradition it was all over inside two hours at an extraordinary general meeting. In one giant step the FA went from the nineteenth century into the twenty-first.

The FA are run from now on by a the board of directors, six from the professional game and six from the counties, now called the National Game. The professionals will run the professional side and the grass roots will be administrated by the National Control Board, whose members are drawn from the National Game. It was a huge step. Crozier adds:

'I don't think that many people realise that every penny of profit this organisation makes, and last season it was between £15 and £18 million, goes back into football, at every level. We get no credit for doing that and the message has to be got across that we do care, we are helping everyone. We must bring the sport closer the FA. So often we are thought of as just a disciplinary body. There are so many players and yet the only contact they get from us is likely to be a letter saying "You owe us £5" for some disciplinary situation. That is not a good image. Not one that I want.

'My target is to make sure that the FA leads the way in the

successful redevelopment of football. There are so many people, and so much being done behind the scenes that the public are not aware of. In the past the FA has been reactive and never set the agenda. That must never happen again, we have to get on the front foot and lead in every way. When there is a FIFA meeting about fixtures, we must not go there to listen and accept, we must go there and say, "This is what England wants and what it intends to do." If we do not want to do something, we must not be put off and persuaded against our will.

'The same goes with television. When the next deal comes and this is going to be the biggest and most important television deal in football's history, we must not be railroaded. The FA must say to TV, you can have our product but we want a say in how it is going to be presented and when it will appear. For instance the FA Cup, with every round spread over four or five days, has lost its momentum. I want the competition to go back to its old traditions. I think that is what the public want.

'It is a vital TV deal because there is going to be so much money at stake and we have to make sure that the money goes into the right areas of the game. The grass roots of the sport, for instance, is so important. We have to get that right.'

Crozier's passion comes out when you talk about all subjects. The FA, the England team, grass roots, television, the image of the game, the foreign import and what can we do about it and the prospect that England is in danger of losing the David and Goliath aspect of the sport, when big falls to small, when the minnow cuts the giant down to size. I have banged on about this for many years and can not bear to think of the day when we do not have a rainbow for the small clubs to climb. The day that money means no more giant-killing because the big are too good for the small, is the day that football will not mean the same for me in England.

'It would be dreadful if David was never around in football,' says Crozier. 'It is the reason why other countries struggle, like Scotland and Holland, is because there is no strength in depth. It means we have to make sure the money is spread and enough gets down to the smaller clubs to have a future. There will always be a gap and we are not going to be able to close it, but we can make sure that it does not get too wide. In Scotland Rangers and Celtic have even thought of redistributing some of their own money to less successful clubs so that competition becomes harder. That kind of situation must never happen in England.

'I do believe however that clubs can market themselves better, sell themselves more. The opportunity is there although not always taken. I certainly don't want Manchester United, Arsenal and Chelsea to win everything all the time because that would be unhealthy for the sport.'

Keegan's involvement in everything going on is immense. The FA took advice from their coach over the TV deal with Keegan also having an input into when Internationals should be played. That is the first time that has happened and shows the respect he has inside Lancaster Gate. As I have said before, he is sitting on a job for life. Only he can blow it.

Keegan has also spoken to his bosses about the England players becoming bigger and better role models in the game. Image is extremely important to the FA and they have asked superstars like David Beckham, Alan Shearer and Michael Owen to help them improve the image with on-pitch behaviour levels.

'Kevin is very keen on the players becoming greater role models,' says Crozier. 'We support that because I am alarmed at the number of reports we get about youngsters misbehaving because they have been influenced by their heroes on television. Beckham and other England players have a huge influence on these kids and they can help us so much. We called on their help for the campaign to clean up the image of football.'

One of Keegan's biggest concerns heading towards the European Championships was the development of young players in England, or the lack of them. Keegan is worried that whoever takes over from him will be left with a completely bare cupboard because the natural growth has been stifled by the foreign invasion. Nothing can be done to prevent the foreign players being signed but there are moves to restrict the number of them playing in any one team. Five seems to be the favoured number, as they do in Spain.

Crozier says: 'I share Kevin's worry about the lack of English talent coming through. There are some clubs, like Manchester United, Leeds and West Ham, where there is a superb crop of young players emerging. If we can encourage other clubs, if we can make sure that new talent does develop and that talent has the right habits, on and off the pitch, and if we do make sure that there is a new England emerging we will have done a damn good job. For that to happen there might have to be a period when we have to wait for that talent to break through. We may have to struggle for a period, while we wait. The fact is we have to get it right in the long term, in 15 years' time, say. It means that kids of eight, nine and ten today are brilliantly developed for our future. That is what I see. That is what I want, indeed, what the FA wants.'

They are sound words, of course, but are we are nation who can wait? Are we, and I include my own profession in this, able to stand back when we don't qualify for major tournaments and play meaningless friendlies, while we wait for today's ten year olds to mature, and not moan and complain? And, of course, there is no guarantee that they will be good enough and bring the success that is so desperately needed.

It is a puzzle that can not be solved. Do we carry on hyping it up and being let down? Do we carry on allowing in the foreign players to stifle the youth? Do we change things and wait? Would we be able to wait? If England lost at home in a World Cup qualifying match to Sweden would we say, as one: It does not matter because in five years we will be World Champions. It does not work like that I'm afraid and we remain a nation who wants results yesterday. We live in a society who do not like waiting. Be at a traffic light minding your own business and there will always be someone who wants to race away and be first out of the blocks. 'I want it now' is an English expression.

That is the same in football. England wants to be first now, and in the future. I understand completely where Crozier is coming from and applaud his thinking. But it will not happen. Yes, we must coach and encourage the kids, change the rules to help them, but we – the FA and the England coach – must also expect a bumpy ride while we wait.

The public and, OK, the media, have some justification in thinking that a coach, earning £1 million a year, and a bunch of players earning more, should be able to do well in the major tournaments. The coach holds the key. If he is astute, clever, has the respect of the players, picks the right team and gets the best out of them, knows his tactics and can outwit the best coaches in the world, then we are in business. That is the bottom line.

Is Kevin Keegan that man? Going into the European Championships we have to say the Jury Is Out. He got us to the finals and that is what he set out to do. He talks a good game and firmly believes that we have the players to win it. The test is the Championships, how England play, how Keegan reacts. Would he keep cool if things go wrong? If he gets through the group then all will be well. If we do not qualify for the knockout stages then the FA will be in trouble. If Keegan was to quit then everything said in this chapter would not make much sense. Because everything the FA do now is based on continuity, with everyone inside Lancaster Gate working together.

Keegan is the Pied Piper. The flagship. The leader. The public figure. His head is the tip of the iceberg and everyone else at 16 Lancaster Gate are paddling their little legs under the water. Without Keegan they have no one else, which they have admitted.

As Kevin Keegan's England headed towards the European Championship Finals there were a lot of men crossing their fingers behind him. Success was absolutely vital, for the short and long-term future of English football. Over to you, Kev. The Messiah.

CHAPTER 11

A FUNNY THING HAPPENED TO KEVIN KEEGAN IN TOKYO

There is no question that Kevin Keegan at times tries too hard with the media. He is superb to interview, knows what journalists want, says the right things and co-operates more than most. He has the knack of saying what people are feeling and that is a key to anyone in the public eye. If you can get people to say 'yes, he's right' then you are more than half-way there. Keegan's press conferences can often be a performance. There he is, up there in lights, and when the spotlight is on him people listen. 'I am trying to give you the answers you want' is one of his favourite sayings at press conferences.

Of all the England managers I have worked closely with Keegan and Bobby Robson were and are the best to interview. For different reasons. I first covered England when the late Sir Alf Ramsey was in charge. He hated working with the media and it showed. But it was a different game then, a different world when it came to media. He did not co-operate and there was no pressure on him to change. Journalists might have moaned behind his back but never in print.

The late Don Revie had his favourites in the newspapers and never got close to us as a unit. Joe Mercer was a respected character who you listened to but realised that his was only a part-time, holding appointment. Ron Greenwood came from a culture of a closed-shop atmosphere with journalists waiting outside in the cold for a scrap of information. There was a them and us attitude. The public relations at the 1982 World Cup in Spain, for instance, was a disaster. It never fails to amaze me just how badly organised England and all that surrounds them can be. For instance, in Spain Ron and his staff thought that it would be good fun to invite a few local dancers in to entertain the players. They didn't realise that the dancers were local prostitutes, who loved every minute of showing off. The national newspapers got hold of the story and, as they say, the rest is history. Just imagine what exposure that kind of story would get today.

The Kevin Keegan affair in Spain was not exactly handled well. Keegan has to take a lot of responsibility for it. He went into the World Cup with a back injury – although he denies this now: 'I was not injured going into the tournament, I hurt my back in the first training session,' he says – and it was never admitted. Keegan at one stage drove back to Germany to see the specialist he had faith in. Again it was not admitted and we had the bizarre situation of England saying that Keegan was OK and yet the captain not even in the country. The story came out through the back door and Greenwood and Keegan were very grumpy for a long time. They were made to look foolish. Keegan, in fact, hardly talked to the media throughout the tournament.

Bobby Robson was a dream, simply because he loved the job so much. He enjoyed everything about it. He put his foot in it, often right up to the ankle, with things that he said, he could not remember some players' names and got others wrong. But here was a character you warmed to because of his love and passion for the job. He was criticised more than any other England manager but ended a hero and there is not a journalist who does not have a warm spot for Bobby Robson. Ask him today if he would return to the job, at his age, and he would say yes like a shot. 'It is the country and you can not turn them down,' he says. England got rid of him too soon.

Graham Taylor was also good with the media, who again tried too hard, but there was never enough respect for him as a coach at the highest level for the relationship with the media to mature. Terry Venables was clever, on and off the pitch. He knew exactly what to say and when to say it to a pack of journalists. He was also one of the rare managers who knew what a story was and what would interest us.

He also had his favourites and was good to them. He was always available to them and off the record conversations took place many times for card marking and a pointer in the right direction. I ended up having a lot of respect for Venables, despite one or two fall-outs along the way. The bottom line for journalists, surely, is results, regardless of relationships.

Glenn Hoddle, as we have already said, was a disaster for the media. He simply could not work out why we wanted to talk to him. And when he did talk he would inevitably come out with weird and wonderful sayings. 'Them Boys' or 'So and so has got his different head on today.' It did not make sense and, in the end, nor did he. Glenn and I used to be close, but not any more. That is the profession, those are the pressures. He could not take criticism and we will never have a relationship again. It is a shame because, as a coach, I have high regard for him. I suspect that as tactical brains then Hoddle and Keegan are a long way apart. My own thoughts regarding Hoddle are that in all walks of life you have to take criticism, accept it, and not react negatively to it. You have to rise above it.

And so to Keegan. He does not go into press conferences with rehearsed lines and angles, like Taylor did, and he thinks he knows what journalists want. The longer he sits in front of us however the more it becomes apparent that Keegan does not really understand journalism. He tries with what he says but no England manager can have a concept about what is a story. 'Please don't make too much of that,' he says. 'Make of that what you will' is another comment. He also uses, 'I would not be afraid to do that' too often for his own good. I hope the FA brief him and there is no harm in a press officer saying to journalists, 'What do you want to talk to the manager about today?' and then go away and warn the coach. That is common sense.

It is frustrating for certain journalists because there are others who do not have any ideas as they go into an England briefing. They just sit there and gobble up everything and anything that goes. There are other major irritations, including agency reporters who get access to all England press conferences, without a question or idea in their head. Early in 2000 a group of us went up to Newcastle to interview Alan Shearer, a press situation organised by sponsors Nationwide. One agency guy just sat in the corner, taking notes, and then asked us afterwards when he could put the copy out.

I also can't stand radio or TV journalists who begin an interview with the phrase 'The tabloids have been hard on you this week.' Well, what is that person's opinion? Why does he or she have to live off what has been written? Why do they not say 'What made you do that?' rather than rely on others for their ammunition. And what about the reporter who stands at the back of a player interview and simply pushes his tape recorder as close to the player as he can, often straining on tiptoe at the back of a gaggle of media, especially in the mixed zone area? It happened to me after England had played Brazil at Wembley in the final build-up the European finals. About four national journalists were interviewing David Seaman, after TV, radio and the Sunday newspapers had finished with him. I wanted to ask him about his future and he admitted that he had no intention of quitting after the finals and expected to be around for the next World Cup. The agency reporter, without a clue what had been said, or an idea of his own, listened to his tape later and thought 'that's interesting' and it was on the Press Association the next day before I had filed my story to the *Sun*.

Venables knew who those kinds of journalists were and I wonder if Keegan will discover the same when he goes through his first major tournament. He does, I believe, try hard. Too hard in some situations. A good example came when he went to Tokyo for the draw for the 2002 World Cup qualifying rounds. It was soon after we had qualified for the European Championships with our mixed performances against Scotland. Tokyo was Keegan's first public appearance since the stick and criticism he had received, especially from the *Daily Mail,* following the home defeat by Scotland.

In that first interview he must have known what was coming and did he have his answers ready? If he did they were the wrong answers. It was reported that Keegan said: 'After the Scotland game it became very obvious to me that if we had gone out I would have had to have gone.

'I believe that one hundred per cent. Looking at the way it went, I said to my missus that if they had scored another goal at Wembley that would have been me finished, without a doubt.

'I want to be England manager for as long as I can but I am a realist. If things don't go fantastically well at Euro 2000, to then take England into the World Cup would be difficult. My contract expires in 2002 but I don't suppose it would be me in charge. The days of the England manager lasting six or eight years are long gone. It is so instant now. Here you go, it's your job, get on with it and you had better be successful.

'It is not the public, it is not the FA. The FA have not even said that results must improve, they have been very supportive. But the FA alone won't keep me here. It is not the way it works any more. I am not being unkind, but you underestimate the press.

'I don't think you realise the effect it has on people. The way it is now I would be delighted to get through to the next World Cup, that would be an achievement. I am not a fool. There will be some who will be just waiting for something to go wrong, and then bang. So much is turned into a negative it is sad.'

Whether it was true or not, what Keegan said made sense. The pressure on him to go from some quarters if the European Championships are a disaster would be tremendous. As Noel White has said, it is not the FA who control when the England managers come and go any more. The other thing that Keegan is acutely aware of is the power of the media. Hoddle underestimated it and there is no question that the media wanted Hoddle out. Not just because so many of us thought he had lost his way and the dressing room, but because he had splintered the media.

For the record, England in the World Cup qualifying group were drawn against Germany, Albania, Greece and Finland. The headlines went from 'I'll Quit If We Fail' to 'Keegan Faces the Old Enemy' in the space of a couple of days. It was an interesting trip for the new England coach. He told the FA people that he is close to that he learned a lot in Japan. About many things ...

Within a few days he was denying that he had ever used the word quit or that walking out on England had not entered his mind. He was angered, he said, by the interpretation of the remarks he had made about the perils of the position. 'I never said that if we do not do well in Euro 2000 I would quit,' he rebuked. 'I said that the World Cup is a great competition and one that I was really looking forward to. But at the moment I have to be focused on Euro 2000. That is the priority. If I do not do well in Belgium and Holland then maybe the World Cup would be beyond me. I also said that I want to keep the job for as long as possible. But I am a realist and the only way I am going to do that is by getting good results. That is the only way any manager in football keeps his job.' So, you pay your money and take your choice. The journalists in Tokyo, of course, and quite rightly, stick by their stories.

He strongly denied that he had ever walked out on anyone. When reminded that as a player he once walked out on England, and then turned his back on Newcastle as manager, he answered: 'OK, that's twice. But it will not happen with my job as England coach.'

I hope he is right although there are many, and some who know Keegan well, who believe that when the going gets tough, the tough walk out. They expect Keegan to say thanks, but no thanks, if England fail in the Euros and the criticism starts to fly.

His mood was certainly relaxed and confident when he went to Brussels in December 1999 for the European Championships draw. He remains a world star and the media follow him around, certainly when England are drawn against Germany, as they were again. It meant that Keegan, in the biggest year of his life, had to get past his country's greatest rivals if the year 2000 was going to see him successful or, indeed, stay in the job.

Keegan made a joke of meeting the Germans again, although he knew that a group of Germany, Portugal and Romania in the Euros was not easy, especially with only two going through. He said to Germany manager Erich Ribbeck: 'We should go on holiday together.' But Keegan knew that these were massive matches for him. They were matches that meant the difference between his continuing in his job or going back to the golf course.

'The most important game for me in the European Finals will be the first, against Portugal. Lose your first match in a major tournament and you could be on your way home,' he said. But get past Portugal and then it was on to Germany, whom England have not beaten in a competitive match since 1966 and all that. And Portugal had not lost to England in a competitive match since our victorious World Cup campaign either.

'On paper I know people will say I am the coach of the weakest team,' said Keegan. 'Yes, this is also the toughest group. But that is not the way I look at it. I know my players will not be the weakest at the European Championship.'

He also repeated his 'I will quit' denial, insisting that he had been misrepresented in Tokyo and that he had no thoughts of walking away from the job, whatever the outcome in Brussels and Holland, and whatever the stick he would take. He got the complete backing, once again, of FA Chairman Geoff Thompson.

'There is no point in giving a man the job if you also give him a gun with a bullet in it,' said Thompson. 'He has the backing of the Football Association and, I believe, the complete support of the people in this country.

'His first job was to get England to the Finals. If he had not done it there would not be any pressure on him. Kevin Keegan has lifted the nation, got us to the finals and now is confident of success. We always thought that his main job was to concentrate on the World Cup in 2002 and these finals have been something of a bonus. Don't forget that when he took over he had one hand tied behind his back because of the results he inherited.

'If I could have one wish it would be for everyone, supporters, players and the media to get behind Kevin Keegan. He is the best man for the job, everyone wanted us to appoint him and we delivered. Now Kevin has delivered by getting us to the European Championships. This is a massive year for English football, a massive year for Kevin and the players. Let us make it easier for him by supporting him right the way down the line. Kevin says that England has the players to become European Champions. Why do we have to deny him that prediction? I support him. Just imagine what it would be like if England were to win a major trophy. The repercussions for the game would be fantastic. We would all benefit. It would be the start of a new era. A winning era.'

In football terms that is a massive vote of confidence. They are usually given by a chairman when his manager is under pressure, and the manager ends up by being sacked a few days later. That is not the case for Keegan. The FA are right behind him. They want him to succeed and he is desperate for glory. As a player he never flinched when it came to the ultimate challenge. Mighty Mouse grew in stature. How tall can Kev grow this time?

Turning into the year 2000 every football eye was on him. First four big friendly Internationals to bed down his final squad of 22, then the European Championship Finals and on to World Cup qualifying matches all in the space of one year. The biggest year of his life? Yes. Would he emerge a hero or with his reputation in tatters? 'I am ready for everything,' he said. 'Success, failure and what goes with failure.'

But as Kevin Keegan peered into the future, as he raised his glass on New Year's Eve, as he looked into the Millennium, not even he could have guessed what chapter was about to be written in the history of English football. It would certainly be his chapter. The twelve months that would make or break his career as England coach. The twelve months that would shatter the image that is Keegan, or make it for the rest of his days.

CHAPTER 12

THE FINAL COUNTDOWN

'Why are the media so negative?' Kevin Keegan groaned. 'In press conferences I actually have to ask them the positive questions I think they should be asking me. I try to help them, I want to and I just wish they would really get behind the England team.'

Keegan was reflecting on his first press conference of 2000 after naming his squad to play against Argentina at Wembley on 23 February, the first of his four warm-up matches. In that press conference he had grown tired and despondent at the level of questioning about discipline and player behaviour, on and off the pitch. 'Let's draw a line underneath this now, shall we boys?' he asked at one stage. Then the lights went out in the conference room at London's Metropole Hotel to ease the tension and allow Keegan a natural break. 'There are two kids been picked today (Aston Villa's Gareth Barry and Steve Gerrard of Liverpool) and why can't we talk about them?' Afterwards he added: 'I know what the tone of the pieces they will write in the morning and I can't say I am thrilled about it.'

There were signs at that press conference that Keegan was over-reacting to criticism. At one point when we were discussing Chelsea skipper Dennis Wise, who had been kept in the squad despite his terrible disciplinary record and who had been charged that same week with misconduct for his alleged part in a tunnel bust up at Stamford Bridge, Nigel Clarke of the *Mail* whispered something to me. Keegan broke off from answering another question to demand to know what Clarke had said. 'Wise is on a misconduct charge because the referee reported him and the FA acted,' said Clarke. 'I know that,' said Keegan. 'But no one knows what went on in that tunnel and are we going to be the judge and jury? Does a man not have the right to defend himself? When I pick an England player I pick him warts and all.'

Keegan also voiced his concern over the FA's crackdown on discipline not being in line with other countries. 'We don't want this to damage us,' he said. It was an interesting start to the year by Keegan. You got the impression that he wanted to be friendly but that his frosty side was not far away. His questioning of the FA's stance over discipline was interesting, especially coming at the end of a week when his bosses charged four clubs, Chelsea, Wimbledon, Leeds and Spurs with failing to control their players, and four players and a coach with misconduct. On top of that Stan Collymore and his Leicester teammates were sent home from Spain after a boozing spree, climaxing with Collymore letting off a fire extinguisher in a hotel bar in La Manga.

Keegan later complained that there were too many negatives reported when it came to England. The old chestnut about his lack of tactical knowledge was also brought up. 'It goes back to my days at Newcastle when we were so far ahead in the Championship and did not win it. People will always find the vulnerabilities. But we almost did it at Newcastle playing marvellous attacking football. Playing like that is my belief and we are getting that way with England. I will not change. I have always been positive. I remember writing in the first Newcastle programme of the season "And now for the Premiership" and the chairman coming to see me and saying that it would get the public too expectant. "That is the whole point," I said.'

Keegan expects. The country expect. He doesn't mind that. He thrives on it. Can he cope with it? We would find out in 2000.

He again voiced his love of doing the job and his determination to do it for many years to come. 'I would like to go beyond the next World Cup although I accept that results will determine that,' he said. 'The players too will have a big say in what happens. But, yes, I want to go on a long time. I have no idea what happens after England, or when that will be. Something will crop up that tickles my fancy. I was enjoying myself at Fulham and heading towards the target that we set. In a way it was a shame that the England job cropped up when it did.

'But, like I have said many times, you can not look back. I am not scared to say that I think we have a great chance of becoming European Champions. And I am not scared of the backlash if we don't. Tell me, are Germany really better than England at this stage?'

Keegan lined up four big friendlies for the build-up, at home to Argentina on 23 February, then a big gap until Brazil on 27 May, again at Wembley. Then came Ukraine at home and a short trip to Malta just a week before taking the squad of 22 to Belgium and Holland. He had to name a provisional squad of 35 by 10 May and then cream it down to 22. That deadline, incredibly, was midnight after the match against the Ukraine. It would mean Keegan going into the game knowing that he would have an hour afterwards to make a decision on a final place in the squad or, more drastically, make a verdict on a player he wanted to take to the final who was injured against Ukraine.

'I would have to say to the medical people, "Will he be fit to play in 12 days?" and take their judgment and make a verdict. When I first heard what UEFA wanted I could not believe it, but those are the facts and it is going to be a hairy one hour and a bit after that match. I will not have time for a press conference or anything like that, just to be with the players before faxing the choice to UEFA.' Keegan will also have to tell players who are not in his squad as they sit in the dressing room, some having played against Ukraine. A squad of 35 on 10 May also made the Argentina match hugely significant. It was the coach's one and only game for real experiment.

Keegan certainly faced big decisions. In his 24-man squad for Argentina there was no place for Darren Anderton, a hero under Terry Venables and Glenn Hoddle, or Teddy Sheringham, who had been in good form for United. 'Teddy needs to play more consistently and not just be in and out of the United team,' said Keegan. Also missing was Steve McManaman, who had not set the world alight since his Bosman move to Real Madrid on £52,000 a week. If you added the not selected Anderton, McManaman and Sheringham plus injured Robbie Fowler, Michael Owen, Tony Adams, Ian Walker, Stuart Pearce, David Batty and Graeme Le Saux plus Joe Cole and Frank Lampard, who were with the Under 21s, it proved just how hard Keegan's job was.

Keegan's squad against Argentina was:

Seaman, Martyn, Wright, G. Neville, P. Neville, Barry, Southgate, Campbell, Keown, Ferdinand, Beckham, Ince, Froggatt, Wilcox, Dyer, Gerrard, Parlour, Scholes, Sinclair, Wise, Cole, Phillips, Heskey, Shearer. Owen, Fowler, Le Saux and Redknapp were all missing through injury. *Match*: 23 February. *Score*: 0–0. *Team*: Seaman, Keown (Ferdinand 46), Southgate, Campbell, Dyer (P. Neville 59), Beckham (Parlour 72), Wise, Wilcox, Shearer (Phillips 78), Heskey (Cole 79).

It followed these squads in his first nine matches as England coach:

Match against Poland (Wembley, 27 March 1999)
Score: 3–1. *Squad*: Seaman, Ferdinand, Campbell, Southgate, P. Neville, G. Neville, Adams, Keown, Anderton, Le Saux, Hinchcliffe, Sherwood, Beckham, Scholes, Parlour, Batty, McManaman, Redknapp, Shearer. Owen, Fowler, Cole, Sutton. *Team*: Seaman, G.

Neville, Keown, Campbell, Le Saux, Beckham (P. Neville 78), Sherwood, Scholes, (Redknapp 84), McManaman (Parlour 70), Shearer, Cole. *Scorer*: Scholes, 11 minutes, 21 and 70.

Match against Hungary (Budapest, 28 April)

Score: 1–1. *Squad*: Martyn, Seaman, Ferdinand, Campbell, Keown, Le Saux, Southgate, P. Neville, Brown, Woodgate, Gray, Lampard, Sherwood, Scholes, Butt, Batty, McManaman, Redknapp, Shearer, Cole, Phillips, Heskey. *Team*: Seaman, Brown (Gray 73), Keown, Ferdinand (Carragher 61), P. Neville, Sherwood, Batty, Butt, McManaman (Redknapp 85), Shearer, Phillips (Heskey 82). *Scorer*: Shearer, 21 mins, pen.).

Matches against Sweden (Wembley, 5 June) and Bulgaria (Sofia, 9 June)

Squad: Seaman, Walker, Wright, Campbell, Southgate, Keown, Ferdinand, P. Neville, Le Saux, Woodgate, Gray, Batty, Beckham, Sherwood, Redknapp, Scholes, Parlour, Shearer, Sheringham, Cole, Heskey, Fowler. *Team v. Sweden*: Seaman, P. Neville, Keown (Ferdinand 35), Campbell, Le Saux (Gray 46), Beckham (Parlour 76), Batty, Sherwood, Scholes, Shearer, Cole. *Score:* 0–0. *Team v. Bulgaria*: Seaman, Campbell, Southgate, Woodgate (Parlour 65), P. Neville, Redknapp, Batty, Gray, Sheringham, Shearer, Fowler (Heskey 81). *Scorer*: Shearer, 15.

Matches against Luxembourg (Wembley, 4 September) and Poland (Warsaw, 8 September)

Squad: Seaman, Martyn, Walker, P. Neville, Adams, Campbell, Southgate, Keown, Ferdinand, Woodgate, Pearce, Batty, Dyer, Anderton, Beckham, Sherwood, Redknapp, Scholes, Parlour, McManaman, Shearer, Sheringham, Owen, Sutton, Fowler, Phillips. *Team v. Luxembourg*: Martyn, Dyer (G. Neville 46), Keown, Adams (P. Neville 64), Pearce, McManaman, Beckham (Owen 64), Batty,

Parlour, Shearer, Fowler. *Score*: 6–0. *Scorers*: Shearer 12, pen, 28, 34, McManaman, 30, 44, Owen 90. *Team v Poland*: Martyn, G. Neville (P. Neville 13), Keown, Adams, Pearce, Beckham, Batty, Scholes, McManaman (Dyer 80), Fowler (Owen 66), Shearer. *Score*: 0–0.

Match against Belgium (Stadium of Light, Sunderland, 10 October)

Squad: Seaman, Martyn, Wright, Gray, P. Neville, Le Saux, Adams, Keown, Southgate, Woodgate, Guppy, Sinclair, Dyer, Lampard, Beckham, Parlour, Ince, Redknapp, Wise, Scholes, Shearer, Owen, Heskey, Phillips. *Team*: Seaman (Martyn 46), Dyer (Neville 58), Southgate, Adams, Keown, Guppy, Lampard (Wise 76), Ince, Redknapp, Shearer (Heskey 86), Phillips (Owen 58). *Score*: 2–1. *Scorers*: Shearer 6, Redknapp 66.

Match against Scotland (Hampden Park, 13 November and Wembley, 17 November)

Squad: Seaman, Martyn, Walker, Campbell, Adams, Keown, Southgate, Ferdinand, P. Neville, Groggatt, Sinclair, Guppy, Ince, Wise, Redknapp, Parlour, Beckham, Scholes, McManaman, Heskey, Shearer, Phillips, Cole, Owen. *Team at Hampden*: Seaman, Campbell, Keown, Adams, P. Neville, Beckham, Ince, Scholes, Redknapp, Owen (Cole 67), Shearer. *Score*: 2–0. *Scorer*: Scholes, 21, 41. *Team at Wembley*: Seaman, Campbell, Southgate, Adams, P. Neville, Beckham (Parlour 90), Ince, Scholes, Redknapp, Owen (Heskey 63), Shearer. *Score*: 0–1.

Players had been used, looked at, spoken to, analysed, dropped, brought back, axed, discarded and watched closely in training, something that Keegan put an emphasis on. Keegan, before and after the Argentina match, was now homing in on the players he wanted and needed for his biggest trial. Nothing would damage his optimism and Keegan's confidence about one of the biggest years in England football history was shared by his skipper, Alan Shearer. There is a natural bond between the two men. It was Keegan who signed Shearer for Newcastle, indeed persuaded him to 'go home' from under the nose of Manchester United, and they have always been close in their football outlook. 'Talk is cheap,' said Shearer. 'You can predict and hope all you like, the reality is winning, achieving something. It is about time England did that.

'Who knows what is going to happen? We know we will prepare properly, have good enough players and everything will be in place by the time we go to the finals. There will be no shortage of confidence from the players. It might come down to luck. Who knows if this is meant to be our year?'

Shearer and the England players made similar noises before the World Cup in 1998. Glenn Hoddle was positive and that spilt into the squad. They honestly believed that they were going to win it (Hoddle, some say, thinks he did!). This time there was a hidden agenda for Shearer for, three days after the match against Argentina, he announced his retirement from International football. He would play, he said, up to and through the finals and then call it a day. It led to all sorts of speculation surrounding who would take over as captain, and also as the number one striker. Shearer said that his dream ticket partnership for the World Cup qualifying matches would be Emile Heskey, who played against Argentina as a Leicester player and then went quickly to Liverpool, and Liverpool's Michael Owen.

The captaincy is more difficult. Tony Adams of Arsenal is the logical choice but heading towards the finals there were question marks over his fitness. Would he be fit enough to sustain the Championships as a key player, let alone start the new season off as skipper? Tottenham's Sol Campbell was mentioned and yet for some Sol is not a big enough personality to carry the responsibility of being captain of your country. The name of David Beckham was mentioned and making the temperamental and hugely talented Beckham skipper would be controversial and yet, I believe, not too much of a gamble.

One thing that Campbell and Beckham have over Adams and that is they are guaranteed a regular place in the side for years to come. Making one of them captain would bring stability to the England side.

Shearer said that his reasons for retiring after Holland and Belgium were to spend more time with his family, and that he wanted to go out at the top. Fair enough, you can not argue with that. England will miss him. So too Keegan. And who is going to score the goals when the matches are at the highest level? Shearer has his critics but I am not one of them. To me he has never let his country down, has a terrific scoring record and there is always a sense of relief when the captain is around.

One message for Keegan came from his captain. 'I want to play in every match up to the finals and through them,' he said. 'I don't like to miss any games.' That was a poser for the coach. Shearer was an automatic choice, the first name on the sheet and yet if he played in four friendlies where would be the time be for experiment, the chance for someone else to establish himself? An opportunity for Heskey, Kevin Phillips, Owen or Andy Cole to get a foot in. Phillips, when hearing of Shearer's decision, admitted: 'I would be lying if I did not feel, when Alan said he was going, that it was an opportunity for me to get a game and make a stake for a regular spot.'

There was a lot at stake and Keegan was his usual positive self prior to the Argentinian match, especially behind the scenes with the players. How he loves being with them; once again there were race nights after dinner, with the manager leading the betting, and losing most of his money, much to the delight of the players. Whoops of joy greeted every race and it was man-management at its best as Keegan mixed socially with the team. Does it win you matches though? Of course not. Yet he is no fool. He knows that keeping the spirit up in the dressing room and having the players on his side was vital in the countdown. Some of the players at this stage had misgivings about his tactical knowledge but it did not trouble them unduly.

It did others. On the Tuesday afternoon in the press area, after

Keegan had named his side, an Argentinian journalist went from one pack of English journalists to another, with the same question. 'Excuse me,' he said. 'I am confused. Has Kevin Keegan not seen how we play? Is this really his team and why has he not taken into consideration that Argentina will play with three forwards?' The South American view was quickly seized upon by those in the England camp who had begun to look upon Keegan as nothing more than a cheerleader. By the time Keegan sat down to explain his selection and tactics the mood in the room was extremely negative. You could smell it, feel the tension as Keegan looked into the eyes of the journalists who, he knew, were his biggest critics.

He had selected Dennis Wise. It was controversial and foolish according to most newspaper men. Emile Heskey was Shearer's partner and David Beckham would play in a more central midfield role with the freedom to run the show. The coach also opted to play with a three-man defence. Keegan quickly picked up the mood. It had been the same feeling that had spread through the selection press conference. Keegan said: 'If things don't work out I will be answerable for my decisions. If things don't work out then you will have your day again.'

He again defended Wise, knowing that most journalists would not have had the little Chelsea captain anywhere near the team. 'I can not defend Wise's disciplinary record if I put it down in front of you but this is a fresh start for him and it is up to Wise. I have said that I trust David Beckham and the same applies to Wise. I trust him otherwise I would not play him. I do not know what is going to happen when he crosses the white line. To be honest with you, if they are not aware of how some of you people feel about them ... and I don't just mean Wise and Beckham. You have expressed things about other players in and out of this squad. They have the chance, on a football pitch, to answer those doubts you have. And you have the opportunity, if they do not get it right, to say "We told you so" and that is fair enough. But I pick my sides on ability, nothing else.

'I am happy with the side I have picked and it is perfectly capable of doing well against Argentina. This is a great chance for a lot of players. I am giving it to them and they can take it. You talk to me about the temperament of Beckham and Wise, well you can throw Paul Scholes in as well, if you like. Why not look for positives and not negatives? We can meet for alibis afterwards, if it goes wrong, and, as I say, you can have your day again.'

These kinds of press conference were becoming commonplace. Keegan defending his players, their reputations and also defending his selections against a backdrop of doubt. He was appalled by the headlines that greeted him on the morning of the match. The *Mirror, Mail* and *Express* were particularly heavy on the coach and his selection.

Keegan knew that his players had seen the papers and he was embarrassed and saddened for little Wise. The Chelsea star later told the story of how, when travelling on the coach to Wembley, he was confronted by a teammate holding up the *Mirror*'s headline. 'It was nasty,' said Wise. 'I don't mind being criticised but why does it have to be personal and nasty? There I was on my way to represent my country and all I got was negatives. Surely it was a time for getting behind the team, regardless of what anyone thought of individuals.' I have to agree with Keegan and Wise. I have always felt that newspapers should act as proud flag-wavers on the day of Internationals. Then if things go wrong be critical and constructive.

How the mood had changed after the game! It was only 0–0 but England played well and you could feel the pleasure in Keegan, and the relief, when he talked afterwards. What pleased him most? 'The players answering the criticism,' he said. 'There were so many negatives before the kick-off it was good to see them brush it aside and produce a performance like that. They did not deserve the publicity they got before the kick-off and I don't understand it. This was the perfect answer.'

I found it strange that he should not go into raptures about individuals and the team performance and instead level his thoughts at the newspapers. There are some odd things going on. It either indicates that Keegan is concerning himself too much about the media or that we really do feature in his thoughts. Yes, he tries to be helpful but this was not a time to gloat. Silence would have been far more golden.

It was a good display by England. Not sensational but encouraging. Especially Emile Heskey, playing up front with Alan Shearer. Heskey was a revelation, using his pace, power and skill to frighten the Argentinians. He is not a prolific scorer though and that is a concern to Keegan as he pieces together his squad of 22. At this stage of the build-up there appear to be six strikers involved with five certain to go, Shearer and Michael Owen being certainties, then comes Robbie Fowler, if he is fit, Heskey, Andy Cole and Kevin Phillips. Injuries may decide in the end although it is not an easy choice for Keegan.

Dennis Wise was superb at Wembley against the Argies. He knew he was under pressure and admitted later that had he not performed he (and Keegan) would have been slaughtered by criticism. He responded superbly, often bossing the game from midfield, and his passing was excellent. The Wise selection came off handsomely for Keegan. It was not long before the critics who had rounded on Wise now had him as a certainty for the Euro squad of 22. 'That has not gone unnoticed,' said Wise.

There was talk after the game of 'if the match had meant something then Argentina would have stepped up a gear' and this is such an old chestnut when England play well in friendlies. The fact is that England produced a performance that allowed Keegan to kick-start the biggest year of his life in confident mood. It allowed him to plan ahead without doubts in his mind. He firmly believes that he has the players to win the European Championships and Heskey and Wise, out of nowhere, gave him other options.

The coach knew that he had big decisions to make. As he said 'Take this squad, add the players injured and whom I have not chosen, and you see how tough it is going to be to water it down to 22.' The biggest name missing was Manchester United striker Cole. On fire for his club, he had been brought back by Keegan earlier in his career and now overlooked. It would be a gamble by Keegan not to take a striker so confident and deadly in the Premiership. Kevin Phillips too offered him a dilemma. The Premiership's top scorer, the Sunderland man, remained desperate for a chance at the highest level to prove to Keegan that he was worth a place. 'The trouble is they can't all go,' said Keegan. 'Picking the squad is like selecting the team. I have to get it right.'

The mood in the banqueting hall after the match was understandably upbeat too. FA councillors and Committee men, in their little huddles, slapped each other on the back and went home satisfied that no new crisis was to envelop them. FA Chairman Geoff Thompson was just heading home when he stopped to chat about Keegan, England and the future of the game. Thompson is a sound bloke and much tougher and more switched on than many give him credit for. 'I am delighted we played well because it allows the year to start on an upbeat note,' he said. 'It is a huge year for England. How will we do in the Euros, will we win the right to stage the World Cup in 2006 and can we qualify for the World Cup in 2002? It will not be long before all those questions are answered.'

He missed one out. Will Keegan still be the manager after the European Championships? He wants to be, the FA are desperate for him to stay on, yet will his pride allow him to ride failure and inevitable criticism? It is an interesting year.

CHAPTER 13

ENGLAND v BRAZIL, WEMBLEY, 27 MAY 2000

Kevin Keegan declared his hand early. We know that he likes to be bold and brave and yet he took everyone by surprise by announcing five players who would form the backbone of his starting line-up in Euro 2000. With still three warm-up matches left and loss of form and fitness to take into consideration, Keegan was still happy to give away some of his plans more than two months before the first game against Portugal.

Talking live on TalkSport Radio and answering questions on a fan phone-in Keegan said that his five heavyweights to form the strength of his European Championship team would be skipper Alan Shearer, Arsenal's Tony Adams and David Seaman, Sol Campbell of Spurs and David Beckham of Manchester United. He also confirmed that it would be Adams who would be the captaincy replacement for Shearer, who had announced his retirement from International football after the finals.

The big five were no surprise to anyone. Regarding Shearer,

criticised by so many people, but who remained England's best hope. Keegan has always supported the player he signed for Newcastle and he was not going to start back-tracking now. Shearer in my mind remains our best bet to score the important goal. 'Let us hope Alan bows out of International football in a blaze of glory,' said Keegan and you would not bet against him. It was surprising, therefore, when Keegan said a few days later, when he was in Barcelona to watch the England Under 21 team beat Yugoslavia 3–0 to qualify for the Under 21 Championships, that he would not be scared to axe Shearer if the captain lost form in Euro 2000. What was the point in committing himself to Shearer on Monday and threatening him with the axe by Thursday? It was just another case of Keegan putting his mouth before his thoughts. Good copy, but unnecessary.

Adams, clearly, is vital to Keegan. He even said that he would take the Arsenal defender if he wasn't fit enough to play in the first game but would be OK for the second against Germany. 'I want Tony in the dressing room,' said Keegan. He came down on Adams for the captaincy after Shearer, a popular choice. Most of the England team, while respecting Shearer, believe that Adams is the best captain in the Premiership. He is the man they look to when the chips are down. A great inspiration and a real leader in every sense of the word. Keegan said that Campbell would step up as skipper if Adams was ever injured. There have to be doubts, however, about Adams's long-term availability for the England team. No one would put money on him being fit enough to lead England if we reach the World Cup in 2002.

Campbell is a regular although I am not sure about his captaincy credibility. He leads by example and has the bonus of being a defender, to back up the argument that defenders make the best leaders, but is he a captain in the true sense of the word? Does he make players want to play for him? Towards the end of the season there were also alarms about his form. He clearly did not enjoy himself playing in a struggling Tottenham team and it began to show with England. At times he looked nervous and vulnerable under pressure.

Seaman in goal is again no shock. The European Championships will surely be his last major tournament. Age is against him and there have been signs of wear and tear with the form. 'Seaman is still my number one although Nigel Martyn of Leeds is now right up behind him,' said Keegan. Like Shearer, you can always rely on Seaman when the going gets tough.

David Beckham had been pushed in some areas of the media to be the next captain. I would not have been against that. Here is a world-class player who is feared by opponents. He has never been captain before but there was a case of giving him the responsibility of the armband to help his suspect on-pitch temperament. Beckham heading towards the finals was never out of the media, on front of newspapers and glossy magazines with his wife Victoria. The business people behind Victoria and the Spice Girls loved the publicity. Beckham's United manager Sir Alex Ferguson hated it. Fergie has never liked things out of his control and that is why, quite rightly, he had to win a spat with Beckham over missed training because of his son's ill health. Significantly, Beckham's form jumped into another gear when the dust had settled on the row with his manager. Keegan watches from afar and has only praise for Beckham. 'He has a lot to handle and he does it well,' says the coach. 'The spotlight is right on him and I have never had a problem with David Beckham. Never. And don't expect to.'

Keegan quickly added Paul Scholes to his Fabulous Five to make it a Sensational Six. 'I named five on Monday and Paul Scholes should have been in it,' he said. 'You know how much Scholes means to me and the England team.' The England coach also said that he knew 18 of his squad of 22 and, sadly, wrote off David Batty and Graeme Le Saux. 'Injury has robbed them of playing in a major Championships and I feel very sorry for them,' he said. For Le Saux it meant missing his second successive European Championship Final and his absence caused Keegan all sorts of headaches.

Keegan favours a 4–4–2 formation but without Le Saux he has no recognised left back. 'Who can play there?' Keegan asked. 'It has been a major headache for some time, for a number of England managers.' There is Phil Neville of Manchester United but is he International class? And Neville does not get into the first-choice United side when everyone else is fit. No Le Saux would surely mean a switch to a 3–5–2 system for Keegan with wing backs used. The right side of the midfield is easy, Beckham selects himself and Keegan and Ferguson both prefer the biggest name in English football playing wide on the right, firing in those spectacular crosses, rather than moved into central midfield.

On the left? Stephen Froggatt of Coventry and Steve Guppy of Leicester had been used without impact and surely would not be in the final 22. Jason Wilcox of Leeds was impressive against Argentina and is the favourite. What about Steve McManaman of Real Madrid? 'Two good performances against Manchester United in the Champions League quarter-final would do him a lot of good,' said Keegan. McManaman was outstanding in the first leg in Madrid and Keegan was in the ITV studio watching.

Keegan's problem positions two months before the finals were at full back, the left side of a midfield five and which striker to leave out. He repeated that he would be taking five forwards and there were six to choose from: Shearer and Michael Owen, who were certain, then Emile Heskey, Kevin Phillips, Andy Cole and Robbie Fowler. Cole looked to be the odd one out although Fowler's injury could solve the problem for Keegan. 'Robbie will be fit,' said Keegan, again in Barcelona with the Under 21s. The rest of the squad seemed to pick itself with Liverpool's Steve Gerrard making a late challenge with a series of impressive midfield performances in the holding role, particularly in front of Keegan in Barcelona.

Emile Heskey was also impressive in the Under 21 game. He received terrible racial abuse from one or two ignorant Yugoslav fans and responded with an outstanding contribution. His normally laid-back temperament was pushed to the limit by the abuse, and on-pitch spitting, pushing and verbal attacks and, again, Keegan was quick to acknowledge how well Heskey had done. It was significant that after the match Heskey, Gerrard and Under 21 skipper, West Ham's Frank Lampard, were encouraged to attend a press conference to explain what had gone on on the pitch. They all said yes and here was a lesson to the senior players. The conference was organised quickly and without fuss by the FA's Adrian Bevington and it was refreshing to have such co-operation after the fuss and fights with the senior team. I know that Under 21 football does not carry the same pressure or demands and yet all this emphasised was that the media are simply looking for access and help.

Shortly before he announced his squad to face Brazil, Ukraine and Malta – a squad that would indicate more than any other his thoughts for Euro 2000 – I caught up with the England coach at the launch of a Play Station game that he was endorsing. The conference was at the Sports Café in London's Haymarket and I was told to report at a certain time because I had an allotted ten minutes. The *Sun* were the only newspaper granted an exclusive interview in return for helping to promote the game although the interview rules were laid down as soon as I reached the venue. He will not talk about individuals and you must keep it general, they said, and don't forget to mention the game. These people do amuse me. They step into football with no idea how football journalists operate.

'Do you know Kevin?' one asked me. Yes, I do, surprisingly. 'Did you know that he is naming a squad soon?' Er, yes I do. 'He will not name it now.' No, I wouldn't expect that. 'Your time is now,' was their next instruction and there he was, the England coach. Sitting behind a desk and surrounded by Play Station gear.

'What are you doing here?' he joked. I said it was like coming for a job interview and Keegan was soon talking about himself and his players, his thoughts and dreams. Nothing changes. He was upbeat, confident and looking forward to the finals. He said that the public were with him. 'I get stopped in the street by members of the public. Taxi drivers wish me luck and they ask how are we going to do,' he said. 'And I tell them, we are going to win it, and I really mean that.' He said that he already knew his squad of 22 for the finals, which would come from the 28 he was soon to reveal.' Time up, Mr Woolnough, and I was out of there, blinking into the daylight.

Keegan's involvement with this project was interesting. It was a commercial deal separate from any of his commitments as England coach. He organises all his own commercial output. There were increasing demands on the coach and it was significant that Keegan was doing more and more away from his coaching. On the Friday following his Play Station appearance he played football with some executives in a behind closed doors publicity stunt. Nice work and money if you can get it but these things do come back and haunt you if you are not successful as England coach. Interestingly, the man by his side at the Play Station presentation was Neil Rodford, the Fulham Managing Director who had left his post at Craven Cottage to work with Keegan and his business interests.

There was another row in his ongoing dispute with the *Daily Mail* before he announced his squad. The *Mail* dominated their back page on Friday, 12 May, with a headline which screamed: Who needs to practise penalties? They revealed that Keegan, in a soon to be screened TV interview, admitted that England would not practise penalties in Euro 2000. It followed heartbreak penalty shoot-out defeats at the hands of Germany in 1990 and Euro 96.

Keegan was furious and took the unprecedented step of issuing a statement the next day, actually naming the newspaper and condemning them for trying to undermine him. He pointed out that what he said was that it is impossible to recreate the atmosphere of a match shoot-out situation. The *Mail* responded with a 'Keegan backtrack' story and it is safe to say that there is no love lost between the newspaper and the coach. Indeed, in press conferences Keegan is just about holding on to his temper when confronted by questions from the *Mail*'s Nigel Clarke and Martin Lipton. We have seen him explode before. Is there another eruption coming?

'I don't think some journalists even listen to the answers I give,' he moaned. 'I know I am just keeping this job warm for someone else but I do think that the papers could be more supportive. In my first press conference I was asked what vegetable would I like to be and I answered a cucumber. Why? Because I am determined to always stay cool. I really would like to stay around for a long time and I know that depends on results. The critics are always having a go about my tactics. Give me a break. I have set up sides before. Do you honestly believe that I do not know what I am doing? I also put a lot of trust in players. Judge me on my results. I was brought in to get us to the finals and we have done that. We didn't play well against Scotland at home but we are here. I am excited and feel privileged to be here as coach. I wish I could be playing again. If I could roll back the clock it would be great to jump into a player's shirt just for one minute, until I got knackered. I am positive and so are the players. I know the nation is behind me. Yes, I can handle the stress. I have good people around me.'

Part of Keegan's planning was a scouting system at the finals. He employed a team of scouts to watch every European Championship game. Martin Hunter, who is involved in the England Under 18 set-up, and who masterminded the operation from the team's hotel in Belgium, headed his network. The four scouts were Mike Pejic, the former Stoke full back, Nigel Spackman, former Liverpool and Chelsea star and Sheffield United manager, who is now a Sky TV pundit, Malcolm Crosby, who took Sunderland to the 1999 FA Cup Final and Kenny Swain, the former Chelsea player. Not high profile men, but people Keegan trusted. It was also typical of the England manager. He does not have hugely experienced men on his staff, certainly no big names, unlike Bobby Robson and Terry Venables but similar to Glenn Hoddle. It is worth pointing out that when England reached the semi finals in 1990 (World Cup) and 1996 (Euros) Don

Howe was on the England bench. Experience, a shoulder to cry on and a vast mine of information to call on. Also, a superb defensive coach.

Keegan ordered a room at the team hotel to be turned into a video cutting room where, within an hour of receiving a video of teams and players in the competition, they would be cut down for player information. 'We will know within an hour the strengths of an opponent at free kicks, how he takes a corner, a throw in, his body movement, everything,' said Keegan. But would he miss an experienced head alongside him? Keegan's backroom boys for the finals were Les Reed, Derek Fazackerley and Arthur Cox as coaches (Cox is experienced but with no International pedigree), and Ray Clemence as the goalkeeping coach. 'I don't think there is an outstanding team in the Championships,' he added.

There were no real surprises in his squad, apart from the recall of Nick Barmby of Everton. There was also a spot as the fourth goalkeeper for David James of Aston Villa. The squad was: Seaman, Martyn, Wright, James, Ferdinand, Campbell, Neville, Neville, Adams, Keown, Southgate, Beckham, Wise, Ince, Redknapp, Dyer, Barmby, Parlour, Scholes, Wilcox, Gerrard, McManaman, Shearer, Owen, Cole, Heskey, Phillips, Fowler.

The first casualty, and it came before a first training session, was Jason Wilcox of Leeds. Everyone had been asking about Robbie Fowler, well short of match practice after a season of injuries and frustration, and Michael Owen, with his hamstring strain, but it was Wilcox who dropped out. He turned up on the Sunday night with a swollen knee and was immediately ruled out and ordered to have an operation.

It was a huge blow for Keegan. Not because Wilcox is an outstanding footballer, but because he gave the team balance down the dreaded left-hand side. The coach revealed that Wilcox would have been a definite for the 22 and you can only feel sympathy for Keegan. No Le Saux, no Pearce and now no Wilcox. It left a half fit Fowler as the only left-footed player in the squad. He quickly called in Villa's

Gareth Barry, and Nick Barmby of Everton emerged as the favourite to go instead of Wilcox. On the Monday before Brazil, Owen announced that he had seen a specialist and was fit and Keegan again indicated that he was ready to take Fowler, despite his lack of matches. That had to be a gamble. There was also a concern over Andy Cole's fitness and suddenly the six strikers that Keegan had called the best group in the Euros were looking a bit thin.

His seeming determination to take Fowler, a player Keegan has always admired, drew an interesting comparison to his own World Cup experience in 1982 in Spain. It was then thought that Ron Greenwood, the manager, had gambled on taking two injured players, Keegan himself and Trevor Brooking, of West Ham. I was in Spain and although time numbs the brain, I always thought that Keegan had been injured going into the finals.

'Not so,' says Keegan. 'I went as a fit player and did my back in during the first training session. So it is not the same as Fowler and you can't compare it. I want to put that record straight. The rest you know about. Trevor did have a pelvic problem when he went to Spain. But my situation is nothing like Robbie Fowler's.' It was a remarkable memory record by Keegan, considering that he can not even recall how many caps he had. 'There will be no gamble on fitness when I name my 22,' he added. But he did say that an important player, such as Tony Adams, would be taken even if he was not fit enough for the first game, against Portugal, but would be fit to face the Germans in the second game.

Keegan was not involved but one worrying aspect of the finals has to be the threat of hooliganism. In Copenhagen, before the UEFA Cup Final between Arsenal and Galatasaray, there was terrible fighting and scenes that could wreck England's bid to stage the 2006 World Cup. There is also a real threat of violence in the European Championships, something that would be terrible for the bid and also the concentration of the England players.

It is a cancer of our society, the urge to go abroad, get drunk and fight. In Copenhagen it was more sinister, crime organised on the Internet and controlled by mobile phone. Innocent families were caught up in the mayhem, young children so frightened that they didn't even want to go to the game itself, and that is my fear if the World Cup comes here. The argument is that we can control our own hooligans. That's great, isn't it. We know there is going to be fighting so bring it here and let us try and control it.

Steps have to be taken. Passports taken away from the mindless scum who ruin it for so many others. Heavy prison sentences for the caught and proven and if that does not work, then the only alternative is to withdraw the England team for major Championships. No one wants that to happen and I just hope that this particular argument is not used during or after the Euros. How many times have we said this? Don't travel, don't fight and enjoy the football. They do not listen so why should we think they will listen now? It is a huge problem for English football. We thought it had gone away. It hasn't. It was the two Leeds fans stabbed to death in Istanbul that brought it back again. It allowed anger and frustration to rise and crime to be organised. Turkey are in the Euros and when we play Romania, in our third group match, the Turks are themselves playing only an hour away in Brussels.

There is also concern ahead of the Germany match about the wisdom of playing the game in the town of Charleroi and at its tiny stadium. The FA are backing the local authorities who say that the game is safe, and that they can control any hooliganism. I do hope they are right. Keegan himself visited the stadium and gave it his seal of approval in a glowing PR exercise organised by the FA. A measure of how small the stadium is that UEFA received almost 500 requests from photographers to attend the game. Only 150 could be accommodated.

The problems surrounding Charleroi were highlighted by the *Daily Mail* in the build-up to the match against Brazil. The newspapers now were full of Keegan and the European Championships, plus the problems on and off the pitch, something not gone unnoticed by the England coach. The *Mail*, certainly, seems to be getting to Keegan. On the Tuesday before the Brazil game an FA official contacted me to ask what the coach had said to me about Andy Cole and had I passed the quote on to the *Mail*'s Martin Lipton? There had been confusion over Cole's fitness at the press conference on the Monday and I approached Keegan after all his media work to clarify the Cole situation. He explained it ,to me and stressed: 'I have told Andy not to worry about getting fit for the match against Brazil, but to be completely fit next Wednesday, May 31, when I will name the squad.'

It appeared in the *Mail*, in a direct quote, that Cole would miss the Brazil match and Keegan took exception. He complained to the FA and they in turn asked me for what had been said, and done. The only thing that this did for me was to reveal some of the pressure that Keegan is feeling heading towards the tournament. This, surely, was not an issue to take stock of. We knew that he and the *Mail* were at loggerheads and that their campaign to unseat him was gathering momentum. But a slight misquote was not something for the England coach to get his knickers in a twist about. He really has to learn to ride these things, and become bigger than them. A serious issue, OK, then he should react. But Cole's fitness, and the fact that Keegan admitted that he needed to see a specialist, was not a major issue for him to think that the media were turning against him.

Clearly, however, the temperament, and that explosive temper, are going to be tested to the full, if things do go wrong and the temperature is turned up once the England squad get to the finals, and the media circus starts to focus completely on one thing alone. And that target is undoubtedly Kevin Keegan.

He would not let the *Mail* thing go and, the next day, this time the Thursday before the Brazil game, 25 May, he rounded on the paper's Martin Lipton, who was sitting bold as brass in the middle of the front row at the press conference. As one FA observer, who knew that Keegan was unhappy with the reporter, said: 'Is Lipton stupid or is he looking for a fight, sitting right in the coach's face?' Keegan was clearly waiting to have a go and when the subject of the injuries came up he said: 'I think Martin, you misquoted me again. I never said Andy Cole definitely would not play against Brazil. Martin, I have every right to say to you "Go out". That is why we have got the lady here (nodding at the stenographer). You can sit down with me for ten minutes afterwards. I never said that. You can't quote me saying it. We have been down this road before. I have every right to ask you to leave. Don't put quotes that I didn't say.

'I don't mind you criticising and things like that but, please, you made that as a quote. I had to go and apologise to Andy Cole. I should not have to do that. Martin, it is not the first time. Please not again. I promise that I will do what I am entitled to do, and that is put you outside. That is why we give you these sheets (again nodding at the stenographer). What I said was that he had to prove his fitness by 31 May. So there is a difference in that, you know. So please, get it right. Sorry everyone, I am whinging now.'

It was controlled anger again from Keegan. Had Lipton decided to retaliate strongly and stand up to the England coach, I suspect that there would have been an explosion. Instead it died away with a few smiles from the other reporters, with Lipton treated like a naughty schoolboy who had forgotten to hand in his homework. But, again, the signs were there.

Keegan didn't like some of the headlines, or the fact that we, the national reporters, were calling the England injuries a crisis. I pointed out to him in the Thursday press conference that an England player visiting a specialist before the naming of a squad of 22 for a major Championship did represent a story. 'Look, I am telling you that it is not a crisis.' I am afraid the England coach and the press will never see eye to eye on that one. It was interesting that in Friday's papers there were more reports of Cole struggling. The *Mirror* reported on their back page that he was definitely out of Euro 2000. Now that is a crisis. But at Friday's press conference Keegan didn't mention the new development. I wonder if he would have done had Lipton written it in the *Mail?* He also insisted that Cole was fit for selection for Euro 2000.

I had a long telephone conversation during the build-up to the Brazil game with Geoff Thompson, the chairman of the FA and Keegan's boss. He was at home playing with his new laptop. I have always got on well with Thompson and find him a straight, honest man who is no fool when it comes to judging people. Deep down he knows that Keegan may be a volcano waiting to erupt. It was Thompson who gave the *Daily Telegraph*'s Football Correspondent Henry Winter the famous 'It will all end it tears' quote soon after Keegan had taken over. He told me that he was quietly optimistic about doing well in the finals and would be pleased just to get through the first group phase. He said that Keegan simply had to cope with criticism if it came. He revealed to me that the FA would give Keegan a new contract if there was success in the finals. 'By success I mean getting to the final,' he said.

Keegan is certainly not fazed by such challenges. Indeed, he enjoys them and, heading for the Euros, nothing, it appeared, seemed to trouble him on the football front. Little things, small signs, however, were developing that the pressure was getting to him. The national newspaper photographers had a taste of that explosive temper at Wembley on the Thursday training session before the match against Brazil. They were kept waiting in the tunnel for more than an hour and didn't enjoy it when they were allowed in and told to take photographs of Keegan and some England players who were also promoting the NSPCC charity. They refused and got a curt 'I am not here to make your job easy' answer from the England coach.

The NSPCC charity is, of course, a good one, but here was another PR disaster. Why not allow the photographers in at the start, let them get their pictures done, pose for a couple of charity photos and everyone is happy? Keegan would have been left alone to get on with his build-up to Brazil and the cameramen would have gone away happy. Simple. It seems that the bigger the business, the more complicated the simple of art of public relations becomes. No wonder the FA is searching for a man to head up their public relations department at Lancaster Gate. About time.

David Davies, the FA's Executive Director, wants to recruit someone to work alongside him with complete responsibility and power to run the media side of the FA. It is a big, powerful job and Davies, who did not advertise for the six-figure post, instead sought advice, talked and interviewed in the build-up to the European finals, with a view to the appointment being in place for the start of the 2000–1 season.

The team that Keegan sent out to face Brazil was: Seaman, G. Neville, Keown, Campbell, P. Neville; Beckham, Ince, Scholes, Wise; Shearer, Owen. Emile Heskey and Tony Adams would both have played but pulled out of training with back problems. Keegan insisted that neither of them was a long-term problem. Crisis, what crisis? Oh no, not that road again. The selection of Heskey would have been interesting. It is known that Alan Shearer prefers playing with Heskey to Owen and it threw up the old rumour that the England captain picks the side, especially his front partner. Both men deny the allegation. 'No player influences me over team selection, other than through his performance,' Keegan said.

Going into Brazil, Shearer had a possible nine matches left. 'I want to play and score in them all. My dream is to finish as the European Championship top scorer and lift the trophy as my farewell present to the country,' he said. He said that he would miss the England get-togethers and, I am sure, we will miss him. I am not sure who is going to score the important goals for us when it matters most?

Shearer was not on trial against Brazil. Michael Owen certainly was and he passed with flying colours. Owen scored England's goal in the 1–1 draw and looked to be back to his sharp and confident best. It was good news and good timing for Keegan, who called England's performance honourable. It was more than that for Owen, who seems certain now to be Shearer's partner up front in the opening Euro 2000 game against Portugal. 'This is the fittest, mentally and physically, I have felt all season,' Owen said. 'I have got all my old confidence back now. I don't just want to be an ordinary pro, I want to be the greatest striker in the world.' The goal was a weight off Owen's shoulders. He had lived with the boy-wonder tag since the France World Cup and that stunning goal against Argentina and here he was, looking ready to take his career on to a new level at Euro 2000. Emile Heskey and Robbie Fowler were waiting for their chance but it looked like Owen as the first choice. He had forced the issue.

There were good performances from Paul Ince and Dennis Wise, playing in the problem left-sided role, and the players were all happy with the display. 'What is the point of peaking now and then not being at our best at the finals?' said Arsenal goalkeeper David Seaman. It was the defence, however, that caused the most anxiety. Brazil's equaliser on the stroke of half time was a combination of mistakes from Sol Campbell, Seaman and Gary Neville, although Keegan refused to point the finger at any of them. Campbell's form however is a worry. He is not the commanding central defender we have seen in the past and looks to be nervous. A concern for me is that Tony Adams, Campbell, and Martin Keown are not comfortable when they have got possession moving out of defence. Their distribution is suspect, especially under pressure.

Keegan didn't appear to be worried at all. Even an injury to Arsenal's Ray Parlour, after he had come on for Paul Ince, didn't seem to dampen the enthusiasm of the England coach. He smiled and said all the right things after the game before heading back to England's hideaway in Burnham Beeches. Next Ukraine at Wembley followed by the naming of the European Championship squad about an hour after the match.

Parlour was a major doubt for him at the start of the week, so too Jamie Redknapp, both with knee injuries, and injuries were making Keegan's job of naming the 22 easier. If they were both ruled out, and a goalkeeper had to be ditched, Keegan only had to find three players to break the news to. 'I am not looking forward to it,' he said. 'I will do it quietly man to man on Wednesday before the Ukraine game.' He decided not to name his team, as he usually does before a friendly, because he thought it unfair on the players who were being sent home. 'It would give the game away completely if I named a team on the Tuesday before telling the players on the Wednesday' he said. 'It would not take a rocket scientist to figure out who was not going if I named the team.' No one expected a surprise, certainly not of Gazza 1998 proportions.

A surprise visitor to the England camp on the Tuesday before the match against Ukraine was FA Chief Executive Adam Crozier. He arrived announced in the media tent alongside David Davies who, interestingly, had reverted to being Keegan's right-hand PR man throughout the build-up to the tournament and at the Championships. It is the first time we had seen Davies in a high-profile position since the sacking of Glenn Hoddle. Crozier wore no tie, as usual, nor did Davies and you don't often see the new Chief Executive dressed formally. I have spotted him in a tie and I am sure he does not turn up for dinners and speeches dressed with his top button undone. Maybe he is setting a new fashion inside Lancaster Gate. From blazers to no buttons. He is certainly pushing a new image, a good one too.

Crozier sat in on the media press conference, perched at the back of the room and listening intently. I recall former FA Chairman Bert Millichip arriving once for a Terry Venables press day, and Graham Kelly, the former secretary, was a regular visitor to the England managers' press conference. But it was the first time that Keegan had been observed by one of the powers of the game. Crozier caught the England manager in relaxed mood, sitting alongside Davies and dressed smartly in his England track suit. His grey hair was pushed back and there are no tell-tale signs to the face that the pressure is mounting, whatever is going on inside the England coach. Are there a few more worry lines around the eyes? Perhaps. But that is understandable. It would be interesting to see pictures of the England coach on the day he took over, and now. There would be a change. There has to be. Bobby Robson almost changed overnight, so did Graham Taylor. It is inevitable. Just look back at PM Tony Blair on the day he swept into Downing Street and note the change today. You can't keep the stress and strain away and they say that an England football coach gets more publicity than the top politicians.

Crozier heard Keegan explain how he was going to tell the six players who would not make his squad, face to face, after the last training session on Wednesday lunch time. He spoke in glowing terms about the return of Steve McManaman after his glory of winning the European Cup with Real Madrid. Keegan clearly has McManaman pencilled in for a key role in Euro 2000 and said that against Ukraine the former Liverpool star would be given a free role.

'He can go anywhere, do anything, Steve has got a completely free role,' said Keegan. But when questioned further he added: 'I totally agree with what you are saying. When you talk about a free role, no one gets a free role. Any player still has to do a job for the team.'

Confused? I wonder if Crozier was. Had Glenn Hoddle said it when the knives were out and he was at his most vulnerable, he would have been slaughtered in print for such utterings. There is something different about Keegan. He is a little tough nut and, of course, he has not yet stepped completely out of the honeymoon period. That is to come at the Euros.

I thought the most interesting thing that Keegan said at his pre-match press conference was this, in answer to the question whether there was a lively debate with his coaches about tactics and the best way to go into the tournament. 'Are you all of one mind?' Keegan said: 'To be honest, I don't discuss it too much with the coaches. Other than when I sit down and say "This is the way I am going to play" and then we put that into what we do. Obviously we talk about and discuss things over meals and at training. We talk about certain players. That is what you do every day of your life when you are here because, to be honest with you, there is not a lot else to do.'

It is what a lot of people thought, and some feared. Keegan does not confide in anyone deeply when it comes to making decisions. He has no old hand with him and doesn't want one. In the thick of the Championships, when it is good to draw on experience, I hope he doesn't regret not having an old tournament campaigner around him, or regret his own stubbornness.

Tuesday night was busy if you were a journalist chasing against deadlines. Keegan had told us at his press conference that Jamie Redknapp and Ray Parlour had been sent for scans on knee injuries and the result of those examinations would be announced at 4.30pm. That was put back to seven and when it go close to eight o'clock there was a lot of panic going on with journalists chasing information, the FA and one another. 'Have they announced the decisions? No. What the bloody hell are they playing at' or words to that affect. Steve Double, the FA press officer, eventually rang me to say that Parlour and Redknapp were both out of the Championships and he rang back a little later with some Keegan reaction to the news.

There was an interesting development when Sunderland striker Kevin Phillips revealed his own heartache by saying that he thought he would be one of the odd men out. 'I think the manager has made up his mind, especially with Robbie Fowler and Andy Cole proving their fitness,' said Phillips. The striker who got 30 Premiership goals also groaned at not getting more than six minutes against Brazil on Saturday. 'I needed the second half, or at least 20 minutes to make an impression,' said Phillips. All would be revealed at around 11pm on Wednesday night after the friendly against Ukraine. Keegan was keeping everything crossed that no one would get injured in the match. It would throw his plans into turmoil.

CHAPTER 14

ENGLAND v UKRAINE, WEMBLEY, 31 MAY 2000

This was Kevin Keegan's longest day as England manager and by the time the clock ticked towards midnight the strain was beginning to show. He complained later to FA officials that he had taken on too much and would not put himself through it again. 'It was not right and I have told the FA that it will not happen again,' he said later. 'It got to the stage by the end that I could not give any more.'

Keegan's day began with speculation in the newspapers over which players he would leave out of his Euro 2000 squad of 22. Ray Parlour and Jamie Redknapp were out injured and David James was a probable third after Keegan had admitted that Richard Wright would make his debut against Malta on Saturday. That left three. He had to take training and then after lunch tell the three players who they were.

He went to their rooms and did the dreaded knock on the door. Who is it? It's the boss? Oh shit. He spent fifteen minutes with James, Rio Ferdinand and Keiron Dyer, with all three players taking the pain well. Rio was bitterly disappointed even so. 'I just have to take this on the chin,' he said. 'I thought I would go.' He will come back strongly next season. James, called in late, told Keegan that deep down he thought it would be him but a little bit of his hope was still there until the knock came. The Andy Cole situation was not so clear and it was why the stress and strain began to show late in the day. Keegan said that he spent two half an hour sessions with Cole, one in the morning, one in the afternoon. Why? He said that it was to break the news to him and discuss an ankle injury that was to keep him out of the squad. Confused? You should be. The media had been told repeatedly that Cole was fit after visiting a specialist about his toe injury.

Before the 11pm press conference Keegan had the match against Ukraine and he found the whole package of the day too tiring and stressful. Fair enough, you and I would have done too, but it was of his own making. The media certainly did not want the press conference an hour after the Ukraine game despite Keegan saying two days later: 'I only did it for the media.' We would have preferred it the next morning, or lunchtime, we would have fitted in with his arrangements and those of the squad as they flew to Malta for the last build-up game.

But it was 11pm and a room at Wembley Conference Centre was put aside for a press conference involving print, radio and television media. Before that most national newspaper reporters had found out two of the names, those of Dyer and Ferdinand. The third had to be a forward as Keegan had said that five of the six he had in his squad of 28 would go. The man missing also represented the biggest story of the night. Would it be Cole, but being fit why would Keegan leave him behind? Kevin Phillips had just scored 30 goals in the Premiership and might just get a key one in the finals; Emile Heskey looked the part every time he played for his country while Robbie Fowler was not match fit but we knew that the manager liked and favoured him.

The breakthrough in the story, allowing all papers to get the squad in their first editions (which would have missed the squad had we relied on Keegan's announcement at 11pm) came from Sky Television and their dressing room reporter George Gavin. Sky went live to Gavin in the Wembley tunnel who had the teams to announce. He said that Cole was not in the starting line up, not even on the bench and, he reported, it is thought that the Manchester United player was not actually at Wembley. Bingo. It meant that Cole was out, definitely, but why was he not at the stadium?

Another twist was that Ferdinand and Dyer were among the subs announced by Keegan. Even stranger. Phone calls were made by reporters and it was a member of the FA staff who confirmed the story. Off the record (without quotes) we were told that Cole had been asked if he wanted to be involved in the game after he had been told that he was out and he had declined. He had gone back to Manchester. Cole had walked out on England. The stories were written and the headlines roared for the first editions as Keegan was masterminding the impressive 2–0 victory.

As soon as Keegan walked into the press conference and sat down next to David Davies he was very matter of fact and precise about what he wanted to do and how he wanted to handle it. To a live television audience first he read out the squad, which brought sighs of relief from the front row, which was filled with reporters who had already filed the squad and Cole's absence. 'What's funny?' asked Keegan as the sighs turned into stuttered laughter. 'We are just delighted with your squad,' was the answer. It was Keegan's next statement that took the meeting into a controversial area.

Keegan glanced at the paper alongside him on the desk and said: 'Andy Cole. I have written this down because I don't want anyone to get it wrong. Andy is suffering from a minor foot injury and it has stopped him training recently. We have decided that it would have been too much of a risk to take him. He would have gone had he been fit. I wrote it down because I guess Andy Cole is the biggest issue here.'

It was a complete contradiction to the information we had received a few days earlier, which was that Cole was fit and completely OK to be involved in Euro 2000, if selected. Keegan, clearly, knew that he was stepping into controversial water and almost had his speech rehearsed. He kept repeating that Cole was not fit, as if to make sure that we understood. We felt as if a veil of secrecy was being pulled across our eyes. We had sometimes thought that Hoddle had not been up front with us with and this was the first time we had had to question it with Keegan. 'I am the most honest and open manager you have had for ages' is one of his favourite phrases. Well, Kevin, perhaps not this time.

The longer the press conference went on the more uncomfortable he seemed. The more he was pushed on the subject the more frustrated and annoyed he became. It was the closest to a blow-up we had seen since he took over. When I said to him that he was the third successive England coach to drop Cole from a major Championship, following in the footsteps of Terry Venables in 1996 and Glenn Hoddle for the World Cup in France, he stopped me and said: 'I have not dropped him, don't put that, Brian, I never said that.

'Shall I read it again [no, don't do that Kevin, I said, we understand what you are saying] because I really don't want you to get this wrong. I know the difference between dropped and rested. I am telling you he is not fit.'

He didn't like being asked whether, if Alan Shearer had suffered a similar minor injury, would he have been told to go home too. 'I am not answering that,' he said. 'I am not going down that line.' He didn't like being asked whether Kevin Phillips had been the striker to benefit by Cole's omission. He then started to talk about Cole as a person. 'Don't underestimate this guy. I know he is difficult to get to know and I know him more than most.' I could not understand why Keegan went down this road. We were not interested in Cole the person here, we were trying to establish whether he had been dropped or not, and whether he had been fit to go?

Keegan also punctuated his statements with phrases like 'I know you will make of this what you want' and 'You will put your own stamp on it' or 'The truth or not, it will be your reasoning' and 'Some of you will always say there is something dishonest about what I say.' Keegan could not have been further from the truth. We didn't want a slant or stamp, we wanted the truth from him. 'This is the truth,' he repeated.

Then there was Cole's injury. We were told that it was a toe problem that had cleared up. At the press conference it became a foot injury, or the top of the foot as Keegan called it. To me the whole thing smelt of a big rat that scuttled in and out of the England camp in the build-up to the squad announcement. Why, for instance, say that Cole was fit when he wasn't?

'You know what it is like,' he said. 'We have to come in front of you people and say whether a player is fit or not. A lot happened between last Friday and today with Cole's injury.' Keegan, clearly, should have told us originally that Cole had a problem that was causing concern. It would have stopped us writing that he was fit and misleading the public. And why did Keegan need an hour with the player? If the player is not fit you meet him, chat about the injury and that is it. Fifteen minutes, like the other players got. Why didn't Cole go to Wembley like the others who had not made the squad?

I suspect we will have to wait some time to get to the bottom of the saga. Some people have suggested that Cole is not popular with the other players. It has also been suggested that Shearer, a huge influence on the England camp, does not like Cole around. The allegations are dismissed by Keegan. 'You have got to get to know him,' he says. Cole, the next day, made a statement saying that he was definitely injured.

Keegan and I clashed again in the press conference when he started to talk about the atmosphere around the camp. 'I don't care what any of you say, you are good at gloom and doom.' Not so, I called out. We want England to do well, we want you to win the European Championships. I really mean that. I get my leg pulled all the time for predicting that England are going to win a major competition and certainly my newspaper, the *Sun*, in the build-up to the Championships, could not have been more supportive to Keegan and the players. 'OK,' he conceded. 'It is not gloom with all of you. But why not get behind us first and then see what happens?'

It was an extraordinary performance by an extraordinary little man. He has the energy of a horse and the mental capacity of a scientist but here was Keegan trying too hard again. Instead of walking into the press conference, calling out the names, making a statement and heading off home, he tried to double-guess the stories, mood and questions. He came with his answers before he had been asked anything and he quite clearly protested too much. It smacked of guilty conscience and my guess is that Cole was upset and chose not to go to Wembley. It was a pity that Keegan's comments made newspapers change first editions from 'Cole Walks Out' to just 'Cole Out' stories. The only paper who stuck with their original was the *Telegraph*, written by Football Correspondent Henry Winter.

Keegan was also upset with some of the questions. He told us later that the one about Shearer was 'stupid' and 'uncalled for' and repeated that he had been annoyed with himself for allowing the conference to go on so long.

His mood the next day however was completely different. By the time we all got to Malta, the media circus arrived before the players and met up at a building opposite their hotel, Keegan was smiling, relaxed and back in his 'OK, boys?' mood. You have to appreciate, of course, that England were in Malta for two reasons. First, to play a game of football, but a close second was to use Malta's Centenary celebrations as a PR exercise for the two votes Malta hold for who gets the 2006 World Cup. A lot of wining and dining went on and the FA had all the bigwigs out, including former chairman Sir Bert Millichip and his wife Barbara. Millichip is hugely popular and still influential with UEFA, and his appearance was significant. On the Saturday after the game the VIPs and their wives all stayed behind for a banquet. FA Chairman Geoff Thompson is pushing for a place on the UEFA

Executive Committee and, again, Saturday night in Malta was important for canvassing. Promises over the best champagne. It is the same in any business. I suspect to certain members of the FA Saturday night was more important than Saturday afternoon.

Keegan revealed that Richard Wright of Ipswich would make his debut and play for the entire 90 minutes but that David Seaman remained his number one goalkeeper, despite Nigel Martyn's brilliant display against Ukraine on Wednesday night.

The security around the England management and players is extraordinary and in Malta it was no different. It is understandable, I suppose, as these players today are worth millions. As soon as Keegan or any of the squad stood up from being interviewed by the media they were followed by police and the FA's own security. It was strange, therefore, that so many locals were allowed into the building where the interviews took place. Local children were everywhere on the Friday before the game. Security was tight but were all the local kids and their friends searched? Any of them could have been carrying a knife or other weapon. PR again. 2006 again.

My own newspaper signed up David Beckham for the duration of the European Championships. This is not uncommon at major tournaments; most papers get involved and if there is success the player can be a great flag-waver as support and interest back home grows. Beckham, of course, is the biggest name in English football. The only problem is that there are so many agents and business advisers involved these days that doing an interview can become a nightmare. It is not a question of getting a good piece out of the individual. It is the problem of the agent liking what the player wanted to say, or indeed what was written. Beckham is not the best player to be interviewed, but he has his views and it is at that level that when he speaks, people listen.

The *Sun*'s first column was still hacked around with a great big red pen by the people who control his business life. You can't say that, can't put that it, let us make it happy, happy. No, guys, let us make it a PR exercise for you. You like the money it brings in but you don't like it when there is a headline that goes against the grain. Beckham was happy with my colleague Steve Howard's handling of the article, the agents were not. It was pathetic. Equally pathetic was the *Daily Mirror* the next day. Beckham did a general interview for all newspapers on the Friday. It was nothing special, but it was Beckham. The *Mirror* billed it as Beckham speaks exclusively to us. It was doubly funny because their Football Correspondent didn't ask Beckham one question.

I have banged on about this method of interviewing before. You can't beat the system, I'm afraid, player is wheeled in, player is spoken to by three or four journalists, the others take notes and fill their boots and then tell their offices 'Great stuff from Beckham.' Cheats. Also, if the agents are so worried about what he says on a Thursday, how come he can be interviewed on a Friday without their raising an eyebrow, let alone a red pen?

Keegan named his team on the Friday – it is the last time we will see a side on paper before a match this season – and it was Wright, G. Neville, Keown, Campbell, P. Neville, Beckham, Wise, Scholes, Barmby, Shearer, Owen. The side picked would play 4–4–2, Keegan said, which was a clear indication of how he planned to play at Euro 2000. There was no point in playing this system in Malta if he wanted to go with a three-man defence in Belgium and Holland, especially as he said that he had no plans for a behind closed doors practice match with the first team of his choice.

Keegan's preparation was hit late on Friday night when Steve Double, the FA Press Officer, was rung by the *Express* newspaper and told that they were running a front page story saying that Keegan would join up with ITV to be a pundit once England went out of the Championships. That was not new because a week earlier Keegan had attended ITV's Euro 2000 launch in London. What hurt him was the way the story was written. The headline said that loser Keegan would go to television and there was a strong implication that the England coach was going to cash in on any England failure. It was mischief-making and Keegan was furious when he saw the story. In fact he went berserk and top FA officials got involved with the protests. He has however simply got to ride these things if he is stay focused on the job, the only job that matters to him. Bringing success to the nation.

The match was something of a disaster and a farce. England played poorly, they didn't appear that interested and Malta treated it like an exhibition game, using eleven substitutes so that all players involved could say that they had played against England at the height of their country's centenary celebrations. Typical of their reaction was David Carabott, who had to take a first half penalty twice but then missed a late spot kick that would have given Malta a history-making draw in only their fifth match against us. He said: 'I took three penalties against England, scored twice and missed one. That is the highlight of my career and it doesn't matter that I did not score the last one. Yes, it would have gone down in our history but this match will never be forgotten. It was a huge occasion for our country.' Easily pleased, the old Maltese.

We had seen performances like this before from England on the eve of a major tournament. Tunisia away in 1990 brought similar groans and again China in 1996 had everyone complaining that England did not stand a chance. On both occasions we reached the semi-final. Perhaps it is a good omen. Let's hope so.

The only player to take any satisfaction out of the game was Everton's Nick Barmby. He is a good, intelligent footballer and has played for some time down the left side for Spurs, Middlesbrough and Everton. 'If you had asked me a month ago I would have told you that Barmby was nowhere near the 22,' Keegan said. Yet, here he was, on the fringe of the team and ready to replace the enigma that is Steve McManaman. I hope he does. I have no faith in McManaman, certainly at this level. He has yet to take International football by the scruff of the neck.

The strikers seemed to be sorting themselves out. Alan Shearer plays, despite form or lack of goals; he did not score in England's 2–1 victory and that is six games now without a goal. It was twelve before Euro 96 and looked what happened then, Shearer finished with five and as the competition's top scorer. Against Malta he looked like someone saving himself for one last push. The European Championships offer Shearer six last games as an England International.

'I have never won anything with England. Been close, but that is not enough,' he said. 'Talk is cheap. Losing a semi-final on penalties is not success. You have to come first. What I want to do is leave the country with the European Championship trophy. I want to hold it aloft and say goodbye.'

It is who plays up front with him that carries the debate back home. Michael Owen is the favourite with Emile Heskey on his shoulder. Robbie Fowler can not be match-fit, while Kevin Phillips, who missed two easy chances against Malta, is the odd man out. Flying back to England after the victory – for the record Martin Keown and Heskey scored the goals – Keegan reflected on his last build-up game. It was on him now. Two days' rest, two days off for the players, and then he would be the most photographed and talked about man in England. But would he be the most successful?

Apart from Barmby or McManaman I believe that he knew his team to make or break him as an England coach. He said after Malta: 'If we play like we did against Malta then we can pack our bags, come home early. I am just glad that we played like that now and not at the European Championships.' So are we Kevin, so are we.

The media treated him kindly. No one put the boot in and headlines such as 'We will get it Wright' or 'Don't give up on us now' greeted the England coach when he woke up on Sunday morning. There is just something about Keegan that brings hope and optimism. He is also rated a lucky manager. England on paper should not win Euro 2000. England on form can't do it. Keegan's England might just.

He believes he can and has more confidence in his players than any other man or woman in the country.

As Keegan travelled to Belgium with his players on Thursday, 8 June, just five days before the opening match, he looked back on his 13 months in control. He had got England to the finals, changed his mind about taking the job and got a £1 million a year contract. England had not really played well under his control and he went to the finals with a lop-sided squad, with no first choice left-footed player and one or two players just holding on to their places. In 13 months the media had been kind to him, apart from one or two situations that he didn't like, but generally it had been a smooth approach to his greatest test.

Now, would the real Kevin Keegan stand up and be counted? Is he a good – no, great – manager? Can he match the best of Europe tactically? In the space of eight days all those questions would be answered. That is the span of the group phase. Get through that and anything can happen. Fail and you might not survive. Succeed and Kevin Keegan could write his own contract, and salary. Hero or villain? It was pressure like never before on the man known as the Messiah.

CHAPTER 15

THE EUROPEAN CHAMPIONSHIPS

I had been here before. Many times. The eve of a major Championship. The expectancy high, the excitement building, the injury scares and the hope that could this be England's turn. Maybe, just maybe. It would mean so much to the nation.

Kevin Keegan had helped to build the expectancy. The man is a walking press conference at times and he said all the right things as England flew to Belgium for the start of the tournament.

'If I get the best out of these players, we will win Euro 2000.' Win it, not could win it. It was the closest since Sir Alf Ramsey said in 1966: 'Can we win the World Cup? Yes, certainly.' And England did. Could they do it again?

Since 1966 every tournament has been the same. Can we? My first World Cup was in 1982 in Spain, my first European Championship two years later in France. The nearest to glory came first in 1990 when Bobby Robson took us to the semi finals and that dramatic penalty shoot-out defeat against Germany in Turin. Six years later it was Terry Venables' turn to reach a semi-final, again in the semi-final and another penalty shoot-out heartbreak, again against Germany. I suspect both times we would have gone on to be Champions.

In 1998 Glenn Hoddle and his players got a hero's welcome when they returned from France after that classic match against Argentina. It was a game that had everything, with David Beckham being sent off and yet another penalty shoot-out. But why the heroes' welcome? Gareth Southgate admits: 'I was embarrassed. To me it was just another glorious English failure. We do not want moral victories, we want to be Champions. That is the only thing that matters. I know that my penalty miss in 1996 robbed a lot of people of their last chance of winning something and I regret that. I have got another chance, a lot of players and staff did not get it.'

Even Keegan said: 'I have had a great career. I can show you a lot of medals but I can not put anything on the table that I won with England. I regret that. I desperately want to us to be successful. Really successful.'

On the Wednesday before England flew to Belgium, Keegan was in superb form with the media. Here was the British Bulldog at his best. It was a repeat of his display on the first day that he took the job. Keegan was up for it and it is no wonder that players like to play for him. He makes you feel good. He makes you feel confident.

'These European Championships are the only thing that matter to me now,' he said. 'I have not booked a holiday, I am completely focused on winning. The players are the same. A lot of people have had their say but that does not alter my thinking. That is their opinion. Mine is that we are going to win it. The cupboard has been bare since Sir Alf in 1966. No other England manager can do anything about that. I can. The players and I can do it together.'

There was an amusing moment when someone asked Keegan why he was so confident. 'Are you really, really, really, really, really confident?' Keegan looked at him and said; 'Yes, I really, really am.' You had to admire Keegan's front, his passion and, of course, his patriotism.

Keegan has done everything he can to turn the players into

Champions. He has broken down the barriers of a 'them and us' situation that has existed before. Under Glenn Hoddle there was definitely a stand-offish regime between him and the players. He is very much the boss, a figure that no one really got close to. Keegan is one of the boys with his men. He spends every minute he can with the squad, making them love him, encouraging them and even eating with them. One of his first tasks as England coach was to dismantle the staff table at meal times at the restaurants the players and he share around the world. The players instead are encouraged to eat with the management, something that had never happened before. 'He makes you feel good, makes you feel that you want to do well for him,' said Manchester United's Phil Neville.

Keegan also made a passionate pre-tournament plea for the hooligans to behave. 'Enough is enough,' he said. 'This is our game, it is the biggest and best game in the world and we must not them walk all over it.'

The longer you listened to Keegan on this day the more you agreed with his every word. Hooliganism, however, remained a shadow over the tournament. It would be a miracle if the three and half weeks passed without the minority who cause such embarrassment for the English game striking again. It would put everything at risk, particularly the Football Association's bid to stage the 2006 World Cup. Do the thugs care? Do they hell.

Our own journey to Belgium was dominated by the news that skipper Alan Shearer was injured and could miss the first game. The knee problem he picked up in Malta needed a scan and Shearer was rushed to Stanmore Hospital on the Thursday morning before the team flew out. The news quickly spread and we got to hear about it on the Eurostar train taking us from Waterloo Station into Belgium. A series of phone calls followed and it materialised that Shearer was seriously doubtful for the first game.

The skipper was certainly not involved at England's first training session. He stood back and watched the others. He smiled but behind the expression I suspect there was a fear that he could miss the opening match in what was his swansong as an England player. It would be cruel luck if Shearer were to miss out. The irony was that the only forward that Keegan could call up in an emergency was Andy Cole, whom the coach had already told us was not fit for the Championships.

England chose not to submit an original squad of 35 to UEFA, only the 28 names that Keegan selected his 22 from. It meant that any late call-up had to come from the 28, not the 35. The cut was Monday, the day of England's first game, and UEFA confirmed that only players from the 28 could be called upon. There was a conflict here, even though everyone expected Shearer to play against Portugal. Keegan said that there would be no replacement call-up even if Shearer broke down.

'I have selected the five best strikers and would go with four of them,' he said. The coach insisted that had he wanted to call for a replacement he could ask for any forward, and not just from the original 28. 'That went out of the window a long time ago,' he said. UEFA disagreed.

The first training session in Belgium proved just how contrived the England scene has become. The session we attended in Spa was so stage managed I looked for a floor manager directing the operation. The security is massive and the number of guards you have to pass just to get a glimpse of the players is staggering. It was not long ago when media mixed with players for a chat at the end of each session and there was a feeling of togetherness. Those days will never return. Now it is very much them and us.

By the time the reporters and photographers were let into the La Fraineuse training camp the England squad were coming to the end of a nine-a-side match. There was about fifteen minutes to watch and photograph and then Kevin Keegan led the players over to where the press were standing on a constructed platform, and they did some stretches and made a few comments, just so the photographers could fill their boots again. But it smelt of 'we don't really want to do this but here we are'. It was rather like being at the zoo at feeding time. Here they are, we must not be late or we'll miss it.

Kevin Keegan strutted around making jokes with the players before the squad walked over to where some local kids had been let in to wait for autographs. Good press relations for the local community but it just smelt of being too organised, too precious. What a contrast to the Portugal camp. England's first-match rivals played a friendly on the Thursday against a local team and made every player and the backroom staff available for interview afterwards. They even invited the media to stay for dinner with the players if they so wished.

I doubt whether England will ever return to the days when media mixed freely with the squad and had the opportunity to talk football in a non-pressurised situation. It is just so highly organised these days. The media centre at La Fraineuse had superb facilities - the FA had spared no expense in that department - and there was plenty of room to work, interview and chat. It would have been good to have seen the players there, strolling around and chatting without the stop-watch on them and the heavy presence of security.

The media hotel was a stone's throw from the team's HQ. That was unusual for a major tournament. Spa was ideal for Keegan's build-up. A sleepy town, it offered no distractions, certainly no attractions for the supporters who would soon invade. A big sign had been erected outside their hotel. 'We keep our fingers crossed for the England team.' So do we Kevin, so do we.

The weekend before England's opening match was kept with fingers crossed for Shearer. Despite his critics, and there are many, it would be a major blow to lose the captain. Keegan would be left with a partnership of Owen and Emile Heskey, who had only played together for four minutes, Robbie Fowler, who is not match fit, and the untried Kevin Phillips. Nothing, however, could dent the manager's confidence or desire.

Only once or twice did he drop his guard, when they were away from the cameras and live media conferences. He said that he needed an answer from Shearer on the Saturday, after he had trained for the first time in five days. I suspect that he would give Shearer right up until kick-off on Monday night if the captain asked for it. Shearer was desperate to play. Keegan called for honesty from his players when discussing their knocks and injuries. It would take a huge setback for Shearer not to lead out his country against Portugal. He would play with a niggle in his left knee.

The extraordinary thing to develop from the injury is that Shearer had been playing with the injury – not the knee that he has undergone three operations on – for five weeks. Five weeks! Why then did not Keegan rest him from the match in Malta and nurse him through to the big kick off?

'He needs games,' explained Keegan. 'He needed to get shots in on goal and do all the things that strikers do.' Strange, but it was almost overlooked as everyone waited for the start, willing England to do well. I sensed that we had reached something of the crossroads with this tournament. If Keegan couldn't do it, then who could?

There was a flash of the pressure on Keegan on the Saturday before Portugal when he sat in front of the Sunday newspaper reporters. After a few questions over Shearer's fitness and other points, a *Sunday Mirror* reporter asked Keegan about the sex ban that the Swedish team had imposed on their players. 'That's it lads, I am off to see the wife.' With that he walked out. A funny, quick-thinking reply but a sign that Keegan was on edge. It was also a stupid question. The reporter involved could at least have waited until towards the end of the press conference.

There was no surprise when Shearer declared himself fit after his training session. He did everything asked of him and told the medical staff and, more significantly, Keegan, that he was OK and ready to play. It was the news that everyone had expected. There was more drama to come, however, surrounding Shearer when the first editions of the Sunday newspapers dropped in London. The *Mail on Sunday* revealed that Shearer had received an injection on Thursday following his scan. They also reported that the injection went completely against what Keegan had said in an *Evening Standard* interview back on 26 May and that was that the England coach would never give one of his players an injection to play in a game.

It led to David Davies's being rung that night by the reporters in Spa and Davies denying the story completely. But under pressure he told the reporters to ring back in ten minutes. The FA then released a statement saying that Shearer had undergone an injection but it was not painkilling, and that did not contradict anything the England coach had said previously.

The statement, and the fact that Shearer had been injected, did throw up a lot of questions. Why had the FA and particularly Keegan kept the news from the media? Why too had Shearer told the Sunday reporters in an interview on the Saturday lunch time that he was fit and that there was nothing wrong? It materialised that Shearer had been suffering with the problem, an irritation in his left knee, for some weeks, indeed playing with it. It made the decision to play him against Malta even more ridiculous.

By the Sunday morning the FA had re-grouped and issued another statement, again from Davies, saying that individuals deserved a certain amount of privacy about their fitness. What was technically correct was that neither Keegan or Shearer had been asked whether an injection had been carried out. An oversight by reporters but when you are led to believe that there are no problems and that the player is completely fit your mind does not go down the road of injections.

It was embarrassing for the *News of the World*, whose number one columnist is Shearer. His ghost writer and he had spoken every day since Thursday and indeed Shearer had told him about the injection soon after he had it, but asked the paper not to use the story. No reporter can break that kind of confidence, and only catch up when another paper breaks the news. The FA remained adamant. They took the advice of the specialist after the scan; they sought permission from Shearer's club Newcastle; one of their backroom medical staff carried out the injection; it was not painkilling, simply anti inflammatory – what was the problem, and fuss? You had to have sympathy with them.

By Sunday morning the team was out in the media, even before Keegan had officially told the players. Just as the coach thought it would. In all the private practice matches Keegan had used Steve McManaman down the left-hand side, not Dennis Wise, with Sol Campbell preferred to Martin Keown at the centre of the defence. It was to be 4–4–2, also as expected. It meant that Keegan had gone with his attacking instinct and you could not blame him for that. He has always believed in attacking the opposition and not showing a negative hand. Wise would have offered more security while McManaman gave England more options going forward.

It is not the team I would have selected. McManaman, for me, has never done it for his country. Never taken a game by the scruff of the neck. England's left-hand side, of McManaman in front of Phil Neville, concerned me against a Portugal team who are at their best attacking sides and exploiting weakness, especially down their opponent's left side. We can only hope that Keegan has got it right, and so to McManaman. It was the former Liverpool star's performances for Real Madrid in the Champions League against Manchester United, and then the final itself, that convinced Keegan to put him in.

Keegan and his players left their Spa HQ, the Balmoral Hotel, at around 11 am on the Sunday morning for Eindhoven, the venue of the first game. There were about one hundred fans to see them off, standing behind the security barriers erected by local police. The loyalty of these supporters never ceases to amaze me. They stand outside the hotel, come rain and shine, sometimes for just a glimpse of their heroes through a coach window. It is the same at Burnham Beeches, England's HQ at home. In the build-up to home Internationals hundreds of fans gather hoping for an autograph or handshake and perhaps, if they are lucky, a picture with their favourite player.

Eindhoven on Sunday afternoon was a sleepy, soulless place. Holland were playing that night so the locals were not interested in the England team training, or Keegan's last press conference before the biggest match of his life. As always, Keegan was in confident mood. He wanted to clear up the Shearer situation.

'Sitting up here on this platform allows me to put the record straight when journalists don't get it right. We have to put up with that, and we do,' he said. 'This story has been blown out of all proportion. It was bad journalism,' he said. Keegan repeated that it had not been a painkilling injection and that he had not gone back on his policy. 'I would not give a player a painkilling injection just to get him through a game,' he stressed.

Keegan said all the right things, as ever. 'We want what the country wants. We want the nation to be proud of us. I have looked into the players' eyes and they are hungry. They are focused. We are ready. Let the football start.' He never misses a trick and, in an effort to rekindle that winning feeling, had invited Sir Geoff Hurst to be with the England side in Euro 2000. Hurst, the only player to score a hat trick in a World Cup Final when England won in 1966 – our only success – stayed with the team all day Sunday and Monday, travelling with the players or the coach on the way to the stadium.

It was a good touch by Keegan, for ever the patriot. It was not Hurst, of course, who would make the difference. It was the team, Keegan's tactics, if things started to go wrong, and the form of the players. A key player was undoubtedly Tony Adams. He revealed to a group of us on the Saturday afternoon that his reading matter for the trip was 'Henry V'. It led to Monday morning headlines like 'Stiffen the sinews, summon up the blood … and, upon this charge, Cry God for Harry, England and St. George' and 'Once more into the breach, dear friends, once more.' It was just what we tabloids wanted on the morning of England's kick-off and Adams even allowed himself to be photographed draped in the cross of St George. Adams is hugely popular with the other players and also the media. I have only the utmost respect for him. If anyone deserved a winner's medal it was the Arsenal captain.

So, the talking was over. The battle cries sung, the team picked, Kevin Keegan and England were ready. The country expects. The spotlight was on the little man who took over the job in a crisis and grew quickly to love it. Kevin Keegan was either going to be king of the day, or the fool on the hill. It was massive for him. He took the players for a walk on the day of the game, then rested before getting on the coach for the short drive to the Eindhoven Stadium. He had achieved so much in his career. Nothing compared to these 90 minutes. I managed to get a word with Keegan as he marched out of the press conference, surrounded by security guards and FA staff.

'Good luck,' I said.

'Thanks,' he replied. 'I know you mean it.'

And I did. I passionately wanted England to win Euro 2000. The repercussions for the game next season would be amazing.

CHAPTER 16

ENGLAND v PORTUGAL, MONDAY 12 JUNE, EINDHOVEN

Team: Seaman; G. Neville, Adams, Campbell, P. Neville; Beckham,
Ince, Scholes, McManaman; Shearer, Owen. Subs. Heskey for
Owen, Wise for McManaman, Kcown for Adams. Score: 2–3.
Scorers: Scholes, McManaman.

At around 9.03 pm in Eindhoven the giant screens positioned around
the Phillips Stadium caught a glimpse of Kevin Keegan's face. He was
out of the England dugout, on his feet, as Steve McManaman had just
driven his team into a 2–0 lead. The face was a picture of pleasure and
satisfaction. How much can go through a human mind in a couple of
seconds? Every emotion surely was dragged through Keegan's feelings.
This is it, what I always dreamed of, 2–0 up in our first match in the
Europeans, the team playing well, the crowd singing, we are on our way.

Keegan was on his feet many more times as the drama unfolded, and at the end he quickly marched over to Portugal coach Humberto Coelho for an embrace following a superb match. This time the camera caught a different Keegan. The satisfaction had been replaced by strain. England had lost. Now would come a silent dressing room. Now would come the inquests. Now would come the prospect of failure. There had been many questions asked about Keegan's footballing brain on the way to the finals during his 16 months in control. The system he liked to play, the attacking players he always backed, his ability to change things when things went wrong. Here they all were staring him in the face.

The worst fears of his critics had come true in a stunning football match, the kind of game you love to be at. This was an occasion, but it left the barrels being loaded and pointed at Keegan. No International team should lose a 2–0 lead after 18 minutes. It had only happened to England once before, on the dreadful night when we had played so well against Germany in the 1970 World Cup and lost after extra time. And England had played well here. There were so many pluses. Yet so many Keegan-style minuses too. He had said early in his England career, 'I am not your man for 0–0 games', and he was right. It was Liverpool 4 Newcastle 3 all over again with Keegan throwing himself forward on to an advertising board when Liverpool scored their stunning winner. That is how every Englishman felt in Eindhoven on Monday night.

At 2–0 England looked like going on to punish a Portugal team who were brilliant going forward yet vulnerable in defence. One more goal would have killed them off. Just as long as we tightened up and did not allow them to dominate us. We couldn't control them. Rui Costa and Joao Pinto got a grip of the game and suddenly every time Portugal attacked they looked like scoring. England became stretched and outnumbered in midfield. Where were the changes to the England team and its tactics? They didn't come. The only alteration Keegan made at half time was in attack, changing the disappointing

Michael Owen for Emile Heskey. We were getting overrun and the manager changes a forward. It was a significant moment and a real insight into Keegan's thinking.

There were a number of disappointing performances. David Seaman looked shaky under pressure although he deserved more protection. Tony Adams suddenly looked like an old man as Portugal attacked him at pace, Paul Ince could not hold on in midfield and Alan Shearer, despite not having the service, never looked like shaking a stubborn but hardly top-class defence. Portugal enjoyed the run of the game for long periods and we did nothing to stop them.

The after-match press conference was interesting and for me very significant. Keegan's mood was upbeat and good-humoured while alongside him sat a grim-faced Alan Shearer. Keegan even made jokes, especially when asked to do an interview live in German. 'I will do it in English,' he said. 'Because my German is not very good these days.' But he was pressed and spoke in German, ending it with a joke and a smile. Then when asked what his regrets were he reeled off a few and added, 'I regret that mike hitting the ceiling,' when the mike on a pole was lifted too high.

More laughter and I just wondered how an England manager having thrown away a 2–0 lead could be so happy. Just imagine Sir Alex Ferguson or Arsene Wenger laughing and joking their way through a bad defeat. I suspect that Keegan's mood covered his real feelings. Or his weaknesses as a coach. It was an act. One we had seen so many times. This again was Keegan the motivator, but where was Keegan the coach?

'I do not regret the system I used,' he said. 'It was a system to cause Portugal problems. I suspect that there will be heavy criticism for the defenders. But we defend and attack as a team. We all take responsibility. If only we could have held them for another ten minutes and made them more desperate.'

If only, if only. The bottom line is that Portugal exposed what we all feared. That we do not have the defenders to cope with world-class strikers, in midfield we have to have a system that does not allow the opposition to play and up front only Paul Scholes these days looks like scoring consistently.

It was a depressing coach journey back to Spa, not only for Keegan and his players but the media too. Another glorious failure, another great match, another game to keep the fans back home and here on their feet, but no end result. Shearer was far more realistic than Keegan. If we do not beat Germany on Saturday we can pack our bags and go home,' he said.

You could tell Shearer's mood was black. I suspect that he didn't think much of Keegan's jokes. An incident occurred after the final whistle that dominated the tabloids' headlines and perhaps allowed Keegan to escape heavier criticism. It emerged that an agency photographer had spotted David Beckham giving some England fans a one-finger salute as he left the pitch. Beckham had just exchanged shirts with Figo and was heading down the tunnel when he made his gesture. It was the kind of behaviour that was jumped upon by the FA in our domestic game although the FA this time quickly leapt to Beckham's defence.

It materialised that a group of drunken England fans had been bawling foul-mouthed abuse at Beckham and other England players through the second half. The moment Portugal started to take control of the game it had started and Kevin Keegan was aware of what was going on. He and his staff were appalled by it and England security staff made it known to UEFA security who the culprits were and asked them to be removed. They were not and it climaxed with Beckham losing his cool, not for the first time in his career.

Television captured him walking off the pitch, shaking his head and looking over to the fans in disbelief. You have to have sympathy for Beckham. He is not just a wonderful footballer but is a worldwide public figure because of his lifestyle and is an obvious target for the morons and idiots. You and I would react if we took such continued abuse, but if you are being followed every step of the way then you simply have to behave. One slip and, bingo, the idiots have got what they wanted. The FA were still making statements about Beckham and what happened at one o'clock in the morning, such was their concern over the handling of the incident. They clearly were going to support him all the way and were worried that UEFA would react with a suspension.

Thankfully, they didn't, which was the right decision. What Beckham has to put up with just because he is married to a superstar is incredible. It was the Beckham story that completely dominated Tuesday, the day after England's defeat. You would not have thought that England had played in a superb game and thrown away a 2–0 lead, such was the impact Beckham's one-finger salute had made on the media. Keegan defended Beckham strongly in his press conference.

'The abuse he had to put up was the worst I have experienced ever,' he said. 'If Beckham has to put up with fifty per cent of that on certain days of his life then it shows just how well he handles the pressure.' Keegan revealed that had the abuse been aimed at him, and not Beckham and other England players, then he would have struggled not to have reacted:

'I would have struggled to have held on to my temper,' he said. 'I would have said something had I gone back down the tunnel. If you had heard it, had your sons and daughters been confronted with it, then I think you would have reacted. I take my hat off to the players that they didn't react more strongly. Why does this have to happen? These young men are playing for their country and have the three lions on their chest. I feel so sorry for them.'

Worse was to follow for Keegan. The next day, Wednesday, he awoke to be told that the *Mirror* were actually running what was claimed to have been chanted at Beckham by the drunken morons. Keegan despaired and you can only have sympathy with him. How can journalism stoop so low? Does it really matter what they said and do we want to have it rammed down our throats? We have all heard it at football grounds, the abuse against him and the slogans aimed at his wife, Posh Spice Victoria, and their son.

Keegan knew that when he took the job on he would be faced with such incidents, knew that the criticism would come. The job as England coach is a lonely one. You can spend as much time as you like with the players but the moment you close the door and sit alone in your room, then the realisation is that it is you against the rest. Yes, you can protect the players, say the right things and be in the right places. The bottom line is results. Win and the country laughs with you, lose and you are public enemy number one. Had England beaten Portugal then the Beckham incident would not have been mentioned. You can understand why some men have turned down the England job because they didn't fancy the aggro. Keegan wanted it and was prepared for everything that was to be thrown at him. He was certainly hurt by the defeat and the criticism that followed. Bemused by the treatment of Beckham.

His mood had changed at the Tuesday press conference. On Monday night after the match he had been upbeat and joking, indeed too light-hearted for me. This time realism had set in and the sparkle had left his face. He was still shocked when someone asked why he was so euphoric after the game.

'I didn't mean to be happy, sorry about that,' he answered sarcastically. 'I am a realist and what is the point in me going into the after-match press conference and slashing my wrists?

'I was not "up", I can promise you that. It is my job to tell the truth and the truth is that we can still go through. Whether we are good enough to do it only time will tell, but that is the reality and I am not going to cover that up just because we have lost. I am not one of those people who get depressed.

'We had the chance to do something special against Portugal and could not see it through. The players are down and we are licking our wounds. Funnily enough, at the start of the competition I thought the gap of five days between Portugal and Germany was going to be too long. But it is prime time for us now and we must make good use of it out on the training pitch. The table doesn't look great, I know that. But it is not impossible for us to win the group. We had problems defending as a team and that is what we must work on and improve. We answered some questions, but didn't answer the important ones. We tried and, yes, Portugal caused us problems.'

Keegan fiercely defended his players, especially the spine of the side, David Seaman, Tony Adams, Paul Ince and Alan Shearer.

'The spine is as strong as ever and that spine has the character to overcome any criticism. It is the backbone of our team,' he said. 'We did get carried away with the situation of being 2–0 up and the atmosphere from the fans. You will say that it is typical Kevin Keegan. But, believe it or not, I do like to see teams play with their heads at times. It was the defending of the team that was disappointing.'

Keegan was also stunned when questioned about his own responsibility for England's failure. 'The coach takes all the criticism,' he said. I pick the team and I decide how we are going to play. The buck stops with me and I am happy with that.' He was hurt again when the *Mirror*, on its Wednesday morning back page, said that Keegan was influenced by senior players. He has said many times that he talks to and respects senior players but insists that he is his own man.

'I decide and then we discuss it as coaches,' he said. 'I have never asked you people [the media] to look at me any other way. That is the way it has been since I took over and, please God, it will be for a good while longer.' Pressed on the cavalier Newcastle style he again looked hurt and clearly controlled his anger. 'I am not going to go down that route again because I have done it before.' Was Newcastle a success or failure under my control? he asked the reporter. In terms of winning things, a failure was the answer. 'Was it?' he said, amazed that anyone could think that what he did for Newcastle represented a failure. 'OK, I accept that winner takes all.'

And the winner does. Keegan knew that victory over Germany on

Saturday would change the mood of the nation, the camp, the media and the anti feeling building up against him. He also knew that he had to do it without Tony Adams and Steve McManaman, both injured against Portugal. Keegan took Wednesday off from the media. He needed to. The atmosphere in the camp was one of heavy criticism, often written by reporters of little experience and some who were covering their first major tournament.

There is an atmosphere at times that I no longer like around the England camp. It is one of being too quick to react in a negative way. It is the outcome I'm afraid of too many people under too much pressure. Too many reporters unable to stand up to constant pressure from their desks back in London, too many reporters unable to say 'No, I am not doing that' and too many reporters trying to create a quick reputation for themselves.

There have been many Football Association Public Relations cock-ups over the years, notably the handling of the Glenn Hoddle affair. Wednesday before Germany produced another classic. Keegan was never going to do a press conference and so the FA decided to put up Les Reed, one of Keegan's backroom boys. Reed is a quiet, decent guy who works hard behind the scenes studying the opposition for the England coach and compiling dossiers and videos of information. The longer he sat in front of the media the harder the questions became, regarding England's failure against Portugal. Reed answered them honestly and admitted that the players were unable to deal with the instructions sent out to them when things started to go wrong.

David Davies, sitting alongside Reed, became increasingly uncomfortable as he realised that the mood was changing. Here was an easy target being exploited. But Davies should never have exposed Reed to a media day, even though the coach said that he had enjoyed himself. After the press conference Davies spent much time ringing reporters to go easy on Reed, and not to let him down, he even contacted London to ask the Sports Editor of Sky Sports News to disdain the way he used the interview material. It was PR at its worst.

When will they learn?

It didn't get much better the following day when Davies said that he would take some German questions at Keegan's press briefing. The mike was given to a reporter who started to speak in English only to be told by Davies, 'No, you are not German enough,' and the mike was whisked away from him. The reporter, of course, was German, much to the embarrassment of the FA's Executive Director. Keegan got in on the act a few moments later when he asked Micky Walker of the *Irish Times* where he came from in Germany. 'Belfast,' was the answer. 'Oh, they have moved it since I was last there,' said the England coach. Much laughter and nothing was taken too seriously. There were more serious issues at stake.

Keegan certainly seemed relaxed and the team he announced to the players, which was discovered by various reporters via contacts, showed only two changes from the side that lost to Portugal. Dennis Wise of Chelsea and Martin Keown of Arsenal coming in for the injured Steve McManaman and Tony Adams. The Germans, it was reported, were in disarray with internal politics and players dropping out. We had heard it all before and Keegan was quick to point out that he was not interested in history and statistics. Only results.

'It is about now,' he said, 'The reality is that we have to beat Germany to progress. I am not interested in 1966, '70 or '96, this is about my team trying to reach the quarter finals of the European Championships. I expect to win.'

CHAPTER 17

ENGLAND V GERMANY, SATURDAY 17 JUNE, CHARLEROI

Team: Seaman, G. Neville, Keown, Campbell, P. Neville; Beckham, Ince, Scholes (Barmby), Wise; Shearer, Owen (Gerrard). Score: 1–0. Scorer: Shearer.

It was Alan Shearer who best summed up the feeling of pure joy. 'I was knackered,' he said. 'More tired than I have ever been on a football pitch. But I was not coming off. No way. I wanted to be there at the final whistle when we beat Germany.'

Shearer's mood was easy to understand. He had suffered in 1996 and was fed up with having Germany's record against England thrust down his throat. The captain had scored the goal and this was his moment, one of the best of his career. The final whistle brought scenes of wild celebration from the England players. They hugged each other, raised their fists in triumph at the supporters who had created such a fantastic atmosphere. The substitutes joined them in the middle of the pitch. Sol Campbell could not hide his passion. He just screamed and screamed into the Brussels night. And there was Kevin Keegan, clapping his players on the back and enjoying one of the great games in his life. It is impossible to share this kind of situations with top sportsmen. These are their moments, the ones they will treasure in their careers, for the rest of their lives. We can watch and imagine but never live it properly.

The dressing room was a cauldron of noise, in sharp contrast to the atmosphere after Monday night's defeat by Portugal. Keegan went from player to player congratulating them. 'He is always a happy chap,' Arsenal's Martin Keown said. It was an understatement yet we knew what he meant. As Keegan came through the mixed zone interview area in the bowels of the stadium he just nodded. Two, three, four times. It was a gesture of victory. It was a gesture of pleasure. The feeling in the England camp was such that you would have thought that we had won the European Championship.

But what these players had experienced was something special. Victory over Germany. The old enemy. It was great to be English in Charleroi on Saturday night, for football reasons. Of course there were the terrible crowd scenes in Brussels that had backdropped the match but, thankfully, there was no trouble in the stadium. People will criticise me for saying that, but it is how I felt when I wrote these words the morning after. I too was fed up with losing to Germany. It was great to be able to say, 'I was there,' when we look back in years to come. And, of course, there was much more to come in this tournament. Romania on Tuesday night would not be easy. They have a good pedigree in major tournaments. But England needed a point to go into the last eight and a possible clash with Italy. Surely, after beating Germany, we couldn't fail against Romania?

What England did not realise was that as they were celebrating and enjoying their victory UEFA were growing increasingly annoyed about the fans that follow us whenever we play abroad. I use the term fan lightly. The hooligans are simply the scum of the earth – morons, lowlife whose one aim in society is to get drunk and cause trouble. We watch them on television and shake our heads in disbelief. Sadly, we have become so used to having them around on England trips that we almost accept their presence. What a slur on our society that statement is. Yet it is true. 'Oh the yobs are at it again,' we say and then go on our way. Well, on the Sunday following the victory over Germany, UEFA decided that enough was enough. While Kevin Keegan held a press conference to talk football at the media centre in Spa, UEFA called a 6 pm press briefing about the crowd trouble that had occurred in Brussels, where water cannons had to be used.

The Football Association were taken completely by surprise by the hard line employed by UEFA and tournament organisers. The FA had expected a slap across the wrist, and an attack from UEFA against the British Government for allowing known hooligans into Belgium and Holland. What they got was to transform Sunday from celebrating victory into the most serious situation since our clubs were banned from European football because of crowd trouble. The message from the organisers was simple. Any more crowd trouble, and England will be expelled from Euro 2000. It sent shock waves into the team's hotel. The FA were told by Lennart Johansson, the president of UEFA: 'We are serious. It can't go on, it will kill football.'

The FA had been holding talks, almost hourly, with the Government since they arrived in Belgium and believed they had done everything possible to curb crowd violence. David Davies, the Executive Director, thrown into another crisis, has said many times: 'We are not a police force, we are not a government, we are a football authority and there are limitations to the powers we have.' Davies and Chief Executive Adam Crozier, who had returned to London after a brief visit to Euro 2000, locked themselves in urgent telephone conversation. They were stunned by UEFA's ultimatum and taken by surprise by the quickness of events. They had not been invited to the meeting and Sir Brian Hayes, the FA's Chief Security Officer and former Deputy Commissionaire of the Metropolitan Police, went with a prepared statement. Incredibly, he was not allowed to ask or answer questions and was not present when the UEFA delegate came to their conclusion. One more riot and pack your bags.

What could the FA do? They believed they had done everything in their power to stop hooliganism. They authorised 5,000 official fans from the England Supporters Club, which has a 27,000 membership, and knew who they were and their addresses. Yet in Charleroi on Saturday night there were almost 20,000 England fans and many more without tickets outside. They are the ones the FA can not control. That is why they believe they should have more help from the Government.

Davies, who began this book and the Keegan story in the middle of a crisis, was in the spotlight again. With Crozier back in London it was Davies who had to make the short walk from the team's Balmoral Hotel to the media's Dorint Hotel in Spa to read a prepared statement. The moment he stepped off the street and into the drive the huge lamps that TV cameras use lit up. There he was again. David Davies. He had made the walk to Harrods all those months ago to capture Keegan. Now he was trying to keep England in European football on the eve of Keegan's finest hour. The media had asked for Kevin Keegan and skipper Alan Shearer to be present too, but the request was rejected by the FA. They wanted the coach and the players to concentrate only on the Romania game, which was just 48 hours away.

I believe that Keegan should have been used. The national newspapers and all other media outlets were full of one story and one story only on the Monday morning, the possibility of England being kicked out of Euro 2000. Keegan's plea to fans would have made more impact than one from Davies. Again, it was a missed PR opportunity from the FA. Davies is helpful but he does not carry the weight of a massive name like Keegan. The PR department were in turmoil that Sunday night; praise here for Joanne Budd, one of the FA's press officers. Not for the first time she held things together. Budd deserves a bigger and better platform.

It took the FA more than four hours to prepare a statement and, incredibly, the only weapon they had was to plead again with the morons who had not been listening for years. Why should they listen now? They do not care. To them it is a sport to kill football. They have no feeling for anything, let alone the England football team. They travel to fight and drink. They are a growth of the culture in England. We have let standards drop as a country and this is the result. Standards start at home and once they have been allowed to slip then the hooligan is alive and kicking. I wonder what the parents of these morons caught on camera think. Maybe they stopped caring years ago.

Davies did his best to appear authoritative. He said: 'We want to be part of a safe festival of football, just like we did in Euro 96.' Significantly, Davies quickly turned the heat on the British Government. He added: 'The Government's reaction to UEFA is for them. As far as the FA are concerned it is public knowledge that we called for emergency legislation to remove passports from proven troublemakers. We have worked tirelessly for this tournament. Kevin Keegan appealed before we left for good behaviour. I am repeating that appeal for Kevin, all the players and English football.'

Davies revealed the FA's deep concerns over UEFA's handling of their meeting. They were staggered that neither the chairman (Geoff Thompson) nor Chief Executive (Adam Crozier) were invited to attend the UEFA meeting. Davies said: 'We were surprised how this came about, there is no hiding that. It is for UEFA to explain the process how they went about this matter. I am not surprised by the stance they have taken. I make that clear. We want to work with them to make this a real festival of football.

'How a Football Association can be responsible for fans well away from stadiums is something that UEFA has always rejected in the past and now is a matter for discussion between us and them. We must point out that that a majority of the fans arrested and involved in the crowd scenes did not figure in any of the records we had of proven troublemakers. We understand why trouble happens and all we can do is play our part in trying to stop it to the maximum.

'My message again is help the team, help English football. Football yes, violence no, that is the message. That is the slogan.' We had heard it before, of course, may times. And why should the fans suddenly listen to the FA? Because these morons have no feeling for anything. 'We feel strongly about this,' says Davies. 'There are procedures that have to be taken before a country can be excluded from a tournament. We have confidence that these people will listen. I am not going to fall into language about "it is – this or else". They will listen because this is a very important moment for everyone. One has to be optimistic. This is so important for English football. The England team matters, so much is at stake here. The chances of the team matter. The country recognises that. There is pressure that we can put on these people.

'All I can ask is for everyone to put as much pressure on them as possible. Make them realise what damage they are doing. We have worked tirelessly with anyone and everyone available to combat these people. You have never done enough but we must not let them win. Never. I ask you, what more can we do as the FA? I have to say that I do believe that the people who have the solution to this are the politicians. It is a cultural problem. The behaviour that we have witnessed here we have seen before in society. The legislation was there last year but it was blocked. There were civil libertarians on both sides who blocked it. The politicians must answer the questions. You can't give in to these criminals and I call them that because that is what they are. The FA alone can not stop it. It is however within the country's capability to stop these people. We certainly do not contemplate pulling the England team out of the competition. I refuse to get into an if or what situation.'

With every fight seen on every TV screen around the world England's hopes of staging the World Cup in 2006 diminished. The FA knew that. So did Davies as he stood before the media late on Sunday night and then carried out a de-briefing in the media hotel in a room on the basement floor. 'The issue of 2006 remains to be seen,' he said. 'Clearly the incidents have not been helpful. There are other countries with security problems. Moral judgements have to be made. We are only 17 days away from a result about 2006.'

Davies had spoken with Keegan before making his appearance. 'Kevin's view about this is very strong,' he added. 'But it is very important that Kevin and the players go about their business. They want to go through so badly against Romania and they must remain focused. The manager has to concentrate on team affairs.'

It was desperate stuff from Davies and you had to feel sorry for him. He answered what questions he could and fielded others with such answers as 'you will have to ask them' or 'that is a question for the government'. Secretly the FA are fuming with PM Tony Blair, Home Secretary Jack Straw and Foreign Secretary Robin Cook. They pleaded for the trouble-makers to be banned and nothing happened. What we have seen in Belgium is a result of the most weak-willed and lily-livered authority in the country. These hooligans are scum and they should be treated as such. It does not need some do-gooder standing up in the Commons saying that society should not ban anyone from travelling abroad. Let the people who blocked the legislation come and be with these lowlife for 24 hours. Let them suffer and then see if they change their minds. It is pathetic how we have dealt with hooliganism over the years. The country has a lot to answer for. I am fed up with politicians coming out of hiding the day after a football crisis and blaming everyone but themselves. While they are not as much at fault as the culprits, they clearly should take some of the blame.

One thing is sure. The events of Sunday completely overshadowed the victory over Germany. The carnival had turned into a crisis. Keegan was left locked away inside the team hotel making sure that UEFA's ultimatum had not damaged morale, spirit and concentration. It was an appalling situation for him. He knew he would be under pressure as England coach. But not this kind of pressure. It had all seemed so good a few hours earlier. The terrific atmosphere inside the stadium, Alan Shearer's goal to answer his critics and the battling team performance to secure our first competitive victory over Germany in 34 years. Thirty years of hurt, we had waited so long and it was ruined with the snarl of a hooligan. The contorted face of English support.

Keegan's attitude to the victory was strange. Instead of enjoying one of the great moments of his career, he turned on the media over Alan Shearer. He blamed us, or at least the critics, for forcing him out of International football. 'Alan can't say these things, but I can,' he said. It was an amazing after-match and one that Shearer would not have been happy with. He has always faced the media and deep down enjoyed the crack with journalists. He has always been honest and never blamed the media in any way for his retirement decision. Shearer has always said that it was for family reasons. I suspect that deep down he also knows that his legs will not carry him any more at the very highest level, but for the manager to blame the media, especially on such a day, was wrong.

The players too took us by surprise in the mixed zone interview area. We thought they would be desperate to talk about beating Germany. On the pitch they had openly celebrated, but an hour later a majority of them scuffled through, head down and only stopping to say 'no' when asked for an interview. Paul Ince, Shearer, Sol Campbell and man of the match Martin Keown were the exceptions. Plus young Paul Gerrard, who had made an impressive second-half entrance as sub and gave us an insight into what will undoubtedly be a player of England's future. The players, as the bus pulled out of the stadium, were already deep into games of cards. What an extraordinary bunch they are. England must be the worst team in the world for a 'them and us' attitude. Monday morning only brought gloom and doom. The atmosphere had changed from excitement to helplessness. There was a feeling that the European Championships were no longer in the hands of the players, but the scum.

One good, respectable England supporter told the story of having a knife put to his throat by a Turk. 'I don't need this,' he said. 'I am never coming abroad to watch England again.' Rather than ban

England, UEFA should not allow any England supporter to obtain tickets. It is the only way. It is hard on the majority of good supporters but if we are to continue to play a part in major tournaments then why should other countries suffer at the hands of yobs? The centre of Brussels is an attractive tourists trap, full of cafés and bars. It became a war zone. The trouble is that English hooligans have now become a target for other sectors of scum. An English fan clubbed is a notch on the belt. Also, why do the authorities still allow booze to be sold before, during and after matches? Shut down the bars, close the supermarkets and don't allow alcohol to be consumed within a ten-mile radius of the stadium.

From daybreak on the Monday the FA were busy. A stream of phone calls took place. The central figures were Davies, who had little sleep, and Adam Crozier, who had got an early flight from London to be in central control. Prime Minister Tony Blair spoke with FIFA President Lennart Johansson, and Home Secretary Jack Straw had discussions with top UEFA officials. Crozier met Kevin Keegan at the team's hotel and it was decided to let the players in on exactly what was happening. Rather than their getting snippets from television and newspapers, Crozier called a meeting of the England squad and gave them a full briefing about UEFA's ultimatum and what had been happening overnight. He assured them that England would not be thrown out of the tournament and that their efforts on the pitch would not be wasted.

Keegan listened. He was under pressure to say something to the media. He had made his passionate appeal before the team left and the media wanted him to hold a press conference that morning, The FA said no. It was another PR chance lost. Keegan should have got his thoughts about the hooligans and UEFA out of the way before travelling to Charleroi for training and his official UEFA press conference, where he could have concentrated on football alone. The FA were again unhelpful and how they need a particularly forceful, experienced press officer in these situations, someone to get hold of the situation, with the confidence and knowledge to brief. Davies is looking for one and the new man needs to be in place pretty quickly.

The press conference held in a room at the media centre at Charleroi was due to start at 6.30 pm local time, 5.30 pm in London and close to newspaper first-edition times. Keegan, Davies and Crozier were half an hour late and I thought it wrong that there was not an apology to the world's media who had been kept waiting. Keegan spoke first about football and then turned his attention to the only subject that the 200 people in the sweltering room were interested in.

Keegan looked tired, he was sweating heavily and spoke passionately, as he always does, about UEFA and the hooligans. 'Listen for once' was his message. He called them losers and said that he was only interested in winners. 'If you must behave badly go and do it in your own backyard.' He said that the players would be devastated if UEFA withdrew England and added: 'I can assure everyone back home and here that nothing will let our focus and concentration slip. Nothing.' Keegan had snapped on the Sunday when questioned about the support inside the stadium.

Asked what he felt about the fans singing 'No surrender to the IRA' and the Dam Busters Tune, he answered: 'I have not heard that, I'm sorry.' Then he turned on a reporter. 'Don't shrug your shoulders, why should I take your word for it?' Keegan did not lose his temper and after his speech about the massive problem and answering a few questions he slipped away to be with his players, leaving Davies and Crozier to face the UEFA music. Keegan had said 'what a shame' when advised that the last question about football was being asked, and it was a shame. You would not have thought that England were 24 hours away from a crucial Euro 2000 game.

Crozier was impressive. He talked well and confidently and didn't hesitate when asked questions. Crozier quickly revealed that UEFA, in writing, had confirmed that the Football Association of any country was only directly responsible for the supporters inside stadiums. This was significant and meant that the FA could use it if fighting broke out again. Crozier also said that UEFA delegates had told him that the atmosphere inside the stadium for Saturday night's game against Germany had been the best so far in the tournament.

There was sympathy with UEFA and the people of Belgium and the revelation that, in discussions with the Government, rules had been tightened up at ports, there would be extra British police working with the local authorities and that any offender caught would be banned for life from attending a football stadium abroad. The only question he could not answer with any authority was why had these stricter codes not been introduced before the tournament. I suspect it was because, secretly, the FA are seething with the Government. Crozier said: 'A legislation was in place two years ago to stop known hooligans, we call them criminals, from leaving England. We urge the government to make that a priority.'

The FA were given assurances from UEFA that the England team's forced exit would only come if there was another severe outbreak of fighting. What they termed as severe was not clear. To the dismay of everyone there was more fighting in Brussels on Monday night and into the early hours of Tuesday morning. Thankfully, this time it was not the English, but the Turks. It put UEFA into a difficult situation. If there was more hooliganism from England fans what would they do about Turkey, who had just got through to the quarter finals?

It was a mess. A depressing mess. I have covered football at the highest level for 25 years and thought I had seen hooligans come and go. Football was returning to being a family sport. This is more sinister. It is organised crime. There is Internet organisation, communication between rival gangs by mobile phones, ring leaders who never get involved and the weapons they use can range from knives to baseball bats. They should never be allowed to travel and if they do and then get caught surely the punishment has got to be heavier. These yobs like to fight and a street battle with the police is good fun. A night in prison is a joke punishment. They are no longer afraid of authority and we, as a country, have a lot to answer for.

We travelled to Charleroi thinking of anything but the game. What has covering International football come to when you are looking over your shoulder as much as waiting for the match to start? It is a tragedy and Keegan worked hard on his players to make sure they were focused. If anyone could keep their concentration on the football he could. Romania, of course, would be no pushover. They are technically gifted and needed a victory to have a chance of playing in the last eight. England needed a point. It was a fascinating contest. If only it was just about the football.

CHAPTER 18

ENGLAND v ROMANIA, TUESDAY 20 JUNE, CHARLEROI

Team: Seaman, G. Neville, Keown, Campbell, P. Neville; Beckham,
Ince, Scholes (Southgate), Wise (Barmby); Shearer, Owen (Heskey).
Score: 2–3. Scorers: Shearer (pen), Owen.

'Can't pass, can't keep possession, can't carry out instructions and give
the ball away too much.'

Those were Kevin Keegan's words, not mine. It was the biggest
criticism of any England squad that I can remember from a manager.
Keegan was talking 45 minutes after England had been knocked out
of Euro 2000 and he repeated his thoughts at a press conference the
following morning. He insisted that he was not criticising the players
directly. But what he had done was to expose the problems that
England faces if we are to ever catch up with the top foreign sides left
behind in the European Championships.

England were a pathetic rabble in Euro 2000. We lived on hope, expectancy, and the victory over Germany allowed us to get lost in sentiment. We forgot that the Germans were worse than us. I have always tipped England to win major tournaments, simply because I so much want to see the country hold up its head and look down on the rest. I can't do it any more. We are going backwards at an alarming rate.

It was the match against Romania that brought the depression and, of course, the exit. We only needed a point and didn't have the tactics, the formation, the know-how, the bottle, the players or the coach to do it. Romania outplayed us, outclassed us and deserved to go through.

Keegan didn't duck his own responsibility. 'I failed to get the best out of the players I chose and that is down to me,' he said. Then he said something that perhaps is the biggest self-condemnation of any England manager there has been. 'I wasn't able to get my team to do what I wanted them to do,' he said. It is an amazing statement. I am the manager but I can't make my team play.

Had Glenn Hoddle said it then the English media would have turned on him like no tomorrow. There would have been calls for his head, he would have been ridiculed and blazed across every tabloid newspaper. Keegan got a soft landing after our exit. There were a couple of calls for him to go but it was cushioned with 'Well, who else is there?' The FA, by the end of the tournament, realised that they had employed a cheerleader but not a tactician. That is all very well. Keegan's man-management skills and motivation have never been questioned. Euro 2000 was a test of his tactics and know-how when he was pitched against the best in Europe. How would he cope when England were in crisis? Twice we led, twice we failed to hold on to the lead. Twice we looked for the manager to change things for the good, twice, nothing.

All through this book I have praised Kevin Keegan. You can not help but like the man. His spirit and optimism are there for everyone to see. He carries his heart on his sleeve. It was the fairytale job for him, climaxing in the biggest moment of his career. A major Championship and it was always going to be Euro 2000 when this particular Kevin Keegan story came to an end. He said we would win it if he got the maximum from his players. He failed. We hoped he would be right. We were fooled.

By the time England had gone home there was an air of depression over Spa, where England had stayed, and I am writing this on the Thursday morning. Spain and Holland have just celebrated victories after two fantastic matches, England are left with the usual inquests. The depression comes from years of hoping and now, the realisation again, that we are a lost cause. We are hopeless.

Why? How many times have we asked that question over the years. Every time we go home early the call goes out for better organisation at grass roots level, for coaches to encourage the young to have better habits and the debate about why we can not perform against top foreign players. I am sick and tired of excuses. Keegan, at least was honest. Players were not good enough and he could not get them to play. Great, isn't it. Manager on £1 million a year and players earning more than that and they can't pass the ball to each other. The only hope we have is that the groundwork being done behind the scenes at the FA by Howard Wilkinson eventually produces players of quality. It is going to take years. At the same time every other country in the world will be improving too. At the moment, technically, we are not on the same planet.

In the England team there were players that money can not buy. David Beckham, Paul Scholes, Michael Owen, Sol Campbell. Every week in the Premiership we see them star and produce great performances. We call them world class. It is the most over-used phrase in English football journalism. World class? Take a look at the other players in Europe. Ours seem great in the Premiership because they are surrounded by top foreign players.

Phil Neville, who made the schoolboy error to hand Romania

their last-minute penalty, is not even a first-choice at Manchester United. I feel sorry for Neville because of the stick he is going to take at every ground in the country for the first few weeks of the season but no sympathy for that tackle that will haunt him for the rest of his career. It was desperate. Neville cried when Glenn Hoddle left him out of the World Cup in 1998. He had us crying with the worst tackle of his career.

Of the squad Keegan selected, only a handful of the players could go home with any satisfaction. David Beckham did well although I have still to see him take an International by the scruff of the neck. He made three of the five goals England scored and will be a key player if we are to qualify for the World Cup in the forthcoming matches against Germany, again, Finland, Greece and Albania. Paul Scholes is quality and, again, is one of the few players who offers us hope. Sol Campbell is a top defender and is guaranteed his place. Martin Keown had a good Euro 2000 and is sure to be around for a couple more seasons.

David Seaman, surely, has to hang up his gloves although his replacement Nigel Martyn, forced into action against Romania five minutes before the start because Seaman pulled a calf muscle, is prone to mistakes. His pathetic punch out that gifted Romania their second goal only emphasised the worry. The Neville brothers, Gary and Phil, are not International class and Gareth Southgate, Paul Ince and Dennis Wise, because of their age, can not be considered again. Tony Adams is Keegan's choice as captain for the retiring Alan Shearer, but at 33 can his fitness be guaranteed for a demanding World Cup campaign? I would make David Beckham captain. He does not have the personality but carries the respect of an outstanding player. The extra responsibility of wearing the armband would do him good.

Keegan insisted that he would pick all the same players again. That is nonsense. There must be new faces. Players like Steve Gerrard, Scholes, Beckham, Michael Owen, Emile Heskey, Steve McManaman, Gareth Barry and Nick Barmby can form the basis of a new-look England. There are other younger players like Keiron Dyer,

Rio Ferdinand and Joe Cole who have to be encouraged. Keegan said: 'There will be younger players coming through but if there was a tournament in a month's time I would pick this squad again. They are the best players in England. I don't think that I am too loyal to my players. Particularly someone like Alan Shearer, who has taken so much criticism. Next season, when we start all over again, all these players will be with me.'

We have reached the stage in English football when the established players are not good enough and the young ones are not ready. We have been here before. Many times. Yet if the players are not good enough there must surely be a team plan, a tactical awareness, a system that makes up for our individual failings. Players not outstanding at International level need a brilliant coach. Keegan is not that man. There is no question of the FA wanting him out. He rescued them when they needed him most and there is no move to oust him. They will do everything they can allow him to get us to the World Cup in 2002, and be successful beyond that. They realise now that Keegan is a perfect front man for them. He is public relations on wheels and can do so much for them as an ambassador. He does, however, need coaching help and it is something that FA Chairman Geoff Thompson admitted as he went about his UEFA duties when Keegan and the players had gone home. 'He may need help,' Thompson said. 'He would be the first to admit that himself.'

Thompson was a busy man during Euro 2000. He was on UEFA business, as well as fulfilling his role as FA Chairman. A place on the UEFA executive committee was one of his targets, and he got it. It was that committee who gave England their ultimatum on hooliganism and the FA were appalled that such representation could be made without their input. A lot of work went on behind the scenes to get him elected. Thompson's views are always worth listening to because he is honest. He said that England not getting through the qualifying group at Euro 2000 was their rightful spot in world rankings. 'We are one of the best 16 teams in Europe, but certainly not in the top six.'

He was dead right, of course. At this moment, Keegan as team manager and Howard Wilkinson as the coaching overlord – the two men had become friends and talked often about players and tactics - did not look like the dream ticket.

The Romanian match was a roller-coaster ride of hopeful attacking, careless defending and throwing away a lead. It was just like watching Keegan's Newcastle. At half-time there was hope because at 2–1 we were more than on our way into the quarter finals. Keegan's lucky. Is it meant to be? These were the kind of questions being thrown around. Then came Martyn's mistake, then came Romania outplaying England in every department and then came Phil Neville's ridiculous challenge. Out. Once again in despair. In 1990 missed penalties and Gazza crying, six years later Gareth Southgate's tears, more spot kick drama in 1998 and now this. It would have been easier to take had we lost 3–0. To lose again with minutes to spare and another mistake, it makes you weep.

Keegan's after-match interview was honest. 'No excuses because we deserved what we got. We did not play and that is why we are heading home.' He refused to blame Nigel Martyn and Phil Neville. 'We lost this together and I take responsibility. I am the coach and the buck stops with me.' The morning after, unshaven, sweating and looking tired, Keegan and Alan Shearer did the rounds of TV, radio and newspaper interviews. 'Still no excuses,' he said. 'These players ran everywhere to try and put it right. At the end of the day it proved beyond us.' Keegan said that he had learned a lot in Euro 2000. What did you learn? He could not really answer.

The worrying thing is does he understand what he has learned. Next time will he be able to make the tactical changes that have to be spot on when the clock is ticking? Know what you are good at. It is the best bit of advice I have ever been given. Keegan is good at motivation, fronting the ship. This does not necessarily make him the best man when it starts to sink. He is brilliant with the players. There are stories of race nights, card schools and sing songs with them. He is with them all the time. Keegan is a racing man and there was an unconfirmed story that he once let Michael Owen out of the team's hotel in Bisharn to watch a race at the local bookmakers. Is he too close to them? Not if he has their respect. I believe he does as a man. As a tactician some senior players agree with Thompson. I think he does need help, but I suspect that Keegan's pride may not allow him to bring in a high-profile coach to work alongside him.

So, it's over again. The hype, the dreams and the expectancy. Gone for another major tournament. The rest of the world laugh at us again. Keegan talks of passion, commitment and English determination being the base of success. There has to be more than that. Portugal and Romania showed that skill, technique and tactics are just as important. Take away David Beckham and Paul Scholes and our technique cupboard is bare.

Kevin Keegan went home for a holiday. 'I will be back next season refreshed and raring to go,' he told us. Do we want him back? There is of course no one else. But you can not win European Championships and World Cups on passion alone. If you could then Keegan would have won everything by now. Once again the wounds have been opened up and it will take, I suspect, more than Kevin Keegan to repair them.

I so desperately wanted to cover England winning a major Championship. Nearly in 1990, close again in 1996, hope in 1998 and England went into Euro 2000 with optimism high. It was put there by Keegan himself. 'If I get the best out of my players we will win,' he said. He meant it. He thought it. We got swept along on his talk. What Keegan probably learned at his three matches is that he just ain't good enough, not on his own and with his current staff. But it would be hard for a proud man like Keegan to admit it.

Will it be different at the 2002 World Cup? What about 2004 and then 2006? ... And on we go. England has always been a Land of Hope and Glory.

With the England team it is always hope. This Keegan story couldn't change it.